WILLFUL NEGLECT

The Dangerous Illusion *of* Homeland Security

CHARLES S. FADDIS

LYONS PRESS
Guilford, Connecticut
An Imprint of Globe Pequot Press

Copyright © 2010 by Charles S. Faddis

Lyons Press is an imprint of Globe Pequot Press.

Text designed by Sheryl P. Kober

Library of Congress Cataloging-in-Publication Data

Faddis, Charles S.
  Willful neglect : the dangerous illusion of homeland security / Charles S. Faddis.
     p. cm.
  Includes bibliographical references and index.
  ISBN 978-1-59921-906-6
  1. National security—United States. 2. Civil defense—United States. 3. Public
safety—United States. 4. Terrorism—United States—Prevention. 5. United
States—Defenses. I. Title.
  UA23.F28 2010
  364.3640973—dc22
                                    2009048395

Printed in the United States of America

10 9 8 7 6 5 4 3 2 1

This book is dedicated to my wife, Gina, whose love and patience allowed me to write it; to my children, who so often were pressed into service to help me with fieldwork; to the numerous unnamed "associates" who assisted me with my research; and to all the many dedicated Americans who, often at great personal sacrifice, have the courage to stand up and point out security problems when they see them. I met a lot of unsung patriots working on this project who, true to the American spirit, still have the fortitude to "speak truth to power." We all owe them a debt of gratitude whether we know it or not, and this book would have been impossible to complete without the support of those brave men and women.

Contents

Introduction *vi*

1: If Even the Military Is Not Safe, What Chance Do the Rest of Us Have? *1*

2: A Very Slow-Motion Train Wreck *22*

3: Nothing More Hideous Could Be Imagined *43*

4: It Has Happened Before *66*

5: From the Frying Pan into the Fire—LNG *95*

6: Noah Knew *116*

7: Remembering Caffa *133*

8: We Have Been Warned *164*

9: Making It Safe *193*

Endnotes *205*

Index *221*

About the Author *228*

Introduction

ON DECEMBER 7, 1941, AIRCRAFT OF THE JAPANESE IMPERIAL NAVY launched a surprise attack on the U.S. Navy base at Pearl Harbor in Hawaii. The results, well known to every American who has attended school in this country in the last sixty years, were catastrophic. Over 2,000 Americans were killed; four battleships and numerous other vessels were sunk.[1] Only by sheer good fortune were the aircraft carriers of the American fleet at sea at the time and thus spared attack themselves. It was by any measure a disaster for the United States and a brilliant victory for the nation of Japan.

News of the attack stunned the population of the United States. President Roosevelt, in seeking a declaration of war against Japan days later, famously referred to the day of the attack as a "date which will live in infamy." Demands for accountability began almost immediately, and within weeks both Admiral Husband E. Kimmel and General Walter C. Short, commanders of the Pacific Fleet and the Army forces on Oahu respectively, were relieved.[2] The controversy surrounding their relief and the debate over how the United States could have let itself be caught flat-footed by the Japanese has continued to this day.

At 1230 on December 8, 1941, roughly eight hours after the attack on Pearl Harbor, the Japanese launched an air attack on Clark Field in the Philippines. Clark Field was a critical strategic American air base and housed the only concentration of large four-engine B-17 bombers in the Pacific other than those located in Hawaii. The attack caught these B-17 bombers and the bulk of the fighter aircraft assigned to Clark Field on the ground, still parked in neat, peacetime rows for ease of maintenance and accountability. Twelve of the seventeen B-17 bombers were destroyed. Three more were seriously damaged. Only three U.S. fighter aircraft made it off the ground. A simultaneous attack on another airfield at Iba to the northwest destroyed all but two of the fighters based there. Fully 50 percent of the American aircraft in the Philippines were eliminated in these strikes. The remainder suffered the same fate in follow-on attacks over the next few days.[3]

The general in command of the defense of the Philippines, then still an American colony, was Douglas MacArthur. MacArthur had received word of the attack on Pearl Harbor roughly thirty minutes after it had occurred, at about 0300 hours on December 8, 1941. Despite constant attempts by the commander of the air forces assigned to his command to see him and to get authorization for offensive action, MacArthur had done exactly nothing to prepare for the Japanese attack, to disperse his air units or to seize the initiative by launching attacks of his own on Japanese air bases in Formosa.

MacArthur's inactivity is all the more difficult to understand in the context of the overall strategic military picture. One of the reasons the Japanese achieved surprise at Pearl Harbor was because it was believed impractical for them to strike so far from Japan against American forces. In short, with tensions rising between the two nations, a Japanese attack was not considered inconceivable; it was simply believed they could not reach Pearl.

By contrast, the Philippines had been considered to be one of the first Japanese objectives in any war with the United States for many years. The overall American plan for such a war, in fact, dealt in detail with how to defend the Philippines and hold on against Japanese forces until such time as the American fleet could come to the "rescue." When and if the political situation between the United States and Japan escalated to the point of war, every American officer worth his salt knew absolutely that the Japanese would strike, and would strike hard against the Philippines.

How then to explain MacArthur's failure to act? If it was almost impossible to believe that the U.S. could be caught by surprise in Hawaii, how was it even remotely conceivable that with eight hours' notice, its forces in the Philippines could also be caught napping?

It was almost impossible to fathom, and, in fact, in pondering this very question, the eminent naval historian Samuel B. Morrison later concluded it was "completely incomprehensible."[4]

In truth, I must admit I am among those who share his views. That the United States allowed itself to be caught unawares at Pearl Harbor is a damning testament to the power of preconception and complacency. That it allowed itself to be struck yet again eight hours later with another devastating, disarming air attack smacks of gross incompetence. That MacArthur was not himself cashiered for this failure is perhaps more a testament to wartime politics than anything else.

Eight hours had elapsed—eight precious hours during which preparations could have been made. Air patrols could have been organized. Aircraft could have been dispersed to secondary fields. Preemptive strikes could have been launched against the Japanese air bases in Formosa, from which additional strikes would originate. Instead, nothing was done. Even after all these years it is almost sickening to contemplate.

How much more sickening will it be, then, when we look back and contemplate what we have done, not with eight hours, but with the eight years that have passed since 9/11? How much more incomprehensible will it be for future generations, when they ponder the aftermath of a series of devastating attacks on the U.S. rail system, the bombing of a water treatment facility which releases a toxic chemical cloud over a major U.S. city, or the seizing of a nuclear power plant and its deliberate, systematic meltdown on our soil?

We had, on a strategic scale; plenty of warning that 9/11 was coming. Al-Qaeda told us they were coming, and they launched a series of preliminary attacks on targets such as U.S. naval vessels and embassies. Across the globe there was chatter about the idea of attacking U.S. aircraft and of using those aircraft as flying bombs. We did nothing. Like the commanders at Pearl Harbor, we sat with our hands folded and assumed that when and if the attack came, it would come elsewhere—certainly not on our soil.

Three thousand people died as the result of that complacency. Now, in the aftermath, it is our job to do what MacArthur did not do, to prepare for the next wave of attacks. There is no longer any possibility of avoiding the conclusion that we are at war. There is no question about the brutality of our foes, their level of creativity, or their willingness to strike us inside our own borders. It is incumbent upon us, therefore, to move as fast as is humanly possible to block any and all future attacks.

Amazingly, though, as you tour this nation and examine the prime targets which beg to be defended from terrorist attack, what you find, eight years later, is that virtually nothing meaningful has been done. True, large new bureaucracies have been created and huge shiny, new office buildings constructed, but in terms of concrete measures which will stand in the way of determined, evil men, there is very, very little.

Will this, too, be deemed incomprehensible in the not-so-distant future?

I spent twenty years of my life overseas working counterterrorism. During that time I was often in the company of dangerous men and women who were members of organizations dedicated to our destruction. I convinced many of them to work with us against their own comrades, understanding all the while that allegiances among such individuals often shift suddenly, and there is no such thing as a "friendly" terrorist.

What I learned from this experience, more than anything else, was how to think in the way our enemies do. I learned to see as they see and to plan, scheme, and attack as they do. I learned to ignore any enemy's strengths, to refuse to give battle on his terms, and to strike only at his weaknesses—and then, only when and where I chose. All of this I had the opportunity to put to good use when during the last Iraq War, it was my turn to play the role of the guerrilla and the insurgent against a much larger, conventional force: the Iraqi Army.

Having learned in this "school," it was with shock and horror that I came home from my last overseas assignment in 2006 to find that in the midst of the "war on terror," and years after we had effectively lost the World Trade Center, nothing had been done to prevent the next wave of attacks. I remember vividly, in fact, riding Amtrak to New York City from Baltimore in 2007, and, as if I was in some sort of dream state, attempting to comprehend the total absence of security of any kind on a rail line that ran directly into the heart of New York, and carried much of the industrial lifeblood of America.

I chose to write this book as a wake-up call, in hopes that it would attract attention, force some debate, and, perhaps, save some lives. That said, I did not begin this project without reservations. I do not pretend to be the world's foremost authority on terrorism. I also do not pretend that I know nothing of the craft. It was not lost on me that in writing this book, there was a danger that what I would end up producing would be less of a warning and more of a primer for individuals wishing to do harm to our country.

I chose, therefore, to do two things during the preparation of this book to obviate this danger. First, at critical points in the narrative, I chose to avoid the provision of certain details. Nothing I have done in that regard was intended to mislead, and nothing, in my judgment, impacts on any of my conclusions. I have simply chosen at certain junctures to "fuzz" the picture a bit and reduce the resolution, in the interest of making this narrative of less utility than it might otherwise be to "the bad guys."

Second, in advance of the publication of this work, I sent the relevant chapters to those individuals charged with the security of the installations and facilities discussed. For example, chapter 1, which deals with military installations, was sent directly to the commanding officers of all of the bases discussed. Obviously, what they choose to do (or not do) with the information presented is their business, not mine, but my objective was to ensure that they had an opportunity to review my analysis of their security deficiencies well in advance of that information being made public. I assume that by this point, they have either corrected the problems noted or they have satisfied themselves that I do not know what I am talking about and moved on.

I also knew going into this project that there was no way on earth I was going to be able to examine every aspect of homeland security. Considering every element of the threat posed to our nation by terrorist forces would be a monumental task and would call for a team of individuals with a range of backgrounds, resulting in a product many thousands of pages in length.

I chose then to stick to a certain select number of topics— principally, high-value targets and critical infrastructure. These were by and large fixed, tangible sites which lent themselves to examination and scrutiny. I deliberately stayed away from targets and topics about which I knew very little and where I thought I lacked the expertise to add anything to ongoing debate and discussion. A case in point is the terrorist threat to our cybersecurity. This is a huge and important topic, but not one about which I know enough to be able to make key judgments.

This is not a game. We are at war. We do not get to quit, pick up our ball, and go home when we lose interest. We do not get to define the playing field either. Our enemies have almost infinite patience, and they are fiendishly creative and inventive. The fact that we have now put in place a whole host of measures to prevent another terrorist attack like the one launched on 9/11 means only that, as long as those measures are in place, an attack on commercial aircraft using precisely the same techniques is less likely. It does not mean that we will not be attacked elsewhere in a thousand different ways. It does not even mean that our foes will not find some other mechanism to attack our commercial airlines.

Similarly, the fact that we have declared the central battleground in this "war" to be Iraq or Afghanistan, or any other nation 10,000 miles away, does not mean that Al-Qaeda has agreed to abide by that understanding. Their goal is to inflict as much pain and suffering on us as they can in hopes that they can make the cost of this conflict more than we will bear and force us into retreat. If they can find a way to kill thousands of Americans on our soil, they will gladly do so rather than attempt to kill handfuls at a time on the streets of Baghdad or Kandahar.

We cannot afford continued inactivity. We cannot afford continued deliberation, hesitation, and indecision. We do not need more studies, more conferences, or more experts thinking deep thoughts about the problem of terrorism. We need action. I am sure MacArthur was thinking some very deep strategic thoughts on December 8, 1942, when the Japanese attack began. That did not stop the destruction of the bulk of his air force.

Whatever excuse there was for being caught by surprise on December 7, 1941, there was none when the attacks came the next day in the Philippines. Whatever excuse there was for being caught by surprise on September 11, 2001, there will be none when the next attacks come.

CHAPTER ONE

*If Even the Military Is Not Safe, What Chance Do the Rest of Us Have?**

On April 18, 2008, I was sitting in the bleachers at the parade deck on Parris Island, the Marine Recruit Depot in South Carolina. My son, along with several hundred other very fit young men with shaved heads, was graduating from boot camp. My wife and two younger children were with me. My brother and his family had come as well. The sun was out. The temperature was mild. The stands were filled with the families of the other new Marines. It was in all respects a grand day, one of those events you remember for a lifetime.

I was horrified.

Around me were smiling parents, gushing grandparents, and proud girlfriends dressed up to welcome their Marines home from a grueling three months of training. The well-choreographed graduation ceremony was humming along. We had rented a large house on the water nearby for the weekend, and were planning a barbecue for later in the day.

And all I could think about was the absolute, terrifying, stupefying lack of any security of any kind. It was, from a terrorist's viewpoint, a dream come true.

Parris Island has taken the business of graduating Marines and made it a science. The Marines understand full well the public relations impact of the spectacle, and they have done a masterful and commendable job of involving parents and other family members, drawing them to attend "graduation weekend." I had been in the Army. I had graduated from a whole bunch of schools over the course of my service. I don't

---

* I finished the final edits on this chapter in October 2009. Days later, an active-duty Army Major named Nidal Malik Hasan opened fire on Fort Hood, Texas, killing 14 and wounding 31 before being shot by a female security guard. It was an unfortunate and tragic demonstration of just how inadequate security is on American military installations. I would rather have been proved wrong.

1

remember my parents showing up for a single such graduation, and, more importantly, I don't remember anyone else's parents showing up either. At Parris Island, everybody's parents come.

As a consequence of this focus, boot camp graduation from Parris Island has spawned a whole industry in the local community. Motels, restaurants, vacation rental homes, and souvenir shops all do a brisk business by catering to this crowd of graduation ceremony attendees. Beaufort and the surrounding towns fill up for days whenever a new class is ending its training cycle.

To facilitate the making of travel arrangements and to help answer the questions most families have, several different Web sites have been established. The Marines run their own, but there are also Web sites run by private organizations dedicated to promoting the commercial business that now accompanies the graduation cycle. These sites provide the exact schedule for graduations at the depot, as well as the designations of the units which are graduating. These Web sites also explain the procedures for gaining entry to the facility and give directions to the location of the graduation itself. Via these sites, as well as others on the Internet, detailed maps of Parris Island are also publicly available, as is imagery on Google Earth, which is so good that you can count the number of parking spaces in the lot next to the parade deck.

Parents preparing to drive down to South Carolina for the weekend can access all of this information on any computer connected to the Internet from anywhere in the country. Just as easily, all of this same information could be accessed by a terrorist in the Persian Gulf, Pakistan, or anywhere else on the planet where there is an Internet café. The provision of all this information is intended to help parents and other guests to fine-tune their planning for the "big day." It is also, unfortunately, a terrorist's fantasy, because it means that a huge amount of the information necessary for planning an attack on Parris Island is readily available and reliably verified. Al-Qaeda can, in short, do a huge portion of its casing on the Web.

Much of this would be irrelevant if there was a meaningful plan in place for securing the installation.

There is no such plan in place.

If you show up at the gate of Parris Island uninvited and wish to attend the graduation ceremony, you will be required to show a few basic pieces of documentation. Assuming you can produce such basic documentation, you will be allowed entry to the base, regardless of whether or not you were invited, know anyone who is graduating, or have any other legitimate business there. There is no requirement for you to apply for permission in advance. There is no background check of any kind. In essence, if you have a vehicle, a registration, and a license, you are probably going to be allowed to drive on to the base and then proceed to pretty much anywhere you want to go on the installation. There will be no check of any kind on your movements.

That is the good news. It gets worse.

A few weeks in advance of the actual graduation, the Marine Corps mails out invitations to the graduation ceremony to whomever each recruit designates as his desired guests. Usually, this means an envelope is sent to the parents of the recruit, but it is, ultimately, the recruit's decision as to who is invited. The invitations include an explanation of the events surrounding graduation, a schedule, and a vehicle pass for entry to Parris Island.

The pass which is provided is a piece of colored paper with printing on it designating it as a permit to enter the base. It is the type of thing which could be duplicated by a grade-school child with a computer and a printer in about two minutes. Just as easily, of course, it could be duplicated by someone with nefarious intentions, almost anywhere. In fact, given the proliferation of laptops and their peripherals, it literally could be reproduced in the backseat of a car once a sample or an image of a sample was procured.

The only thing that is changed about the visitors' passes from one ceremony to the next is the color. If I was given a blue pass for my son's graduation, then the pass for the next cycle would likely be yellow or red or green. Everything else about them remains static— meaning that in order for a terrorist to manufacture a false pass, all he needs to know in advance is the color.

These passes are sent out by the hundreds for each graduation ceremony. They are thrown on the dashes of hundreds of vehicles, which drive on and off Parris Island continuously throughout the entire graduation weekend, as a whole host of activities take place. Most of these vehicles are then parked in the lots of motels within a few miles of the front gate. Not surprisingly, more than a few people simply leave the passes on the dash where they were thrown, rather than stowing them away somewhere. This means that if you really want to know what color the parking pass is for any particular ceremony, and you don't have any other way to find out, it is probably going to take you all of five minutes strolling through motel parking lots near the installation to get the information.

Once you have that piece of colored paper sitting on your dash, something marvelous is going to happen. You are not going to have to stop at the main gate at all. You are simply going to be waved through, as I was, by a lone, bored sentry with a sidearm, and, after that, you will have the run of the entire recruit depot. This is a great convenience for Mom and Dad and all the siblings who have just driven down from Richmond to attend graduation. They do not even have to stop their vehicle and provide identification. They sail on by the guard post and head for the bleachers to try to get good seats.

Just imagine what a wonderful convenience it would be for a team of terrorists who had decided that it might be a cool idea to attack the United States Marine Corps at home, on one of its most storied installations. No one would have to worry about showing identification. No one would have to worry about supporting a cover story. Perhaps most of all, no one would have to worry about the possibility of having to explain why their van or camper was loaded not with luggage and snacks but explosives and detonators.

From the front gate to the parade deck is a relatively short distance. There are no further checkpoints of any kind. In fact, there is not even any meaningful physical barrier separating the parade deck from the roads that run immediately adjacent to it. A terrorist team driving a VBIED (a vehicle-borne improvised explosive device) or a car bomb would not only be able to drive to the parade deck, but they could also literally drive directly out onto the parade deck before activating the device.

Imagine the scene—the carnage and the international impact. A typical graduating class at Parris Island is several hundred Marines. They are brought out onto the parade deck and stood at attention for inspection at a time and place which has been announced weeks in advance to the entire Internet-using world. How magnificent would it be for Al-Qaeda to strike such a ceremony, in the heart of Parris Island, on what is considered by the Corps to be "hallowed ground"? I can see the proclamation taking credit for the attack now, replete with references to the Marines' actions in Fallujah, and labeling the attack as God's just retribution upon them for their sins.

We are eight years into a war against a group of very evil and very dangerous men who have demonstrated time and again their willingness to take extreme risks and to employ bold and inventive tactics. Their use of suicide bombers is well known. Their skill in the construction and employment of VBIEDs of enormous power is beyond question. They have infiltrated our nation in numbers before—witness 9/11— and we know without question that they continue to do so today.

It is, therefore, to use the word, *incomprehensible* that a U.S. military installation could be left in the security posture that Parris Island is today.

It would be a simple matter requiring the expenditure of only very limited funds to radically change the current situation and make an attack on a graduation ceremony a much more difficult prospect. My suggestions would include:

- Eliminate the provision which allows non-invitees to attend the ceremony. We are at war. Sacrifices have to be made. No one goes to the show who was not invited.

- Invitees all have to stop at a visitor center of some kind, present a written invitation mailed to them by the base, and then produce photo IDs and vehicle registration information to prove their identities. Parris Island has lots of junior Marines, so if there is no money for a formal visitor center right now, an awning of some sort, a few enlisted "volunteers," and a couple of card tables on the side of the road would still satisfy the requirement quite nicely.

- All vans, campers, and SUVs are searched. Select other vehicles are searched on a random basis. Searches should include inspection of the interior of the vehicles and, by mirror, inspection of the bottoms of the vehicles.

- Once cleared, visitors should be given passes for display while on base. These passes should have to be returned upon departure from the installation. This procedure should be repeated each time a visitor enters the installation.

- The guards at the gate should be beefed up and provided with weapons which might actually allow them to stop drivers of vehicles who choose not to comply with the rules.

- Some sort of barrier should be put in place to allow the guards at the gate to physically bar entry to the base should they need to do so.

- Physical barriers should be put in place around the parade deck so that it is impossible for vehicles to be driven out onto the deck itself.

There is nothing magic about any of the suggested measures, nor are they exhaustive. They are basic physical security steps. They will not make it impossible to stage an attack against Parris Island, but they will make it a much more difficult and problematic prospect. If they were supplemented by more-advanced measures which brought to bear some of the technical capabilities that exist for physical security today, they could be even more effective.

My primary reason for listing the steps above is not to claim some particular level of skill in security measures, or even to try to provide a blueprint for a solution to the current situation. It is to show how simple and cheap it would be to make a dramatic difference in the security status of the installation. In other words, the problem is not money or resources; the problem is mind-set.

I am sure that the individuals responsible for the security of the Marine Corps Recruit Depot at Parris Island are talented and dedicated individuals. I am also sure that among them are individuals who know a great deal about the techniques of physical security, and, quite likely, have employed those techniques in combat zones like Afghanistan and Iraq. They are not failing to secure the installation because they do not care or because they do not know how. They are failing to secure the installation because they do not believe that there is any reasonable prospect that a terrorist attack using a VBIED could be launched against the installation. They are acting under the assumption that our enemies are incapable of delivering such a blow.

This is precisely what happened at Pearl Harbor, and, incredibly, it is what happened the next day at Clark Field. The Japanese did not devastate our forces on both such occasions because the American military did not know how to defend itself. They devastated our forces because they caught us flat-footed, complacent, and passive.

When I left Parris Island, I began to wonder if what I had seen there was just an anomaly, or if it was representative of the security posture of American military installations as a whole. I live just outside Annapolis, Maryland, so I decided I would start by making a visit to the Naval Academy and looking at what sort of physical security was in place there. I took my fourteen-year-old son along to make the whole visit look a little more natural. I hoped that the remodeling work on the museum at the Academy would be done so I could show it to him.

A first impression of the security at the Academy is, to the casual observer, probably fairly positive. There are gates with sentries. There are walls. There is even a new pedestrian entrance which routes all persons not driving vehicles through a security checkpoint. Other than those cleared in certain categories, vehicles can no longer be driven onto the installation.

That positive impression fades quickly upon closer inspection.

My son and I left our car parked against the curb a hundred yards or so from the main gate and entered through the pedestrian entrance and the covered security checkpoint. There were two metal detectors and X-ray machines inside the checkpoint. Neither was in use. Everyone entering the Academy was waved past them. A single junior enlisted guard with a sidearm was inspecting picture IDs and then allowing entrance to the grounds without requiring any explanation of the visitor's destination or business. No record of any kind was being made of who was entering. There was not even a sign-in log.

My son and I passed through the security checkpoint and out onto the sidewalk beyond where I paused for a few moments to observe the procedure in place for the clearance of vehicles entering the installation.

Vehicles entering off of the public street outside were routed down a single lane of traffic and around a sharp turn, which was apparently designed to force them to slow down, and then stopped by a single sentry, with a sidearm, at a guard shack. There was no barrier in place to require the vehicles to stop; they did so in response to the sentry's hand gestures and directions on posted signs. Beyond the guard shack, there was no barrier to prevent vehicles that did not stop from entering the Academy grounds other than a metal gate, which was secured in the open position. It appeared that it was manually opened and closed, something which obviously would take a little bit of time. In any event, the gate was not constructed to stop a speeding vehicle.

Interestingly, the outgoing lane of traffic on the other side of the guard shack did not even have a curve to force traffic to slow down. It was a perfectly straight, flat roadway leading from the interior of the Academy to the public street outside. Any terrorist willing to commit the crime of driving the wrong way on a one-way street would, therefore, be able to drive a VBIED directly onto the Academy grounds without even the inconvenience of moderating his speed to negotiate the curve in the entranceway.

When I had finished absorbing the scene, I turned to my understandably bored son and asked him what he thought the most likely form of terrorist attack against the Academy was. He, who grew up overseas and understands far more than any fourteen-year-old should about terrorism and security, responded without hesitation: "Car bomb."

"Right," I said. "And what measures do you see in place right here that would realistically prevent a car-bomb attack on this facility?"

"None," my son said without hesitation. He still looked bored, like he was wondering why I had dragged him away from his Xbox for this.

Maybe part of the problem is that people, even those involved with security, do not fully comprehend the magnitude of the threat posed by VBIEDs. I find that hard to believe, but maybe it is true. Perhaps, somehow, in some way, they have missed the last twenty or thirty years and are still thinking that a bomb going off is something that will break a little glass, perhaps injure or kill some folks in the immediate proximity, but otherwise not overly disturb life as we know it.

If so, they are sadly mistaken.

For the American military, the introduction to this horrific new tactic was the attack on the U.S. Marine barracks in Beirut, Lebanon, on October 23, 1983. The vehicle used in that attack was a 19-ton truck. Not a sedan. Not a station wagon. A 19-ton truck. On its run into the target that massive vehicle crashed through perimeter barriers, overran an initial sentry position, crashed through a second guard post, and detonated in the atrium of the four-story building in which close to four hundred Marines were sleeping. That single device killed 3 soldiers, 18 sailors, and 220 Marines. Dozens more were wounded. The building was obliterated.[1]

The force of the explosion was later calculated by the FBI to have been equal to 15,000 to 21,000 pounds of TNT. The particular explosive material was determined to have been bulk-form PETN. Detonation of a device like this on the grounds of the Academy would not kill a few visitors or rattle a few windows. It would take down an entire dormitory structure. Done at the "right" time and the "right" place it could kill literally hundreds of future U.S. Navy officers on the grounds of one of our nation's most storied military installations.

People with some knowledge of explosives might brush this hypothetical attack away. Why? Bulk form PETN is not normal, commercially available material. The material used in the 1983 Beirut bombing was likely obtained directly from a military program of some sort, and a strong link to Iran was presumed.[2]

Is the mind-set that refuses to acknowledge this threat therefore based on the presumption that the construction of such a devastating device on U.S. soil is not possible? If so, then those who hold this belief must not have been paying attention when the Oklahoma City bombing occurred.

The bomb which took down the Federal Building in Oklahoma City was built from scratch by Timothy McVeigh, an angry young man with a basic amount of military knowledge from his time in the Army, but no real specialized training in explosives. He built the bomb inside a normal Ryder rental truck. The bomb consisted of 5,000 pounds of ammonium nitrate fertilizer mixed with about 1,200 pounds of liquid nitrate fertilizer and 350 pounds of Tovex. Combined with the weight of the containers holding the material, it weighed 7,000 pounds.[3] Most of the material used was simply stolen from lockers at a quarry in Kansas.[4]

When the device detonated, fragments of the Ryder truck in which the bomb was contained rocketed in every direction. Every structure in a *sixteen-block* radius was damaged, some so badly they had to be demolished. A 4-foot piece of the truck frame landed on the roof of a building two blocks away. The 250-pound rear axle was thrown 200 yards.[5]

The blast punched a giant horseshoe-shaped hole in the north side of the Federal building, and the face of the structure was blown entirely off. One hundred sixty-seven people died, and 509 more were wounded.[6] The explosion was the equivalent of what would be produced with 3 tons of TNT.[7]

Take a look at Google Earth for a few minutes. Visit the Academy. Stroll the grounds. It will take you no time at all to pinpoint several locations at which a device of this magnitude could do devastating damage and inflict a massive blow to the capability and prestige of the United States Navy.

More than any specific ignorance of what terrorists are capable of doing technically, though, my observations of security measures like those at the Academy tell me that the persons devising them have no clear idea of the nature of the individuals against whom they are defending. It is as if decisions are reached about how to construct a defense without first taking stock of what the actual threat is. It is defense in a vacuum—sort of like deciding how much armor to put on a tank before first determining what weapons the enemy is likely to use against it.

Terrorists do not care much about rules, signs, or procedures. If your mechanism for requiring a vehicle to stop is a hand gesture to the driver, you are likely to secure compliance from all the law-abiding people. You may even get compliance from a broad swath of not-so-law-abiding folk who are just not quite up for arousing the ire of a uniformed and armed sentry. It is, however, not likely that a terrorist driving a vehicle loaded with explosives and traveling at a high rate of speed is going to pay a whole lot of attention to your frantic motions for him to come to a complete stop and state his business.

Similarly, said terrorist is not likely to care a whole lot that you are carrying a pistol or that he is going to have to jump a curb or crash through a metal gate or any other such minor distraction. He is not planning on driving his vehicle much longer, anyway. A sentry armed with a pistol, even if he is extraordinarily alert and is able to unholster his weapon and get a few shots off as a truck charges past him, is capable of doing almost nothing. Unless he performs what amounts to a circus trick and succeeds in shooting the driver of the vehicle and killing him instantly, nothing he does is going to make any difference. His weapon cannot stop the vehicle, and any wound he inflicts on the driver will be very unlikely to prevent that individual from doing what he intends to do in the last few seconds of his life.

In short, if you are designing a security checkpoint that is intended to actually pose any real deterrent to a VBIED, at a bare minimum, it needs to have a barrier in place that can actually prevent the physical entry of a large vehicle moving at a high rate of speed onto the target installation. This means a serious, heavy, solid barrier of some sort—not a metal gate or a pole that is raised and lowered, or anything of that ilk.

Such a checkpoint also should include a weapon which is capable of incapacitating a vehicle. This is usually interpreted to mean something like a .50 caliber machine gun, which can shoot through the engine block of a truck and will stop and destroy anything it engages. Of course, such a weapon also needs to be manned; it cannot be the sentry's job to run to the weapon and get it into action.

Viewed with the kind of mind-set I am conjuring above, the security measures currently in place inside the pedestrian entrance at the Academy are just as useless as the automobile entrance for the prevention of terrorist attacks. Perhaps they have the positive effect of keeping general thugs and miscreants from wandering the grounds, but, realistically, there is nothing there that would serve as any kind of deterrent to an attack.

If I am a terrorist, and, for reasons unknown, I have chosen to gain entry to the Academy grounds to stage an attack on foot, X-ray machines and metal detectors are not likely to mean much to me unless the requirement to pass through them is backed up by some force and/or a physical barrier that I consider to be serious. If the extent of a real deterrent to my free passage through the pedestrian entrance is a lone enlisted man with a sidearm secured in a holster on his hip, then all that means to me is that in pre-attack planning, I need to designate one of my team members to shoot that individual through the head as soon as we reach the security checkpoint. Once that is accomplished, I can do whatever I want; there is nothing that can stop me.

There are a million ways to change this equation, of course, none of them new. If there is a second individual behind bulletproof glass who is observing the checkpoint and has the capacity to lock down the entrance to the grounds if there is trouble, my attack plan will not work. In fact, such a measure—which is standard all over the world in many settings, including prisons—is going to dramatically complicate my life and may even be enough to convince me that the attempt is not worth making.

If there is no money for the Academy to construct such a security setup, then simply the provision of additional sentries, particularly ones armed with more than sidearms, will be sufficient to significantly alter the situation as well. It will not make an attack impossible, but if I know there are other guards present who are armed with long guns, and not distracted by the task of examining IDs, that alone is going to be enough to take an otherwise sure thing and put it into the category of plans that are best reconsidered.

I noted earlier that I am not a physical security specialist. That bears repeating. None of the measures I have discussed, or will discuss, are new, innovative, or sensitive. Such measures are in place all over the world in myriad settings. Anyone who is a professional security officer is familiar with them, along with dozens more that are much more sophisticated and technical. Put simply: If these measures are not in place, it is not because they are unknown or unavailable. It is because someone has decided they are not warranted—that the type of attack against which they would defend is unlikely to materialize.

Yes, we are at war, but these folks believe the attack will come elsewhere.

I did not get into this business of examining physical security at military installations with the idea of doing some sort of exhaustive nationwide review. There are any number of individuals, some of them very good friends of mine, who do that for a living. However, I did leave the Academy thinking that in all fairness, I ought to go check out security elsewhere, just to make sure I wasn't stumbling on some sort of subset of aberrational behavior. I also thought that since I had been picking on the Marines and the Navy thus far, in all fairness I ought to choose a U.S. Army installation for my next visit.

So, I went online and wandered around a bit, looking for an Army installation near my house that I could visit without having to create some elaborate pretext. Within a few minutes, I had identified Fort Myer as a suitable candidate. It was close. It had significant symbolic value because of its proximity to D.C., and its status as the home of the Old Guard, the Third U.S. Infantry, the unit that handles all ceremonial duties in Washington. It also housed a museum which was open to the public, providing me with a logical reason to want to gain entry to the installation.

I drove over to Fort Myer one weekend morning in the early fall. It was a beautiful warm, sunny day without the humidity that so often plagues the D.C. area. The Fort is situated in a lovely location overlooking Washington from the Virginia shore, and I was quite honestly looking forward to spending some time at the museum, which is supposed to house some very interesting historical exhibits.

Unfortunately, what I found that morning in the way of security was significantly less pleasant.

The perimeter of the installation was marked by the usual chain-link fence, topped with the barbed wire seen at military bases around the country. As a measure to keep the general public out and to deter vandals and petty thieves, it was probably sufficient. As a defense against an attack by well-armed and well-trained adversaries, it was useless. There were no guards, guard towers, or cameras along most of its length. Nor were there any physical barriers to prevent the entry of a car or truck bomb. Such a fence could be cut, or it could simply be crushed by a large, heavy vehicle, but in any of a variety of ways, getting through it quickly and efficiently would not prove particularly difficult.

I arrived at the gate to enter the installation and said that I wanted to go to the museum. The private security guard in the shack at the entrance was only vaguely aware that there was a museum on post, but he waved me through and told me to drive to a covered parking area about 50 meters ahead to have my car searched.

I complied with the guard's instructions and pulled into the covered area where vehicle searches were conducted. I noted as I did so that the only thing making me drive to the search area was my voluntary decision to comply. Had I chosen instead to step on the gas and plow through the individuals waiting in the search area, I would have been inside the base proper well before any kind of alarm could have been raised, and a reaction organized.

The two guards working the vehicle inspection area were two of the surliest, laziest security officers it has ever been my misfortune to meet. The tall, male guard responded to my inquiry about the museum by making it clear to me that he had no idea if there even was a museum, and he could not possibly care less. He told me to exit my vehicle and open all the doors, the hatchback, and the hood. He then walked over and leaned against a wall to make sure I knew that he had no interest whatsoever in me, my car, or his job.

The male guard's slovenly female associate then circled my car once, looking in the doors with the same care and attention to detail that one would expect from a bored teenage checkout clerk in a supermarket. Everything about her posture and demeanor was calculated to telegraph her total lack of interest in her job. Having done the absolute minimum possible to fulfill the requirements of her position, she turned and walked away without comment. When I asked her if she was done, she grunted over her shoulder and disdained to dignify the query with an intelligible response.

I closed up my car and drove off.

As I toured the installation over the next half-hour in an ultimately unsuccessful effort to find the museum, I thought about the "security" in place, and wondered again about how it had been designed and what it was intended to prevent. A gate with guards but no physical barriers to prevent forced entry was good for keeping out crooks and rank amateurs. It had no value of any kind in preventing armed fanatics from entering the facility and committing mass murder. I had seen a grand total of four guards. They were armed only with sidearms, and it would have been very difficult for them to have been more inattentive and lazy. In an attack they would either die or hide, but they would impede nothing.

Similarly, I found the search of the vehicle puzzling. What was the value of a vehicle search in which the guards did little more than look at the backseat of my car? Was that done based on the theory that I might construct an explosive device, place it inside my car in a location where it was plainly visible, but then voluntarily stop to allow the guards to locate it? If the device was that discoverable, I never would have stopped. I would have blown past the guards and probably would have detonated my explosive device somewhere on base before the incompetents working security could even raise the alarm.

If, on the other hand, I had decided to conceal the device in any of the many usual ways, how would glancing through the doors of the vehicle discover it? If, for instance, I had packed the entire space under the backseat with Semtex, how would the bored female guard determine this fact during her five-second circumnavigation of the vehicle? If I had packed a couple of hundred pounds of explosive under the car, how would an inspection that did not involve the use of mirrors to examine the car's underside discover that?

Vehicle inspections are not hard. Every embassy in the world uses a set of standard procedures for this purpose. An outer gate is opened. The vehicle drives in. The gate is closed behind the vehicle, and an inner gate remains closed. The car or truck is now contained within what is known as a vehicle trap. Until such time as it is searched and cleared, it does not go anywhere.

The vehicle is then inspected. This may include an examination of its interior, but it also involves an inspection of the car's undercarriage using mirrors and swabbing of the car's exterior with pads. These pads are then fed into an analyzer which alarms at the presence of any compounds suggesting explosives. Bomb-sniffing dogs may also be employed.

Only when and if the vehicle is judged clear is the inner gate opened and the vehicle allowed to proceed inside the compound. If you are trying to get inside with a vehicle-borne explosive device, you are not going to make it. You may ultimately choose to detonate yourself in the vehicle trap and may in the process kill some guards, but there is no way you are getting any further.

None of this is rocket science. None of this is new. I did not invent any of these techniques. They are in use all over the world today, and have been for many years. That they are not in use at Fort Myer does not mean that no one there knows about such measures. It means they have made a very deliberate decision not to employ this level of security.

Yes, this storied installation sits right on the banks of the Potomac overlooking Washington, D.C. Yes, it is home to the President's own Honor Guard. Yes, an attack here would reverberate around the world and allow Al-Qaeda to claim the ability to strike at the heart of our most hallowed installations. But, apparently, we have decided it just won't happen. Of course, there will be another attack. Of course, Al-Qaeda remains dangerous. But it won't happen here . . .

Up to now I have been talking about security in terms of our readiness to deal with threats from Al-Qaeda or other similar groups. My focus has been on the "A Team," if you will—the first string; the guys who are most capable of doing us harm. It is perhaps illustrative of the extent of the problem we face, however, to spend some time considering threats from other less-capable adversaries and our ability to defend against them.

In May of 2007, federal agents arrested six individuals in connection with a plan to stage an attack on the Fort Dix Army Base in New Jersey.[8] All of the men were foreign-born Muslims. Among them were a convenience store clerk, a roofer, a cab driver, and a man who had worked for a period of time delivering pizzas on the base in question. Three of the men were brothers from the former Yugoslavia, one was Jordanian, another a Turk. Three were here illegally. Two had green cards. One was a U.S. citizen.[9]

There was no evidence that this group of individuals was acting under the direction of Al-Qaeda central command. They were clearly ideologically aligned with the organization, but they appeared to have come up with the idea and conducted all planning for the attack on their own.[10] Their desire was to inflict as much damage as possible on the U.S. military, and they had concluded that it would be more productive to stage an attack inside the United States than to travel abroad for jihad. In the words of one of the conspirators, "I assure you that you can hit an American base very easily."[11]

The specific selection of Fort Dix as a target was based at least in part on the fact that one of the members of the group had delivered pizzas on the installation and had a strong familiarity with the layout of the base. This individual was also able to provide a map of the facility for use in planning. That said, members of the group also went to the lengths of physically entering the base and conducting video casing of potential targets.[12] It is yet another measure of the inadequacy of current security measures that this group of ad hoc terrorists, with essentially no training from any formal group, was able to enter the installation and videotape potential targets without any apparent difficulty.

During the course of this case, a number of additional comments were made by members of the group regarding the ease with which one could gain access to an American military installation. Mohamad Shnewer, speaking to an undercover government informant, Mahmoud Omar, stated that Fort Dix was much more accessible than military bases in the Middle East, which were generally in remote areas. "Their noses are up," Shnewer said on a recording that accompanied the video he was shooting. "We are America and no one can hit us. And, we are going to make them think differently, God willing."[13]

Prior to making the final selection of Fort Dix as the target, members of the group also conducted surveillance of other military installations. These included Fort Monmouth, the Lakehurst Naval Air Station, a U.S. Coast Guard base, and Dover Air Force Base. Interestingly, the group took note of what they considered to be extensive security at Dover and crossed that facility off their list of potential targets as a consequence. In contrast, they characterized the Naval Air Station as a relatively easy target.[14]

The conspirators purchased several firearms, including handguns and a shotgun. They also sought automatic weapons, and, in fact, were arrested shortly after meeting with a controlled FBI source and acquiring four M16s and three AK-47s. The members of the group conducted firearms training at two different locations using a variety of weapons, and also used a paintball facility to practice their tactics in preparation for the assault.[15]

A group like the individuals discussed above is not likely to successfully carry out an attack on the scale of 9/11. They simply do not have the sophistication or the resources to pull off something of that magnitude. One wonders, however, what defense the kind of security arrangements in place at most U.S. military bases within the United States would present to such a group. No matter how well-trained or disciplined, what chance would a single, bored gate guard with a sidearm stand against a half-dozen men armed with automatic weapons? How many people would die before a response team could be mobilized which would actually be able to confront such a force?

The death toll in such an attack would be unlikely to come anywhere near that of 9/11. It might be "only" a few dozen people. Leaving aside the intrinsic value of each one of those lives for a moment, however, how shattering would it be to the public confidence and to the image of our armed forces for such an attack to happen on our own soil and within the confines of a supposedly secure U.S. military installation? One can almost hear the congratulatory video release from Bin Laden now, filled with glowing praise and promises of a wave of such spontaneous attacks across the length and breadth of America.

The Fort Dix conspirators are not the only individuals identified as having been involved in planning for attacks on U.S. military installations within the United States.

In August of 2005, four men were arrested and indicted in California based in part on their preparations for a planned series of attacks against military recruiting stations. The intent in this instance, as with the Fort Dix plot, was to inflict the maximum number of casualties.[16]

In July 2006 two individuals in Georgia were arrested and charged with providing material support to terrorists. They admitted to traveling to Canada to meet with other extremists and to discuss possible attacks on a range of targets within the United States, to include military bases. One of the specific targets under consideration for attack was Dobbins Air Reserve Base in Marietta, Georgia.[17]

In December 2006 the FBI arrested Derrick Shareef when he attempted to purchase grenades and weapons for an attack against a shopping mall food court. Shareef was motivated by radical Islamic ideology. In the course of the investigation that ensued, it was discovered that Shareef and other individuals had considered and done some preliminary planning on a whole series of other possible attacks as well. These included a strike against a U.S. military recruiting station in a Phoenix mall and attacks on U.S. military facilities near San Diego, California. Planning for the latter had progressed to the point of including detailed discussion of using diversionary fire to draw soldiers out of their barracks and then shooting them as they exited.[18]

Taken collectively, what these incidents show is that in addition to the possibility of an attack on a U.S. military base, such as Parris Island, which might be directed by Al-Qaeda central command itself, there appears to be a not inconsequential risk of a homegrown operation directed at the U.S. military inside the United States. Not surprisingly, given the actions of the military abroad in recent years, any symbol of the U.S. military has a certain intrinsic propaganda value as a target.

In this climate, when we must consider the very real possibility not only of attacks directed from abroad, but also more-spontaneous attacks perpetrated by local actors as well, the failure to put in place realistic security measures is just that much more difficult to fathom. We spout rhetoric all day about a "war on terror," but our actions do not match our words. It is as if we had the luxury of defining the battle space and declaring certain areas safe and secure. Unfortunately, we do not have that luxury; our enemies do not care one whit about where and when we would like to confront them, and, as we shall see, the targets we have left unguarded are in many cases much more dangerous than military bases and installations.

CHAPTER TWO
A Very Slow-Motion Train Wreck

BETWEEN 0737 AND 0742 HOURS LOCAL TIME ON MARCH 11, 2004, ten separate bombs detonated on four commuter trains traveling from the eastern suburbs of Madrid, Spain, into the capital city itself. Five minutes. Ten devices. One hundred ninety-one people died and over 1,500 were wounded.[1]

In each explosion, the force of the blast was such that the portion of the train car closest to the explosive device was completely destroyed. Doors, windows, and seats became shrapnel. Many of the injured lost one or more limbs. Numerous individuals were thrown completely clear of the train cars.[2] In some cases, body parts were blown through the windows of nearby apartment buildings.

Two hundred and fifty people were given medical attention at the sites of the bombings; 2,002 individuals were hospitalized; 291 ambulances were used to transport the injured; and 70,000 people, including medical personnel, emergency first responders, and members of the Spanish military were involved in the response to the attacks.[3]

It could have been much worse.

Three additional devices failed to detonate. Due to an unforeseen delay, one of the trains was running late and was hit just before it was about to enter Atocha Station, the same location at which one of the other trains was struck. Had the explosions occurred moments later, when both trains were at the platform, the carnage would have been significantly greater. It is even possible that the force of the explosions would have brought down the roof of the station, crushing everyone inside.

All of the devices were contained in normal backpacks. They were manufactured using locally procured cell phones and a type of plastic explosive commonly used in the mining industry in Spain.

Each device was rigged to a cell phone's alarm clock setting and programmed in advance to explode at a certain time. Nothing was utilized in the construction of these bombs that was not available inside the target country.

On July 7, 2005, another round of attacks on passenger trains in a large Western city took place. This time the target was London. At 0850 hours local time, three bombs exploded within fifty seconds of each other on three separate London Underground trains. A fourth bomb went off on a bus about an hour later. Fifty-six persons were killed, including the four suicide bombers who carried out the attacks, and 700 were injured.[4]

In the immediate aftermath of the subway bombings, there was a great deal of confusion regarding how many attacks had taken place. The devices exploded while the trains were between stations, so the wounded began to surface on foot from exits in both directions, leading initial responders to believe twice as many incidents had occurred. The force of the explosions in some cases caused significant damage to the tunnels in which the trains were traveling. While authorities attempted to get a handle on the scope of the attacks, the entire London Underground system was shut down. Bus service to a large portion of the city was also cut. Buses did not begin to run again until late afternoon or early evening. The subway remained closed until the next morning, although the affected stations remained out of service for weeks thereafter.

The actual explosive devices were homemade and used a peroxide-based explosive. The resulting compound was unstable and dangerous to work with but easily manufactured using commonly available materials. The bombers detonated the devices themselves, thereby obviating the necessity for any remote or automatic initiation system.[5] Once again there was nothing used in the construction of the devices or the execution of the attacks that was not readily procurable in the target nation.

On July 11, 2006, it was Mumbai's turn.

Seven bombs went off over a period of eleven minutes during the evening rush hour on the Suburban Railway, which carries large numbers of commuters to and from this massive city, the commercial capital of India. The rail system of Mumbai transports some 6 million persons daily, and the crush of passengers during rush hour is almost unbelievable. There was no question that the attacks had been timed so as to ensure the maximum number of casualties. An eighth bomb failed to detonate and was found later by police during a search of a train station on the line. In excess of 200 people were killed and over 700 wounded.

All of the devices were exploded inside of commonly available pressure cookers, apparently in an effort to enhance the force of the explosion. The explosive compound used was a mixture of RDX, a military plastic explosive, and petroleum hydrocarbon oil. The attack was carried out by a Pakistani militant group called Lashkar-e-Taiba, which has ties to Pakistani intelligence, and the RDX was likely acquired via that contact.[6]

The force of the explosions was such that the roofs of some cars were literally torn open. Bodies were scattered across the tracks. Dazed and wounded individuals were found wandering the tracks or lying on the ground near the train in which they had been riding. Some of the explosions took place while the trains were in motion, some while the trains were in station.[7] The disruption to the overall transportation system was enormous, and huge numbers of individuals were left simply to find other ways in and out of the city.

The three cases above are by no means an exhaustive review of terrorist attacks on rail transportation. India alone has been hit any number of times in this fashion over the last several years. They should be sufficient, however, to make the point that carefully timed and orchestrated terrorist attacks on large passenger rail systems are by now an established feature of worldwide jihad. Should such an attack occur tomorrow on U.S. soil, there would be no possible way any security or law enforcement official could claim to be ignorant of the threat or unaware of the consequences.

So, what are we doing to prevent such an event on U.S. soil?

I noted in the introduction how shocked I was upon my return to the United States from overseas in mid-2006 at the lack of security measures on Amtrak during a trip to New York City. In the time between that trip and my beginning work on this project, I had made a large number of trips on the Washington, D.C., metro system without noticing any indication of a meaningful increase in security, but as with my work on military installations, I thought a more-rigorous look at what measures were in place was in order.

On November 7, 2008, I traveled to New York City by rail. I arrived at the Baltimore Washington International rail station around 0630, parked my car in the garage which adjoins the station, and went to pick up my ticket, which had been purchased for me by a publishing house in another state. I had printed a receipt for the ticket at home, and, using an automatic ticketing machine, scanned the bar code on the receipt and received my ticket without showing any photo ID.

There was no security of any kind at the station itself—no metal detector, no security guard, nothing. Having obtained my ticket, I walked to the platform and stood with the crowd of individuals waiting, like me, to catch the next train northbound. Across the tracks, on the other platform, I saw a lone female security officer. She was dressed in some sort of military-style uniform and appeared to be carrying a sidearm. She was walking away from the passengers standing on that platform and looking down as if searching for something. She had no partner. She had no dog. She did not appear to have a metal detector of any kind with her. At some point, she disappeared, and I did not see her again during my time at the station.

I spent twenty years overseas as an operative trained to evade the detection of hostile security services. During that time I worked a large number of terrorist cases, ran a lot of terrorist sources, and absorbed a lot of methodology and psychology from the sources I ran. While in Iraq from 2002 to 2003, I ran a large-scale sabotage and covert action campaign directed against the Iraqi military. In the course of that campaign, I used a lot of what I had learned from working terrorist cases in carrying out actions directed against Iraqi targets. The rules of engagement I operated under were obviously different than those with which any terrorist would be saddled. My team worked to minimize civilian casualties at all times, and we were very rigorous in our target selection. We struck carefully designated targets of military significance and, even then, were very meticulous in when we struck and what weapons we used, so as to avoid any unnecessary loss of life.

Still, many of the challenges we faced were the same as any terrorist cell would face. We had to do careful casing. We had to assemble target packages. We had to find holes in the defense that would allow us to penetrate to the target and accomplish our mission.

It was also true that in most cases, we relied upon native assets to actually carry out the missions for which we were responsible. Deep inside Iraqi-controlled territory, there was no reasonable possibility that an American would pass undetected for long. We could not, therefore, call upon the services of a highly trained team of SEALS or Army Green Berets. We had to utilize local personnel and, often, local components. Whatever the final plan was, it had to be something that could be carried out given the limitations of the situation and the constraints upon our capabilities.

As I stood there in the cold that morning, I tried to call upon all of my experience and training and evaluate the situation from the perspective of a terrorist operative inside the United States, looking to carry out an attack. If I were the enemy and I was casing this location, what would concern me? If, for the sake of argument, I were part of a team preparing for an attack like that carried out in Madrid, what problems would I see?

I thought about it for the entire time I waited at the station. I thought about it halfway to New York, turning it over and over in my head. And, reluctantly, terrifyingly, I ultimately accepted that the conclusion was obvious, and had been since about thirty seconds after I walked onto the platform that morning.

Nothing. There was absolutely nothing in place that I would regard as a significant concern to any reasonably competent group of operators.

The Madrid bombers walked onto the target trains carrying normal backpacks like those commonly seen on the street. They were in Western dress and comfortable within the society in which they were operating. Nothing about them—their demeanor, their language, or their attire—attracted any attention. Presumably, any group of operators involved in an operation of that type inside the United States would be at least as well prepared.

What then would be the value of a security guard without any type of metal detector, explosive-sniffing dog, or other more-exotic technical capability? Don't get me wrong. Having spent my share of time sweating bullets and dodging other people's security services, I can tell you that it is always a complicating factor to have uniformed security on hand. That said, if we are really talking about serious people, bent on doing serious harm, what is it going to matter to them if there is a bored security guard standing on the platform? That kind of thing scares away pickpockets, perverts, and other scourges of humanity. A pro will stand next to the security guard, chatting him up while holding the backpack loaded with explosives slung over one shoulder, and never break a sweat.

To put it another way, if I am in country undetected and have arrived at the platform with my device, my concern is going to be any measure which threatens to single me out as a terrorist among the throng of individuals around me. If I have schooled myself in my manner of dress and language such that I do not immediately, transparently call attention to myself, and if I have taken even rudimentary measures to hide the device which I am carrying—by placing it in a bag or wearing it under my clothes, for instance—then what am I worried about?

I am worried about any measure which has, in effect, the ability to see through my clothes, my backpack, or my shopping bag, if that is my method of concealment, and see what I am carrying and thereby determine my purpose. A metal detector, even one which is not always in use, or which is moved randomly from station to station, is a big concern. A guard who at least randomly stops people before they enter the station and asks to look inside their bags is also a problem. It is hard to plan with such factors thrown into the calculus. Especially if I am looking to do something of significance, something like Madrid, which calls for multiple actors and coordination, I need predictability.

More distressful to me, as the enemy, are measures in effect once I am on the platform. If I walk up to the station one morning and see a metal detector set up where I did not expect one, perhaps I can just turn and walk away. If I am part of a larger operation, this will mean at least part of the plan is disrupted, but at least I will not be captured and questioned.

Consider, though, what happens if there are measures, again, even random, which are in place on the platform itself. What if I am standing with the other passengers on the platform waiting for the train and a security officer walks by with an explosive-sniffing dog and the animal alerts to me or my bag? I do not have the option of simply walking away. I am done, and, if there is, in my mind, any reasonable chance that this might happen, I may very well have to change my entire plan.

The same would apply to any other unpredictable measure that took place once I had purchased my ticket and arrived at the platform. A security officer who went through the crowd randomly asking individuals carrying large bags or backpacks to open them could be a huge problem. An officer who simply wanded such bags with a metal detector would be almost as much of a concern.

We are talking here, of course, about measures designed to thwart large-scale attacks. If we shift to a discussion of small-scale attacks directed at very small numbers of people, then we have to employ much more draconian measures. A large-scale attack on a passenger rail target, like Madrid, is going to involve multiple individuals and multiple devices. If one of these individuals does not board his train and does not hit his target, that diminishes the scale of the attack, but it is not, in and of itself, fatal to the overall project. If, however, one of the bombers is arrested while attempting to board, i.e., detected and apprehended on the platform, this may, in fact, prove to be the undoing of the entire operation.

Any competent police organization in this day and age, no matter how complacent, is not going to arrest a bomber trying to board a train, congratulate itself on work well done, and go home for the day. It is going to trigger a system-wide alert and begin checking all trains. No service is going to begin again for hours at a minimum. Meaning, if I am planning an attack with multiple actors, and one of them gets nabbed before he reaches the target, I, as team leader, have probably just lost my entire op. If one guy gets made, we are all done.

So, if, in the course of my casing for an attack on a passenger train or subway system, I notice that there are, on any kind of regular basis, guards with dogs walking the platform, this is a big problem. If I see that these guards sometimes come onto trains while stopped at a station and walk the aisles with dogs, this is another huge problem. Random bag checks, with enough frequency to be noticed regularly, are also major concerns. In short, long before we get to the point of having to search everyone's bags, enough of a threat of detection has probably been added to the equation that I, as the individual doing the planning for the operation, am going to start thinking of a new plan.

The above is not an exhaustive review of the kinds of security considerations involved in this situation. Nor are my suggestions regarding possible security measures intended to be definitive. As I have said earlier, I am a trained operator; I am not a physical security specialist. Any real expert in security measures would be able to add a number of other more-sophisticated recommendations to my list.

What this review does highlight, however, is that there is a tremendous amount we can do to improve our security posture that would not cost huge amounts of money and would not require the invention of new space-age technology.

The train for New York arrived a few moments late. I boarded, found a seat and settled down to enjoy the ride. On board there was no more security than there had been at the station. At some point, a conductor came by, checked my ticket and walked on without any attempt to confirm my name. Passengers boarded with heavy bags, dropped them in the first convenient space, and then moved on out of sight, looking for a seat or headed for the snack car. No one accounted from them, their luggage, or their whereabouts.

I exited the train in Penn Station and went upstairs to the street. Along the way I saw no security of any kind other than two bored, overweight National Guardsmen who were leaning against a wall and talking about the New York Giants' season. Better to have them there than not in any event. However, realistically, to anyone who is moderately competent and truly bent on doing harm, their presence was irrelevant.

On December 3, 2008, I had an associate repeat the trip described above. Security at BWI was, if anything, even more lax. My associate did not even see a security guard on the platform. On the return trip, my associate noted that there were more visible security personnel in Penn Station and, also, that there were signs indicating that all bags were subject to search. She also noted, however, that at no point during the hour she spent in the station did anyone actually have their bags checked. Over subsequent weeks, I had other associates repeat the trip on multiple occasions. The results were identical.

The above seems to me to require several comments. First, it is unquestionable that during my work on this book, I saw that New York City has taken a much more proactive stance on counterterrorist measures than other parts of the United States. While the federal government seems focused primarily on paperwork and bureaucracy,

New York City, for obvious reasons, has put real teeth into the steps it has taken. This is to be commended.

Second, unfortunately, all the security measures in the world which are centered inside of New York City are likely to be of little value if they are not mirrored throughout any rail system that runs into the city. If I am a terrorist and I want to detonate explosive devices on trains running into New York City during the morning rush hour, I am not going to carry those bombs into Manhattan by car or foot and then try to board a train in the teeth of security. This gets to a fundamental law of counterterrorism: Terrorists do not stage frontal assaults on your most defensible front. They feel along your perimeter until they discover what you have missed, and then they strike where you are weak.

Finally, putting people on notice that their bags may be searched and then not actually searching anyone is, at best, of marginal value. I have walked through a lot of "secure" areas carrying things I was not supposed to. The theoretical chance of being caught did not mean much to me. I was in the business of taking risks. What mattered to me was an objective evaluation of the real probability that I might be stopped or detected. A terrorist will use the same calculus. He or she will case the target and take note of what security measures are in place. If there are, in fact, people being asked to open their bags and backpacks on a regular basis, this will be a concern. If there are guards with metal detectors passing them over bags, this will be a concern. Explosive-sniffing dogs, or, for that matter, dogs which may or may not really be trained to detect explosives, will be a huge concern because of their capacity to work a relatively large area and significant number of pieces of baggage in a short period of time.

In brief, what matters to me is reality—what you are really doing on a regular basis that will prevent me from accomplishing my mission. All the signs, regulations, and directives in the world are of no moment if they are not backed up by action.

So, how big an issue is this, really? Are passenger railway lines really that significant a target?

Each year Americans make more than 3.5 billion trips on intercity trains, commuter rails, and subways. On a given day in New York City, more people pass through Penn Station than all three major airports servicing the region combined.[8] Nor is New York City by any means the only location with heavy passenger traffic. In 2007, 3.7 million Amtrak passengers boarded or alighted from an Amtrak train at 30th Street Station in Philadelphia, the third-busiest passenger rail station in the nation.[9]

New York City and the surrounding area, however, are home to the most extensive mass transit system, not only in the United States, but in all of North America. So, for our purposes, in trying to evaluate the scope of the threat that a rail attack poses, it is perhaps the best place to focus. In fact, two-thirds of all mass transit users in the United States reside in the New York City metropolitan area. Over 50 percent of New Yorkers do not even own an automobile. In the rest of the country, the bulk of commuters drive to work. In New York City, mass transit is the primary means of transportation.

Inside New York City lies the busiest passenger rail terminal in the country, Penn Station. Penn Station alone serves 600,000 passengers a day, at the rate of 1,000 persons every ninety seconds. Amtrak trains stopping at Penn Station provide service throughout the entire Northeast corridor in the United States. In 2004, 4.3 million Amtrak passengers boarded at Penn Station. Commuter lines such as the Long Island Railroad and New Jersey transit service many tens of thousands of commuters daily. Six separate New York City subway lines stop at Penn Station.[10]

Imagine, then, what the impact would be on New York City, and the entire nation, if the kind of attack that took place in Madrid took place inside the United States and centered on Penn Station. Presume that on a typical workday morning, a dozen different explosive devices went off on half a dozen different subway, Amtrak, and commuter trains, all as they converged on Penn Station. Some would detonate inside the station itself, some as the trains were about to enter the station.

Casualties would be huge. The dead would probably number between 500 and 1,000. The injured would well exceed 2,000. Rail lines would be blocked. Tunnels would be damaged. Penn Station would be closed for days, if not weeks. Throughout a region that encompassed many states, all passenger rail traffic would be brought to a halt. Commuters in the hundreds of thousands (if not millions) would be unable to get to work or to return home. Businesses would be forced to close. New York City would once again find itself in a state of siege.

And, to do this would require less men than were employed in the 9/11 attacks, and, at most, a few hundred kilos of explosive.

On May 20, 2004, on the heels of the Madrid bombings, the Department of Homeland Security issued security directives for passenger rail systems. These directives required passenger railways to:

- Designate coordinators to enhance security-related communications with the Transportation Security Administration (TSA) of the Department of Homeland Security.

- Provide TSA with access to the latest security assessments and security plans.

- Reinforce employee watch programs.

- Ask passengers and employees to report unattended property or suspicious behavior.

- Remove trash receptacles at stations determined by a vulnerability assessment to be at significant risk, and only to the extent practical, except for clear plastic or bomb-resistant containers.

- Install bomb-resistant trash cans to the extent resources allow.

- Utilize canine explosive-detection teams, if available, to screen passenger baggage, terminals, and trains.

- Utilize surveillance systems to monitor for suspicious activity, to the extent resources allow.

- Allow TSA-designated canine teams at any time or place to conduct canine operations.

- Conduct frequent inspections of key facilities, stations, terminals, or other critical assets for persons and items that do not belong.

- Inspect each passenger railcar for suspicious or unattended items, at regular periodic intervals.

- Ensure that appropriate levels of policing and security are provided that correlate to DHS threat levels and threat advisories.

- Lock all doors that allow access to train operators' cab or compartment, if equipped with locking mechanisms.

- Require Amtrak to request that adult passengers provide identification at the initial point where tickets are checked.[11]

Every one of these measures is probably a good idea. There is no sense in making things easier for terrorists than we have to, and railway administrators have a lot of things to be concerned about, not just catastrophic terrorist attacks. That said, how many of these directives, which were transparently prompted by the massive coordinated terrorist attack in Madrid, would actually have any chance of preventing such an event on U.S. soil?

Almost none.

A number of directives concerned administrative issues, like the designation of coordinators to handle communication with TSA.

A splendid idea, and one that no doubt went a long way toward improving the flow of information, but not anything that would prevent a group of fanatics from blowing Penn Station to pieces.

Several of the directives had to do with preventing people from placing bombs in trash cans by making the trash cans transparent. Again, a good idea, but nobody died in Madrid, London, or Mumbai from an explosive device hidden in a trash receptacle.

Several additional directives were based on the idea that passengers and railway personnel needed to be encouraged to be more alert. This also was a superb idea. One never knows what sort of casing activity might be noticed by ordinary citizens. The focus on "suspicious behavior," however, suggests a belief that the individuals coming to attack a major passenger railway or subway system are going to be engaged in some kind of fairly amateurish conduct that would jump out to persons around them as unusual.

In fact, if I am casing a subway line for security measures that may prevent me from carrying on to the train one morning a backpack filled with plastic explosive, blasting caps, and a cell-phone initiation system, I don't really have to do very much.

I go to the station. I get on the train. I get off the train. I leave the station. Along the way I count security guards and police officers, take note of metal detectors, dogs, etc. Then I repeat the process over a period of days and weeks. Unless I am very, very bad at what I am doing, it is going to be extremely difficult to pick me out from the crush of other passengers around me.

Some of the directives concerned things like surveillance cameras and requiring identification from passengers. These are also excellent ideas, but, frankly, surveillance cameras are going to be of more use in post-blast investigation than they are in preventing an attack. Showing IDs is a great requirement as well, and to be encouraged, but it also is something that will primarily help in determining who carried out an attack after it has happened. If I have taken all the trouble to put together a team of terrorists who have entered the

United States with the express purpose of staging a major attack on a rail system, those individuals will not be buying tickets for the train using any name that has previously been associated with any kind of extremist or criminal activity.

Out of the entire list of security directives, the only measures that would actually cause a problem for a team of terrorists attempting to perpetrate a Madrid-style attack in the United States are those regarding explosive-sniffing dogs. Unfortunately, these directives are weakly worded, and, as we have already seen, the actual use of dogs is very limited.

It seemed pretty clear to me from the outset that there had not been any real, meaningful response to Madrid, London, and Mumbai on U.S. passenger rail systems. Given the stakes, however, I thought it would be advisable to be prepared to present more than simply anecdotal evidence of the status of rail security. So, following the trips I have outlined above, I brought into the picture several other associates and asked them to compile information on the following rail systems: the Virginia Railway Express (VRE), the New York subway, and the MARC system in Maryland. They did so over a period of many months, with these results.

VRE

The VRE is a transportation partnership of the Northern Virginia Transportation Commission (NVTC) and the Potomac and Rappahannock Transportation Commission (PRTC), and provides commuter rail service from the Northern Virginia suburbs to Alexandria, Crystal City, and downtown Washington, D.C. It carries in excess of 4 million passengers annually and is growing in ridership at a rate four times in excess of that of any other passenger railway in the United States.[12]

VRE services a number of stations in Virginia and Washington, D.C. One of these is Union Station near the Capitol Building and adjacent to the Mall. Union Station is the second-busiest passenger rail station in the United States, after Penn Station, which we have already discussed.[13] Union Station also contains a large number of restaurants and shopping establishments. Thirty-two million people pass through it each year, making it the single-most-visited site in all of Washington, D.C. [14]

Over a period of eight months, during which time my associate rode the railroad everyday, there were no sightings, ever, of any railway security personnel of any kind on VRE. The only officials noted were conductors on the train. There was never an ID check of any kind done before passengers boarded the train. No bag searches were ever done. No explosive-sniffing dogs were ever sighted. No metal detectors were ever seen.

During this period, there were two occasions on which a large number of police officers were noted standing in the station where my associate disembarked. There was no explanation given for their presence, and they did not actually stop or speak with anyone that he could see. I should note that this associate was an intelligence officer and senior military officer, and familiar in some detail with terrorist threats and security methodologies.

The only security measure my associate noted was an automated message on all trains advising that if passengers saw someone leaving something on the train, they should ask them if it was their package, and, if they said no, the matter should be reported to the conductor. My associate added, however, that the recorded message began by talking about keeping the train clean, implying that this was some sort of anti-littering campaign, not a security advisory.

In short, what eight months of daily observation of VRE showed was that, despite the fact that it services the nation's capital and the second-busiest passenger rail terminal in the United States, there are no security measures of any kind in place to prevent a repetition of a Madrid-style attack.

New York Subway

Casing of the New York subway system over a period of months showed only a slightly better situation. Police officers and dogs were seen with some regularity, but bag searches were rare. Overall, while it was clear that New York City was taking the terrorist threat more seriously than the federal government, there was simply not anything close to enough security in place to really force a rethinking of any plan to stage a Madrid-style attack inside the United States.

MARC

Numerous trips on the MARC system showed it to be on a par with VRE. MARC is essentially the Maryland equivalent of VRE. It carries over 30,000 passengers a day, services forty-three stations, and also runs directly into Union Station in the heart of Washington, D.C. Perhaps fittingly, then, security measures on MARC were determined to be a mirror image of those on VRE. There were no sightings whatsoever of security personnel, dogs, metal detectors, or any other impediment to terrorist attack on this system. It was wide open.

I personally visited several MARC stations during morning commute times over a period of months. All of these stations were in suburban Maryland, north of Washington, D.C., and multiple daily trains ran through all of them, heading to Union Station. In fact, during the early-morning hours, typically there were trains every twenty to thirty minutes heading into the nation's capital. I would like to say that I found at least some sort of security presence— something, anything that would at least cause a terrorist attack team to rethink their attempt to replicate Madrid in the MARC system.

I found nothing.

Laurel Station is absolutely typical. It sits next to what is the historic heart of Laurel, Maryland, about forty minutes' ride from Union Station itself. There are several large parking areas adjacent to the station and walkways from the parking areas to the station platforms themselves. The station house sits next to the track on which southbound trains travel. There is an expanse of wooden platform outside.

There are several cameras on the exterior of the station building offering partial views of the station platforms and of the parking areas. Where these are monitored is unclear, but there is no indication whatsoever that they are monitored live on-site. There are no other discernible security measures of any kind.

Anyone taking the train can make it onto the platform via multiple routes. There is no single point of entry and exit. There are no turnstiles. There is no fence or wall or other barrier. The only individual present, even during rush hour, is a single ticket agent. There are no security officers. There are no dogs. I did not even notice any signs warning passengers of the possibility of bag checks or other security measures. A review of the literature handed out by MARC in the station showed a single reference to passengers taking notice of unattended bags and reporting these to railroad personnel. Even this admonition was buried at the end of a pamphlet dealing with a host of other miscellaneous issues.

Standing on the platform at Laurel Station during morning commute is like taking a trip to another time and place. The building itself is lovely, an old station house like something out of a Harry Potter movie, lovingly restored and quaint. Even the wooden platform has a charm that modern concrete platforms lack. You are only forty minutes from the heart of Washington, D.C., but the site is somehow insulated from the suburban sprawl around it. Commuters shuffle in, reading newspapers, checking their BlackBerries, toting their briefcases and backpacks, but somehow they all seem considerably more relaxed and at ease than their tense brethren fighting their way through traffic on the Beltway nearby.

All of this is, of course, an illusion. It is pretense. It is predicated on the false assumption that because we wish we did not have to worry about terrorism, we do not. If we close our eyes and pull the covers over our heads, the monster will go away.

Just how wide-open the MARC system is was demonstrated graphically on November 19, 2008, when a man carrying a Chinese SKS assault rifle was arrested after boarding a MARC train at a station in Baltimore. The man, carrying the rifle wrapped in a blanket, was allowed to board without interference or notice. He was arrested not because railroad security personnel had identified him as a threat, but because the cab driver who dropped him at the station called police, and officers were able to respond before the train left the station. Were it not for the actions of the cab driver, this individual would apparently have been able to ride the train without difficulty to its final destination, Washington, D.C. The SKS is roughly 3 feet in length and fires rounds capable of penetrating steel and concrete.[15]

How is this possible? How can we have created a new cabinet-level bureaucracy, the Department of Homeland Security, with a budget of $50.5 billion, and still, eight years after 9/11 and four years after Madrid, have done nothing of consequence to defend ourselves?[16] Are the authorities convinced, like the security officers at our military installations, that "it cannot happen here"? The Department of Homeland Security is building itself a massive new headquarters compound just east of the Anacostia River in the Washington, D.C., area. The site encompasses 176 acres and will house 14,000 employees. It will cost $3.4 billion to construct.[17] How can we provide funding of this magnitude for homeland security and still, at the end of the day, apparently not have a dime left over to beef up security on targets of obvious, immediate significance?

On February 13, 2003, five men crossing the causeway connecting the Kingdom of Saudi Arabia to the island nation of Bahrain were stopped and arrested. These individuals were identified as having strong extremist credentials and being in contact with jihadists in Saudi Arabia. The resulting investigation determined that these individuals were involved in a plot to stage a cyanide gas attack on the New York City subway system utilizing a device known as the "mobtaker."[18]

The "mobtaker" is a small, homemade device designed to be constructed inside a container such as a large paint can. I won't go into the details of its construction here—jihadist Web sites have taken care of that—but, when activated the "mobtaker" creates hydrogen cyanide gas and cyanogen chloride gas. If activated inside of a confined space, such as a railway car, the "mobtaker" would be highly effective, and would result in a large number of fatalities and serious injuries. Little or no training is required to construct such a device, and all necessary components are commonly available throughout the United States.[19]

This plot was not simply aspirational. The group involved had already conducted surveillance of the subway in advance of a planned attack, and they subsequently sought formal permission from Al-Qaeda leadership to proceed with the operation.[20] Also, unfortunately, I know from direct experience with Al-Qaeda and other Sunni terrorist groups worldwide that the individuals arrested on the causeway were not the only ones working with the "mobtaker" or similar devices. Cyanide gas is one of the most common chemical agents with which terrorists are currently experimenting and training.

In 2004 a Pakistani man was arrested, and ultimately convicted, of planning to blow up a New York subway station in advance of the Republican National Convention. Shahawar Matin Siraj apparently considered a wide range of targets, including bridges and subway stations, before settling on the 34th Street station in Brooklyn as a target. Siraj and an associate cased the station and even drew diagrams of it as part of their planning for the operation. The station in question is located in a congested shopping district which contains, among other establishments, Macy's flagship department store.[21]

In April 2006, Lebanese authorities arrested Assem Hammoud, a resident of Beirut, and charged him with a variety of terrorism-related offenses. Subsequent investigation revealed that Hammoud and a network of associates on three continents were involved in a plot to attack the Port Authority Trans-Hudson Corporation (PATH) trains traveling in tunnels underneath the Hudson River. This railway carries 227,000 passengers a day. The plan called for members of the team to carry explosives onto the trains in backpacks, and included discussion of how much explosive it would take to breach the tunnel walls and cause flooding.[22]

In late November 2008, terrorist-threat reporting resulted in heightened security throughout the Northeast rail corridor. The intelligence in question indicated that Al-Qaeda was planning mass-transit bomb attacks focused on Penn Station, New York City, and the Long Island Railroad. Sources advised that such attacks could have disrupted rail transportation throughout the entire Northeast.[23]

Do we really need anything further in the way of intelligence to tell us what is coming? Is it really necessary that we wait until the day after an attack when the bodies are being counted and the financial impact tabulated before we take steps to prevent the occurrence on U.S. soil of an attack identical to that which has already been carried out on multiple occasions elsewhere? We may not be able to protect against every eventuality, but, surely, we should be able to protect against a threat as clear, present, and imminent as this.

Unfortunately, we are not protecting ourselves against such a threat today. Worse yet, we are also not protecting ourselves against threats which make even the grim possibility of a rail attack seem almost inconsequential by comparison.

CHAPTER THREE
Nothing More Hideous Could Be Imagined

ON THE MORNING OF SEPTEMBER 1, 2004, THE CHILDREN OF SCHOOL Number One in Beslan, Russia, gathered for the first day of class. They were accompanied by large numbers of family members. The beginning of school is a significant event in Russia, where education is still not taken for granted, and its availability to all is celebrated. Traditionally, in Beslan, school began each year with a formal ceremony, including singing and dance performances. In this small town in the Caucasus, where most of the adult population had attended the same school, the first day was a major social event. Those children unfortunate enough to have parents who could not get off work to attend were, in most cases, brought by their grandparents.[1]

As the children gathered in the courtyard of the school for the opening ceremony, a group of Muslim terrorists suddenly appeared, armed with explosives, grenades, and automatic weapons. The size of the group remains a matter of debate to this day, but there were at least thirty armed men, as well as two veiled women in black, wearing suicide belts. Shooting began immediately, and the bulk of the terrified students, their adult relatives, and the school's teachers were herded into the school gymnasium and held as hostages.

Exact figures for the number of hostages are hard to come by, but something in excess of 1,300 people were held. The gymnasium where they were held was 10 meters by 25 meters in size, roughly half the size of gyms found in average American schools. The hostages would be kept in this room for the next fifty-three hours, deprived of food, forced to relieve themselves on the floor, threatened with death and, ultimately, driven by lack of water to the extreme measure of drinking their own urine. When the assault that freed them finally came, it would be so catastrophic that it left 11 Russian soldiers and 344 hostages dead.[2] At least 188 of the dead were children; in addition, 610 hostages were wounded, 356 of these children. The school was in ruins.[3]

Once inside the gym, the terrorists began to rig a series of bombs and booby traps. Two wires were run from the basketball hoops at either side of the hall. Small explosive charges were affixed to the wires and hoops. The walls and entrances were also booby-trapped, and two large plastic containers filled with explosives were put in the middle of the floor.[4] The explosive devices were packed with nuts, bolts, ball bearings, and nails to ensure the most possible damage if they detonated. The entire system was connected to a battery that would provide the power needed to detonate it. A terrorist stood on a trigger, which had to be kept continuously depressed in order to prevent detonation. If this terrorist lifted his foot, the bombs would explode.[5]

At one point during the ordeal, the adult men were assembled and then herded into a separate room. The two veiled women wearing the suicide vests, who may have been having second thoughts about the taking of so many children as hostages, appeared. The other terrorists left the room. Moments later both women detonated their vests, killing themselves and most of the male hostages. Those men that survived were forced to collect the bodies of their dead comrades and throw them out a window.[6]

It is the stuff of nightmares, but in Russia, it had become a horrible, recurring dream.

In May 1994, six terrorists armed with guns and grenades took over a school bus filled with students, teachers, and parents.[7]

In July 1994, four terrorists seized another bus holding forty-two children and adults.

In 1995, 1,000 hospital patients were held hostage in the Russian city of Budyonnovsk, near the border with Chechnya, a largely Muslim republic in the Caucasus. Russian troops were ultimately forced to storm the hospital. Twice. In the end, 100 civilians were killed.[8]

In 1996, Islamic militants seized control of a hospital in Dagestan. They left only after being granted "safe passage" out of Russia.

In October of 2002, fifty armed Chechen rebels seized a theater in the capital city of Moscow and held it for three days, taking 800 people hostage. The entrances to the theater were booby-trapped, and a large explosive device was rigged in the center of the theater. Hostages were required to use the orchestra pit of the theater as a latrine. Using an unknown gas, Russian Special Forces ultimately assaulted the theater. More than 600 people were rescued; 129 hostages died. All of the terrorists were killed by Russian forces.[9]

The scope of some of the attacks that have taken place in Russia may well be significantly beyond that which can be expected in the United States. It is probably unlikely that any terrorist group, for example, could actually assemble a team of forty armed men and women on U.S. soil unless security and social conditions radically change at some point in the future. There have, however, been other similar types of attacks elsewhere in the world which involved much smaller numbers of attackers, the results of which were also horrific.

On May 29, 2004, four Al-Qaeda terrorists attacked a series of walled compounds in Khobar, Saudi Arabia. Located on these compounds were residences and offices occupied by foreigners working in the oil industry in Saudi Arabia. Khobar is located in the Eastern Province of Saudi Arabia, which is the hub of the nation's vital oil sector.

Subsequent to this operation, the leader of the cell that attacked Khobar, Turki Moteiri, gave an interview to Al-Qaeda's Internet magazine, *Sawt al-Jihad,* published on June 15, 2004. In this interview, Moteiri laid out the planning for the attack and provided a chronology of how it proceeded.

Moteiri said the attack was originally conceived as a suicide bombing operation. Moteiri and his three cell members—Nemer al-Baqmi, Hussain, and Nader—drove a car rigged with explosives to the Khobar Petroleum Center compound on the morning of

May 29, 2004, and, after seeing that there was no significant security at the compound, decided to abandon the car and proceed on an indiscriminate killing mission. The objective then changed from suicide bombing to hostage-taking and the execution of "unbelievers."[10]

After breaking through one of the compound gates and killing at least one guard, the terrorist team encountered an executive of the Arab Oil Investment Company, a subsidiary of the U.S. company, Halliburton. They killed him, dragged his corpse around the compound, and then set about systematically hunting down Westerners and other "unbelievers" and executing them.

The attackers then drove to a second complex, where they encountered similarly light security. Methodically, they moved from office to office, rounding up individuals, identifying and killing non-Muslims, and delivering lectures on Islam as they went. After forcing one Italian to speak to *Al Jazeera,* the Qatar-based Arabic satellite TV network, and demand that Italian troops leave Iraq, they then executed him.

Finally, the terrorist team moved on to the heavily fortified Oasis Resort, a complex of villas, a hotel, restaurants, and spas. Here they took time to have a good meal and get some rest. Then, refreshed, they rounded up some more "unbelievers" and "slaughtered" them.[11] The first significant Saudi security forces began to arrive at the compound in response to the attack five hours after the event had begun.

In the end, having repelled a rescue attempt by security forces and having killed the leader of the assault team, remaining in control of the hotel overnight, the terrorists left the hotel via a back exit. They were only detected outside of the hotel in the compound. Feeble attempts by the security forces to block their path were defeated, and the entire terrorist team escaped. A total of twenty-two people had been killed.[12] When Saudi government forces finally retook the hotel hours later, the terrorists were miles away, watching the event on television.

Most recently, we have seen a similar type of attack in India's commercial capital, Mumbai. On November 26, 2008, there were a series of coordinated attacks across the city by members of the Pakistani terrorist group, Lashkar-e-Taiba. Using automatic weapons and grenades, these attackers killed 173 people and wounded another 308. It took three days for responding security forces to resolve the incident and kill or capture all the members of the assault team.[13]

The targets chosen for the attack included the Shivaji Terminus, a major railway station; the Oberoi Trident Hotel; the Taj Mahal Palace Hotel, the Leopold Cafe; the Cama Hospital; and the Orthodox Jewish Nariman House. There was also an explosion at the Mazagaon docks and in a taxi at Vile Parle.[14]

The team consisted of a total of ten terrorists. They were all young men, dressed in Western clothing. Most of them wore T-shirts and jeans. By all accounts, they smiled as they worked their way through the various targets, shooting and killing.

A review of accounts of the attack by survivors is instructive in that it brings home vividly not only the mind-set of the attackers, but also the sheer horror that an attack of this type can inspire. It is, after all, the objective of a terrorist to "terrorize." He does not simply want to kill. He wants to kill in as horrible and chilling a fashion as possible. His goal is not so much the physical destruction of your forces or your assets as it is the destruction of your will to resist.

The Leopold Cafe, a popular site for foreigners, writers, and artists close to the Taj Mahal Palace Hotel, came under attack shortly after 9:00 p.m. Five men armed with AK-47s and grenades entered the establishment and opened fire. There was no prelude, and no attempt to discriminate between Muslims and non-Muslims.

"All of a sudden there was automatic gunfire. The whole place fell apart. It was tremendously loud. My husband and I were hit, as were lots of people," said Diane Murphy, fifty-eight, from Northumberland, England, who was shot in the foot. Her husband Michael, fifty-nine, was shot in the ribs and hospitalized in intensive care after the attack. Those not killed in the initial assault ran and hid in the kitchen and neighboring rooms. Some were able to escape by ripping down curtains to make crude ropes, and then climbing out windows. Many others were not so lucky.[15]

Shortly after this attack, the assault on the railway station began. Terrorists shot up the reservation counter in the station, killed the exclusively Indian passengers inside the building at will, and then moved on unmolested. Fifty-three people were killed at this location.[16] A worker at a cafe in the station, Pappu Mishra, commented on the demeanor of the attackers. "Their audaciousness was breathtaking," he said. "One man loaded the magazine into the gun, the other kept shooting. They appeared calm and composed. They were not in the slightest hurry. They didn't seem to be afraid at all."

By 9:30 p.m., another element of the attacking terrorist team was inside the Taj Hotel. Security arrangements in place at this location apparently posed no obstacle to the attackers. The first notice of a problem was the beginning of gunfire inside the hotel.

"I was in the main lobby and there was all of a sudden a lot of firing outside," said Sajjad Karim, a European parliamentarian in Mumbai for a meeting. "A gunman appeared in front of us, carrying machine gun–type weapons. And he just started firing at us . . . I just turned and ran in the opposite direction."

Inside the hotel, guests ran and hid anywhere they could. Some took refuge in their rooms. Some made improvised escape ropes and climbed out of hotel windows to safety. In one hotel restaurant, guests huddled under tables hoping to escape detection. Throughout the hotel echoed the sounds of gunfire and explosions. Parts of the building began to burn. Meanwhile, a similar attack had already begun in the Oberoi Trident Hotel. It would take until a little before 9:00 the next morning for security forces to retake the Taj Hotel.[17]

In the aftermath of the attack, the Indian press leveled significant criticism at the reaction of the security forces. Unlike in Saudi Arabia, where a tightly controlled press was unable to really dissect the inept response to the Khobar attack, in India, unrestrained journalists had the freedom to really dig into the details of what had transpired. One such journalist was Padma Rao-Sundarji; I will draw extensively on her account of the attack hereafter.[18]

At the railway station where so many individuals were killed, there are no metal detectors, and only a small number of policemen. These policemen, as is common in India, carried bamboo canes, known as lathi, rather than handguns. These canes are generally used for crowd control. Most of these officers fled as soon as the shooting started. In the entire state of Maharashtra, where Mumbai is located, there are 180,000 policemen, but only 2,221 weapons, of which a grand total of 577 are located in Mumbai itself, a city of 13 million people. The railway special police are armed, but they have to share one weapon for every two officers.

Similarly, at Nariman House, which is Mumbai's Jewish Center, there were no metal detectors or armed guards. It took Indian security forces three days to retake this location from the terrorists who occupied it.

The commandos who ultimately defeated the terrorist attack on Mumbai were drawn from a unit known popularly as the "Black Cats." This is a military unit, not part of the police forces of the country. The Black Cats are headquartered in Gurgaon, south of New Delhi, the nation's capital, and a vast distance from Mumbai. This unit has no dedicated air transport, so in this case an aircraft had to be identified and brought from elsewhere in the country to provide transportation. As a result, it was five hours from the time the attacks had begun before the Black Cats had even left their base for the trip to Mumbai.

The commandos landed in Mumbai a little after 5:00 a.m. the day after the attacks had begun. They were then transported by bus from the airport to downtown Mumbai. By the time they were in position to respond, a full ten hours had elapsed since the shooting had started in the Leopold Cafe.[19]

As of the date of this writing, we have yet to experience a terrorist attack of this kind on U.S. soil. Unfortunately, however, we have experienced at least one incident which provides an unsettling parallel: the attack on Columbine High School in 1999. This was an attack by two high school students on the institution where they were enrolled. Originally conceived primarily as a bombing, it developed into a shooting rampage when the devices the pair had built for the purpose failed to detonate.[20]

At the time the attack took place, there was a full-time sheriff's deputy assigned to the school. This individual engaged the two attackers in a gunfight as they first approached the school. Once the two students had shot their way past him, he did not pursue but remained outside to administer first aid to another student who had been shot.

Once inside the school, the attackers began to work their way through the building, looking for victims. Police officers began to respond almost immediately, but the first members of the local SWAT team did not enter the building until about twenty minutes after the shooting. Even then, rather than seek out the killers, they began to methodically clear the school and evacuate the students inside. Over the next several hours, in fact, police officers continued this procedure, going from classroom to classroom, frisking students, searching closets, and taking students out of the building. This was all done according to the doctrine by which these officers had been trained, which emphasized containment of the situation.

Meanwhile, inside the school, the two shooters proceeded unmolested to kill their fellow students. Throughout most of this time period, the two were upstairs in the school library, where they alternated between taunting and executing students trapped in the room with them. When the shooting began, teacher Patti Nielson, who was in the library, called 911. She was told by the operator to keep the students inside the room and wait for the police. This left these individuals trapped when the two killers arrived and began to slowly murder them one by one.

Columbine High School sits on the side of a hill, so that the library, which is on the second floor, can be directly accessed from the ground. In fact, the library is located about 30 feet down a short hallway from an exit door. A large number of police officers were located outside this exit door the entire time that the two killers were methodically committing mass murder only a few seconds away. No attempt was made to enter the building via this doorway; rather, the officers at this location were directed to maintain containment and allow the SWAT team inside to slowly clear the building.

Ultimately, sometime around 12:30 p.m., the two killers killed themselves. Despite this, and the obvious accompanying cessation of shooting, it took several more hours for police officers to make it to the library. During this time period, in a nearby classroom, at least one teacher bled to death from gunshot wounds.[21]

After the Columbine High School massacre, a great deal of discussion took place within the law enforcement community, and, more specifically, among the members of various SWAT teams across the nation. The doctrine that was followed at Columbine, which emphasized containment, was designed for a situation in which hostages were being held and negotiation was at least possible. It worked well for these kinds of events. In a situation such as Columbine, however, which involved what law enforcement personnel refer to as "active shooters," it ensured that by the time a SWAT team ever confronted the perpetrators, a great number of people would have already died.

What evolved as a result of this discussion was an approach which called for a more-aggressive response, primarily built around something called the QUAD (Quick Action Deployment) concept. I am not a SWAT expert, and I will not dwell on the technical aspects of this approach here, but, at its core, this doctrine is pretty simple. If there is a shooting incident, officers respond to the scene. Assuming shooting is ongoing, as soon as there are four officers on-site, they enter the scene, seek out the shooters, and kill or apprehend them. They do not stop to deal with the wounded. They do not focus on evacuation. They find the "bad guys" and they stop the killing. Everything else can wait.[22]

In terms of dealing with "active shooter" situations and preparing for possible terrorist attacks on U.S. soil of the types I outlined at the beginning of this chapter, this move has been a dramatic step forward. As noted by individuals much more qualified than I am on the topic of SWAT tactics, however, it may not have taken us quite far enough.

The tactics currently being taught to most SWAT Teams and police forces nationwide no longer emphasize containment and control to the degree that they did at the time of Columbine.[23] We understand now that we may have to act much more quickly to stop the killing. We are now, however, effectively training for a repetition of the Columbine massacre. We are working to prepare to confront two shooters who are likely poorly trained, poorly armed, and acting without any kind of detailed tactical plan as to how they intend to proceed.[24]

It is better than nothing, but it is not enough.

Now, by this point in the narrative, those readers who are trained in SWAT tactics and law enforcement are probably screaming in frustration at my muddling of all sorts of categories of attacks. Columbine was an "active shooter" situation, involving attackers moving through an area, killing as they went. Beslan was a huge hostage-taking incident. These are not the same thing. The number of attackers involved and the weapons used were dramatically different. There are all sorts of distinctions to be made that I am simply glossing over.

These are valid points. As I noted earlier, I am not a SWAT expert. I have gone through a fair amount of weapons training in my time, and done my share of exercises in shoot houses. They were all focused on defensive maneuvers—how to extricate yourself from a meeting gone bad, for example—and not on assaulting an occupied structure.

My objective here is not to categorize attacks or organize them into some sort of classification system for future study. It is to take a look at these kinds of attacks—where a number of armed terrorists assault an objective rather than use explosives—from the perspective of the terrorists themselves. Looked at in that light, I believe that all of the incidents share certain key characteristics and tell us a great deal about how we have to respond.

I said earlier that terrorists want to terrorize. As simplistic as that sounds, it bears further exploration. Terrorists want to horrify you. They want to chill you. They want to demoralize you. They do not believe that they can defeat you militarily by destroying your infrastructure, bankrupting your treasury, and crushing your armed forces. They believe that they can make the psychological pain of continued resistance so great that you will quit.

They want to break your will.

As a terrorist, if I walk up to an American diplomat on the street somewhere in the Middle East and kill him by shooting him in the face, this is good. If I kidnap him, kill him later, after days of press play, and then dump his body on a downtown street to be found, this is better. The incident is dragged out. More people notice it. Other Westerners have a chance to identify with the victim, to feel his anguish, and to ponder the possibility of their own abduction.

If I kidnap the American, hold him for days, send you videos of him in captivity, and then execute him on camera, this is even better. I can send you the video. I can post it on the Net. The horror will be palpable. Millions of people will hear the screams of the victim and see the terror in his eyes as he is about to die. No one who sees such a thing can possibly be unaffected.

What if I ensure that I do all of the above, and that I also kill the hostage in the most brutal fashion imaginable? What if I kill him slowly? What if I cut off his head rather than shooting him? What if

I use not a sword but a dull knife, and not so much cut off the head as saw it off, so that the victim dies in the most horrible, graphic, painful, protracted way possible?

From my sick, twisted perspective, as one who has decided to play God, this is all so much the better.

From this perspective, then, all of the terrorist attacks described above are part and parcel of the same thing. At Beslan, I would submit, the objective was not the holding of hostages so much as creating leverage in order to secure political concessions. The things the terrorists claimed they wanted, like the withdrawal of all Russian troops from Chechnya, were clearly never going to happen. The objective was to generate terror by doing something so monstrous and striking at something so precious—a nation's children—that they would demoralize their enemy and force it to lose the will to fight. Exactly how the terrorists at Beslan initially envisioned the ending of the incident will always be a matter of conjecture, but, I would suggest that they never had any intention of negotiating a settlement, releasing the hostages, and leaving peacefully. That attack was always going to end in some gruesome fashion, leaving hundreds dead and an empty shell of a school.

Similarly, let us consider Mumbai. Over three days, the terrorists killed a large number of people. That said, significantly more people have been killed by car bombs on numerous occasions around the world. What Mumbai was about was body count, certainly, but even more than that, it was about the horror generated by simultaneous multiple attacks on prominent locations, and then the horrible, slow-motion agony of the resolution of the entire incident. The whole world had an opportunity to watch and absorb the pain, the terror, and the randomness of the event. Individuals in the United States who could not find India on a map could share the suffering of ordinary citizens, wounded and brutalized, desperately trying to climb to safety from the windows of a broken, burning shell of a once-great hotel.

Looking at these kinds of attacks as the terrorist sees them tells us a great deal about what we need to do to prevent such incidents here, and how to respond to them if they do occur. It tells us perhaps even more about what we are not doing.

First, from a defensive perspective, we need to accept that the number of potential targets for such an attack is enormous. Would it be great, from Al-Qaeda's vantage point, to stage an attack on the Mall in Washington, D.C., during a presidential inauguration? Yes, it would, most certainly. Would shooters walking through Times Square on New Year's Eve have an immense impact? Of course. These kinds of "ideal" situations are not required, however. Beslan was an ordinary school in an ordinary town.

The truth is that the United States is filled with venues that would provide lucrative targets for terrorist attacks of the type under discussion. Even confining the discussion to "major" terrorist attacks, and for our purposes leaving aside single, homegrown shooters, if we start looking at major college and professional sports venues, rock concerts, amusement parks, theaters, schools, and the like, we can see rapidly that we are faced with a huge number of potential targets to defend.

In that light, let me confine my comments regarding defensive measures to those which are practical, cost-effective, and achievable. We all know that we are not going to station a platoon of U.S. Marines outside every NFL stadium next week, and there is no point to proposing the impossible. We also are well aware that, exaggerated corporate rhetoric notwithstanding, there is not going to be any cheap, reliable, effective technical solution to this problem anytime soon. Whatever we are going to do is going to have to rely upon proven, available capabilities.

The stadium where the Baltimore Ravens play footfall is not too far north of where I live in Maryland. Let's assume I am the leader of an Al-Qaeda team of six terrorists, which has been sent to attack the stadium during a Ravens game against another NFL team. My objectives are to gain entry to the stadium, to begin killing fans attending the game, to continue killing for as long as I can, and to drag the incident out for the maximum time period possible. I want lots of dead Americans. I want maximum press play. I want everyone in America to come away from the incident feeling terrified, vulnerable, helpless, afraid.

I want to appear from nowhere and strike without mercy. I want images of terrorists, as in Mumbai, appearing unstoppable and unafraid, contrasted with images of helpless Americans being slaughtered like sheep. When the attack is over, I want every person in the United States to feel like such a thing could happen to him or her anytime, anywhere.

In this context, most of the security measures that I have observed at major sporting events, amusement parks, and the like are useless. The Six Flags Park near my home runs metal detectors at the gate, has restrictions on the types of bags that can be carried in, and employs large numbers of screeners at the entrance to ensure compliance with security regulations by the general public. These are pretty typical of the kinds of security measures we see in place around us at venues that attract large crowds of individuals. They are all good things, and I have no doubt that they go a long way toward preventing vandalism and keeping alcohol out of a park filled largely with high school kids during the summer months.

None of these measures mean anything to me as the leader of the terrorist team coming to the park, intent on mass murder. All of your security screeners are just additional victims to me. I am not attempting to sneak into anything. I am coming to attack. You will know that I have arrived, because there will be automatic weapons fire and people will begin to die.

If you really intend to prevent my entry with a security checkpoint, you need to back it up with something that will stop me. This does not mean that you have to build a machine-gun nest at the entrance to your fun park. (This might well detract from the family atmosphere you are attempting to create.) It does not necessarily mean that you have to arm all your security personnel, or even that armed guards have to be visible. I would suggest, however, that somewhere close by you have armed personnel, and that they are ready to engage if and when called upon.

You hear and read a lot of discussion about training of security personnel and how they should be armed in the context of counterterrorism. These are, obviously, important considerations. On many occasions, in Saudi Arabia and elsewhere in the Middle East, heavily armed military and police guards have simply fled when a terrorist attack began. If this is what your security personnel are going to do, and, most importantly, if the terrorists know this, then you have a problem.

By the same token, however, I, as the leader of the terrorist team coming to commit mass murder, am not going to come to your installation to engage in a gunfight. Shooting my way into your park after a protracted engagement and being able to claim credit for killing a handful of security personnel is not what I want. If I think that I am going to get bogged down in an extended effort to neutralize guards at an installation, this may very well be enough to convince me to move on and choose another target.

Looking past the issue of defensive measures to prevent armed attackers from gaining access to a venue such as a stadium, school, or theater, let's talk for a minute about handling the incident as it unfolds on-site. I am not talking here about first aid or first responders. I am talking about how those individuals present at the venue when the attack takes place should react.

I touched briefly above on how SWAT teams were trained to deal with shooting situations pre-Columbine. Allow me to extrapolate from that for a moment, if you will, to a broader philosophy that I think was applied to a whole set of different scenarios in the past, and which continues to linger to some extent today. I am talking about what I would characterize as a policy of nonresistance and passivity.

On 9/11 the hijackers understood that they could seize airliners with minimal displays of force, because they understood the policy in place for dealing with these kinds of situations. Based on past incidents, in which hijackers wished to hold aircraft and passengers and were open to some level of negotiation, this policy stressed that resistance to a hijacking in air was to be avoided. The goal was to get the aircraft safely on the ground where negotiation could begin, and where, if necessary, hostage rescue forces could be brought into play.

Post–9/11, we understand that this is no longer a viable policy. No planeload of passengers anywhere is likely to ever again cooperate with a group of hijackers and allow them to fly the plane where they want. Therefore, for terrorists, the viability of seizing an aircraft using the 9/11 plan ended the moment the passengers of Flight 93 fought back.

The concept of encouraging private citizens not to attempt to help themselves continues to show life in lots of other areas, however. When the school librarian at Columbine called the police and was told not only to remain in place, but also to keep her students with her, she was given about the worst possible advice imaginable. Had she and her charges run for the exit 30 feet away, some of them might have died. It is virtually impossible to believe, however, that whatever happened would have been anywhere near as horrific as what ensued when they elected to remain in place.

So, first and foremost, I would say, when in doubt, do something. Move. If possible, the first reaction should be flight. As the team leader of the group that is coming to kill you, I am not susceptible to pleas for mercy. You can beg and grovel all you want. It may amuse me. It will not deter me.

Run for your life. Do not wait for the police. Do not hope the situation can be resolved without further bloodshed. I am not there to negotiate or to hold you hostage, gain attention for my cause and then release you unharmed. You will not succeed in appealing to my humanity, because I am so warped and twisted by hate and radicalism that I am barely human anymore, anyway. Flee.

By the same logic, if the ultimate horror befalls you, and you find yourself trapped and cannot escape, fight back. In the library at Columbine, students cowered under desks and tables, begging and pleading for their lives, while the murderers taunted them and shot them one by one. The victims were children, and they were terrified. The fear they felt was understandable. The fact remains that had they, as a group, reacted immediately by rushing the two assailants, some of them would have died, but not nearly as many as were ultimately killed. And once the attackers were subdued, even those who had been shot could have been rushed to emergency care and might have survived. By electing not to resist, all the students did was ensure their own deaths.

Equally important is the impact this kind of psychological issue has on the terrorist planning process. If I believe, as the leader of a band of mass murderers that is attacking M & T Stadium in Baltimore, that I am going to move freely through a crowded stadium shooting defenseless men, women, and children at will while the whole world watches on CNN, then, in my diseased mind, I have what appears to be a great opportunity to strike a blow against America and its allies. On the other hand, if I believe that I am going to get off a few shots, kill a handful of people, and then, like as not, get stomped into a greasy spot on the stadium floor by several hundred very angry Ravens fans, I am going to start thinking of another plan. I am not looking for a fair fight. I am looking for a bloodbath.

We are engaged in a worldwide struggle. Our opponents in this "war" are barbaric and without mercy. Tactics we developed for dealing with terrorists bent on holding hostages for political negotiating purposes are of no value in this conflict. We need to understand this, absorb the implications, and act accordingly. It is not nice or comforting to contemplate. It is reality.

Our citizenry needs to understand this new reality. We need to stop avoiding a national discussion on the topic. We may want to pretend that we can put in place a system which would guarantee that the average man or woman will never actually have to act in his or her own defense. Unfortunately, no matter how much we wish this were true, it is not. If and when Beslan comes to America, the actions of common citizens in the first moments of the attack may well determine their fate.

These same lessons must be absorbed in regard to SWAT and law enforcement tactics. Saying containment is not the goal and that we will assemble a certain minimum force and then neutralize the shooters is a good first step. It is only a first step, however, because we need to truly absorb the implications of the threat we are facing, and understand that we are now faced with something that is absolutely, qualitatively different from what we have ever dealt with before on our own soil.

Everybody in the world these days is talking about the "war" on terror. I have very mixed feelings about the use of this term, because while in some ways it illuminates, in others it invites people to jump to a lot of false conclusions about the nature of the struggle in which we are engaged, and how to define victory. Too many people start thinking about World War II, body counts, fixed battles and surrenders on the decks of battleships. None of these things really apply to a shadowy, multidimensional conflict being contested on political, military, and economic levels.

What the use of the term war does do, however, is remind us that when it comes to attacks of the kind we are discussing here, in essence, we are in combat. This is not a police action in the classic sense. We are not dealing with criminals intent on monetary gain. We are not dealing with an emotionally disturbed individual who has snapped under the pressure of unknown stressors. We are dealing with cold, calculating, trained killers who are bent on inflicting the maximum number of casualties—not on our military forces, but on our civilian population. If we are to defeat them, we need to prevent that. We need to frustrate them in the achievement of their objective.

This psychological dimension was perhaps best encapsulated by John Giduck, an expert on the Beslan siege and SWAT tactics as follows.

"When confronting an international terrorist siege, American police have to recognize that they will no longer be peace officers administering the law to a civilian population, but soldiers in a battle against trained and combat-experienced enemy combatants. It will be a war, not a crime scene, and they will have to be ready to fight it as a war."[25]

So, if we assemble a team outside and go into the building or stadium targeted, hunt down the killers, and eliminate them, that is a great thing. If while we are assembling our team, the killers murder 100 innocent persons, no matter how high-speed our tactics and how light our losses among law enforcement personnel, we have failed. The terrorists may be dead, but they have won, nonetheless.

By the same token, if our whole concept of response is based around the idea that four officers with their service weapons are going to be sufficient to handle the situation, we may be in for a very rude awakening. What we may find when these officers arrive is that they are inadequate in every possible way to confront the attack that is unfolding. They will need not just sidearms, but long guns, bulletproof vests, and lots of ammunition. They will also need to have been trained to use all of this gear and to immediately shift from a law enforcement mode to one in which they are acting much like infantrymen in combat.

What I am saying is that we have to completely redefine the way we think about responding to such possible attacks, and accept that there is not going to be a clean, clinical way in which to handle them. If I am an armed security guard at a sporting facility and such an attack occurs, while everyone else in the place is heading for the exits, I am going to have to draw my weapon and start shooting. If I am the first cop on the scene, and SWAT is still twenty minutes away, I am going to have to make the terrorist with the AK-47 stop murdering children, hunker down behind a wall, and start trying to figure out how to kill me. I do not have to be John Wayne. I *do* have to fight back, and, as soon as I do, and as soon as that terrorist starts having to devote his energies to engaging me, I have frustrated his plans and I am on my way to victory.

I have no illusions about the implications of such an approach. Plain and simple, it means we are going to be asking security personnel and beat cops to go to war. When and if they do, many of them will die. They are not ciphers. They are real people, with spouses and children and lives.

In that connection, however, a couple of points need to be emphasized: First, we have no choice. We may lose personnel, but we will save hundreds of lives. Every second that a terrorist team is trying to work its way around to get a clean shot at stadium security is that much more time for innocent civilians to escape and for reaction forces to arrive.

Second, we must remember that the psychological dimension is key. As a terrorist team leader, I am not coming to attack your facility with the goal of getting into a fight with security personnel or local cops and killing them. I know how little time I have. I understand the window that exists in which I can achieve my objective. Just as I will not now try to seize control on an airliner with a box cutter, because I know what the reaction will be, I will not try to carry out a massacre at a public site when I know I am going to be immediately forced into a firefight with on-site security personnel. I will move on. I will come up with another plan.

A few words on negotiation.

If you are talking to the Islamic radicals holding the student body of the local high school hostage, because you are stalling for time, fine.

If you are talking to them because you are trying to gather intelligence on their numbers, their level of sophistication, their distribution within the school, fine.

If you are talking to them and engaging in negotiations with them because you honestly believe you can talk them into surrendering, or into reaching some sort of accommodation, you are hopelessly delusional. People are going to die because you do not understand what you are facing.

Years ago Denzel Washington made a movie called *The Siege,* about a series of attacks by Islamic radicals on New York City. Some of the details on intelligence work in the film were dead-on. Others were silly. There is one scene in that picture, however, which I think captures the essence of what I am trying to convey.

In the film, Islamic terrorists have seized control of a city bus and are holding the passengers hostage on a street in Manhattan. Denzel arrives, accompanied by a CIA officer, and begins to attempt to negotiate. Almost immediately thereafter, news helicopters begin to arrive and circle the site, and other reporters show up on the ground. The CIA officer counsels Denzel to break off negotiations and assault the bus immediately. She says that she understands the terrorists have no intention of negotiating. They seized the bus to attract attention. Now that the press has arrived and cameras are rolling, they are going to kill all the passengers no matter what. The only hope is to try to kill the terrorists before they can act.

Denzel does not listen. He approaches the bus. Seconds later the vehicle explodes. Everyone is killed except Denzel, who escapes with minor injuries. (He is the star of the show, after all.)

It's a movie. I don't want to make more out of it than it is. Still, it goes to the essence of what I am talking about. If an Al-Qaeda team comes to America, occupies a high school or theater or stadium, holds hundreds or thousands hostage, and opens communication, they are not looking for dialogue. They are looking for attention, and the chance to utilize that attention to amplify the amount of terror they can create. Talk to them if you must while you get your act together, and then kill them all as quickly and efficiently as possible. Any other course of action is going to mean that a whole lot of innocent people are going to die.

Let me make some comments about SWAT teams and hostage-rescue forces above the local level.

We have in this country some very fine individuals who serve in organizations like the FBI's Hostage Rescue Team (HRT) and Delta Force. They are infinitely more capable than any terrorist team will ever be. They have the capacity to bring to the fight larger numbers and more firepower than any local SWAT team will ever muster.

It does not matter.

They are never going to arrive on the scene of a terrorist attack of the type we are discussing in time to prevent massive loss of life. The country is too big, and there are too few operators to cover it. If they arrive on-site in numbers and are ready to move within twenty-four hours, that would be a miracle, and during that time period, terrorists may well have killed hundreds of innocent people.

The task of handling the immediate response to a Mumbai-style attack here is going to fall to local law enforcement. They need to prepare for it, and the federal government needs to help them. Of all the national training scenarios Homeland Security has developed, none of them deals with a Mumbai- or Beslan-style attack. This should change, and money and resources should flow accordingly.

There are a number of very intelligent and very capable individuals like Frank Borelli and John Giduck working this problem as we speak. Borelli has devoted his life to preparing law enforcement officers to confront "fedayeen" attacks, and Giduck has become perhaps the world's preeminent expert on Beslan and its implications. They have called for a range of measures, from training small local SWAT teams to work together in much larger, regional formations, to the employment of significantly more-aggressive combat techniques than SWAT teams typically employ. Leaving aside for a moment debates regarding various smaller issues concerning armament, tactical formations, and equipment, my take would be that we ought to be doing all of the things that are being suggested, and we ought to be doing them as fast as we can.

The unfortunate reality is that at some point in the not-too-distant future, some horrific event on a par with Mumbai, Khobar, or Beslan is going to play out here, and the shooters are not going to be two depressed, lost, and suicidal teenagers looking to get even with their peers. The shooters are going to be a half-dozen or a dozen trained, motivated, and disciplined fanatics employing automatic weapons to commit mass murder. God help us if we find ourselves in the middle of such a nightmare, trying to sort out a response while people are already dying.

CHAPTER FOUR
It Has Happened Before

ON THE NIGHT OF DECEMBER 2, 1984, A MASSIVE LEAK OF TOXIC gases from the Union Carbide factory in Bhopal, India, killed between 16,000 and 30,000 people and injured around 500,000 others.[1]

Think about that for a moment. Think about the scale of that.

This is not something that might happen somewhere in the United States, hold our attention for a few hours, and then fade from the national consciousness. Such a disaster in Washington, D.C., would kill the city. Morgues and hospitals would be buried in bodies and patients. We would have to mobilize on a national scale, and the impact would be felt for a generation. The District would have to be evacuated. It would be a ghost town.

And, to make such a thing happen in a major city would require a terrorist team to bring with them nothing more than a certain measure of training and a commitment to their cause. The weapons are already here.

The specific gas which leaked in Bhopal was called methyl isocyanate (MIC). This is a very dangerous substance. When exposed to MIC, test animals die with frightening rapidity. The substance destroys the respiratory system, causes permanent blindness, and burns the skin.[2] This substance is manufactured in a number of different locations within the United States of America, most of them in proximity to large urban areas.

The incident in Bhopal was not the result of a terrorist attack or sabotage. It was an industrial accident that occurred in a chemical plant designed and operated by Union Carbide, a United States corporation. At the time of the accident in Bhopal, the Union Carbide plant there was not even operating. There was an exothermic reaction in the MIC storage tanks, the result of negligent maintenance and safety procedures, and two geysers of MIC gas erupted from the facility. The released chemical agent formed an initial cloud 100 yards wide. The MIC, heavier than air, then rolled into populated areas with other released chemicals, such as phosgene and hydrocyanic acid drifting above it.[3]

Although I cited figures above for the number of dead, these are just estimates. No one will ever know exactly how many died because the count was stopped arbitrarily at 1,754. Most of the dead were inhabitants of slums around the plant. A large number were displaced peasants from surrounding areas. They had no fixed addresses. They appeared on no rolls. Often entire families were wiped out, so there was not even anyone left behind to petition for restitution or to claim a body from the morgue. Many bodies ended up in the Narmada River, which runs through Bhopal, and ultimately washed to sea. Ships offshore subsequently noted corpses floating as far as hundreds of miles from land.[4]

Another half million Bhopalis suffered effects that were not immediately fatal from the toxic cloud. These included damage to the eyes, lungs, brain, muscles, joints, liver, and kidneys, as well as the reproductive, nervous, and immune systems. Many victims suffered neurological attacks that caused convulsions, paralysis, and coma.[5]

Today there remain more than 150,000 people who are chronically affected by the tragedy. Some ten to fifteen die every month. Symptoms, such as breathing difficulties, persistent coughs, ulcerations of the cornea, early-onset cataracts, anorexia, recurrent fevers, burning of the skin, weakness, and depression still manifest themselves. Cancer and tuberculosis rates are much higher than normal. Large numbers of women suffer from chronic gynecological disorders, and many children show retarded growth and development.[6]

MIC is far from the only dangerous chemical manufactured or stored in ordinary commercial chemical facilities. Phosgene, which is a very common substance used widely in the manufacture of fertilizers, was used as a military chemical agent in World War I, and killed thousands of soldiers. Hydrogen cyanide, which is used in many medicines, is the gas of choice in those states which still execute condemned men in gas chambers.[7] Chlorine gas, which is used for hundreds of purposes, from water purification to the manufacture of paint additives, is another World War I–era chemical agent and has been the substance of choice for Iraqi insurgents who use it to detonate chemical VBIEDs in that nation.

The federal government requires chemical facilities in the United States to submit Risk Management Plans (RMPs) measuring things like the number of individuals who are at risk of death or serious injury in the event of a toxic gas release. There are in excess of 13,000 such facilities currently submitting RMPs to the Environmental Protection Agency per this requirement. Of these, 101 are classified as constituting the highest hazards. Eighty million Americans in thirty states live within the danger zones surrounding these facilities.

Twelve million Americans live within range of a toxic gas release from the Kuehne Chemical Plant in South Kearny, New Jersey, alone.[8] This includes all of Manhattan, Brooklyn, Jersey City, Bayonne, and Newark, among other areas.[9] Thirteen separate Los Angeles–area chemical plants each put a million people at risk in the event of a toxic gas release.[10]

The General Chemical Bay Point chemical plant just outside of San Francisco is one of the most dangerous plants in the country. It produces high-purity hydrofluoric acid for use in California's large semiconductor and silicon manufacturing industries. The concentration of the acid produced is from 49 to 70 percent. Acid at a concentration above 50 percent poses a grave danger of forming a toxic gas plume in the event of an accidental or deliberate release. There are 2.1 million people living within range of such a toxic gas release from this plant.[11]

This pattern is repeated across the country. Tens of millions of Americans live surrounded by what are, from a terrorist perspective, giant, prepositioned chemical weapons. There is no need to construct a weapon and design some mechanism for bringing it onto our soil. It is not even necessary to attempt to manufacture some deadly agent at a covert site inside the United States. The agents exist already. They exist in mass quantities, and they are already in position in proximity to major population centers. All that is required is to set them off.

The dangers posed by chemical plants to surrounding areas are, in fact, significant enough that they have made it into formal Department of Homeland Security planning. The Department of Homeland Security and the White House Homeland Security Council have developed fifteen planning scenarios for use by federal, state, and local authorities in preparing to handle terrorist attacks and natural disasters. These scenarios are intended to represent those incidents judged most likely to occur. Homeland Security training scenario number eight posits an attack on a chemical facility and the deliberate rupturing of a chlorine tank at a commercial facility.[12]

According to the scenario constructed by the Department of Homeland Security, this attack would produce 17,550 fatalities, 10,000 severe injuries, and hospitalize 100,000 persons. In excess of 500,000 persons would have to be evacuated from the contaminated area. All of this is based on the assumption that the terrorist group would succeed in punching a single 16-inch-diameter hole in a standard 60,000-gallon chlorine tank pressurized to 250 pounds per inch. In fact, chlorine is routinely stored in tanks as large as 120,000 gallons in the United States, and many industrial facilities might have a number of tanks this size on-site.

Even assuming that only a single 60,000-gallon tank is ruptured, the vapor cloud would likely reach for 25 miles.

Even without terrorist action, industrial accidents at these facilities are relatively common and threaten surrounding communities. On August 28, 2008, there was an explosion at the Bayer CropScience plant in Institute, West Virginia, about a fifteen-minute drive west of the state capital, Charleston. The explosion produced a fireball several hundred feet in height, killed one worker, and injured a second. Several hours passed before local emergency responders were even advised of the true nature of the incident. Had there been a true release of gas, as took place in Bhopal, thousands of individuals would have lost their lives during those hours.[13] The campus of West Virginia State University sits immediately adjacent to the plant and is separated from it by nothing more than a chain-link fence.

The Institute plant produces MIC, the same substance that was released in Bhopal. Bayer reports to EPA indicate that at any one time, it stores between 100,000 and 999,999 pounds of MIC. Using the higher figure, this is twenty times what was released in Bhopal. The Institute plant was designed and built by Union Carbide, the same company that built the Bhopal plant.

This facility also manufactures phosgene. According to Bayer, anywhere from 5 to 50 tons of this chemical agent are on-site at any given time.[14]

Issues at the Institute plant are not uncommon, nor are they exclusively a recent phenomenon. In fact, incidents of this type have occurred consistently over the years.

August 11, 1985: At least 135 people sought treatment at area hospitals after a leak of aldicarb oxime and four other chemicals from the plant, then owned by Union Carbide.

May 20, 1993: Over a thousand local residents are ordered to shelter in their homes after a release of chlorine gas.

August 18, 1994: Thousands of people living around the plant are ordered to shelter in their homes after an accident involving cyanide gas.

December 13, 1994: Sulfur dichloride leaks from the plant.

February 15, 1996: A fire involving the chemical toluene causes widespread shelter-in-place orders.

July 28, 1997: A small quantity of MIC is released from the plant.

October 15, 1999: Residents living within 2 miles of the plant are ordered to shelter in place after a phosgene leak.

August 13, 2001: A chloroform leak results in medical treatment for ten workers.

November 17–21, 2007: State and federal agencies receive complaints of chemical odors from throughout the area surrounding the plant.

December 28, 2007: Release of unidentified gas into surrounding residential areas.[15]

In 1994, the chemical industry disclosed publicly their evaluation of the danger that would be posed by a catastrophic release of 253,600 pounds of MIC from the Institute plant. According to that report, the result would be the creation of a toxic plume that would drift eastward, enveloping the entire city of Charleston, West Virginia, which at the time had a population of roughly 250,000 persons. Concentrations of the chemical would be at a level which would be fatal if exposure lasted one hour.[16]

Accidents involving chemical facilities are not confined to India or the depths of the Kanawha Valley in West Virginia. They occur all over the country, and they happen all the time. What follows is a tiny sampling.

On May 5, 2008, it was discovered that someone had stolen the brass valve out of the bottom of a storage tank at the Reaction Products facility in Contra Costa County, California. This theft apparently occurred over the weekend when the site was left unsecured. Three thousand gallons of toluene were released, and residents in the area were ordered to shelter in place. Fortunately, the toluene did not ignite, or the consequences of exposure to the resulting vapor would have been severe.[17] Toluene is a highly flammable substance. Respiratory exposure to moderate amounts will produce drowsiness, fatigue, and headaches. Exposure to higher concentrations can cause unconsciousness and death.[18]

In early October 2006, 17,000 people were instructed to evacuate from their homes in the suburbs of Raleigh, North Carolina, after a fire in a hazardous waste plant created a giant cloud of chlorine gas. At least forty-one persons were taken to emergency rooms for treatment.[19]

On October 31, 2004, a release of hydrogen sulfide gas from the ConocoPhillips facility in Contra Costa County, California, resulted in the sounding of sirens and an order to residents of the towns of Crockett and Rodeo to shelter in place.

At the Honeywell Facility in Baton Rouge, Louisiana, on July 20, 2003, 8 plant workers were hospitalized, and 600 people living within a mile of the plant were evacuated following a release of chlorine gas. Nine days later a worker died after exposure to antimony pentachloride. In early August, two workers were hospitalized after a spill of hydrofluoric acid.[20]

On July 9, 2001, an explosion at a Texas oil refinery resulted in the release of a large amount of hydrogen fluoride. A seven-block radius around the facility was evacuated. Once released, this material has the capacity to form a deadly gas cloud that can persist for an extended period of time.[21] Fortunately, in this case such a cloud did not form, but the next time the residents living around the facility may not be so lucky.

All of this is horrific enough. Unfortunately, it is only the beginning of the story.

We have been talking up to this point about a finite number of fixed sites at which dangerous chemicals are made or stored. In fact, the problem is infinitely vaster than that, because all of these materials have to be transported, and most of that movement is accomplished on freight rail lines, crisscrossing the country. We are faced, therefore, not only with the possibility of someone detonating a device at a chemical plant, but also, attacking and rupturing a tanker of chlorine or phosgene or some other deadly material as it sits on railroad tracks many miles away from any chemical facility.

There is little dispute about the magnitude of the problem. In the Government Accountability Office (GAO) report of March 23, 2004, "Rail Security: Some Actions Taken to Enhance Passenger and

Freight Rail Security, but Significant Challenges Remain," the GAO concedes: "The freight rail system's extensive infrastructure crisscrosses the nation and extends beyond our borders to move millions of tons of freight each day . . . The extensiveness of the infrastructure creates an infinite number of targets for terrorists."[22]

Testifying before the United States Senate in 2005, former White House Deputy Homeland Security Advisor Richard Falkenrath stated that chemicals being transported by rail within the United States in fact constituted "the single greatest danger of a potential terrorist attack in our country today."[23]

Hazardous chemicals typically travel on railcars in 90-ton pressurized tanks.[24] This is roughly the size tank discussed earlier in regard to Homeland Security's training scenario number eight. In other words, a single one of these could produce 17,500 fatalities. Many freight trains contain dozens of such cars. The railways transport more than 1.7 million shipments of hazardous materials every year, including 100,000 tank cars filled with toxic gases like chlorine and anhydrous ammonia.[25] Other dangerous materials routinely transported include propane, styrene, ammonium nitrate, and radioactive waste.[26]

As with chemical plants, even absent terrorist attacks, accidents involving hazardous materials are fairly common on freight lines, and graphically demonstrate how vulnerable the system is.

On August 29, 2007, a rail tanker filled with chlorine somehow rolled, unattended, out of a rail yard in Las Vegas, Nevada, and then ran out of control for 20 miles before it was caught and secured. During this 20-mile run, the tanker—filled with enough chlorine to kill well in excess of 10,000 people—ran right through the heart of Las Vegas and several densely populated neighborhoods. Fortunately, despite the fact that the car reached speeds of up to 50 miles an hour on this trip, it did not derail, and none of its dangerous contents were released.[27]

On March 12, 2007, a CSX train carrying propane and other chemicals derailed in Oneida, New York. Twenty-eight of the eighty cars in the train went off the tracks. At least two tankers filled with propane exploded, sending a huge fireball into the sky. Officials evacuated the area within a mile of the incident, including most of downtown Oneida, population 10,000. Four firefighters were exposed to chlorine and had to be decontaminated.[28]

On January 6, 2005, as the result of a switching error, a freight train carrying cars of chlorine collided with cars sitting still on a railroad siding near Graniteville, South Carolina, releasing 11,500 gallons of chlorine. Nine individuals, including the train's engineer, were killed, and thousands had to be evacuated from nearby homes. Hundreds were injured.[29]

On July 18, 2001, a sixty-car train derailed and caught fire while passing through the Howard Street Tunnel in Baltimore, Maryland.[30] Five of the sixty cars on the train were carrying acid, including fluorosilicic acid, a chemical which can cause severe burns to the skin, lungs, and nose. The fire ultimately reached 1500 degrees Fahrenheit and filled the downtown area of the city with clouds of dark, acrid smoke.[31] Many streets in downtown Baltimore were closed for days. Subway service was disrupted as well. Downtown stores were shuttered; an Orioles game was canceled, and classes at the University of Baltimore were halted. It took four days for firefighters to get the blaze under control and return the city to normal.[32]

In 1993, a railroad tank car at General Chemical Corp. in Richmond overheated and released sulfuric acid into the air, sending 24,000 people to doctors' offices and hospitals.[33]

In November 1979, a Canadian Pacific train derailed in Ontario, Canada. Six of the derailed cars contained propane, styrene, chlorine, caustic soda, and fiberglass insulation. These cars ruptured and the materials being transported mixed, producing a dangerous and highly caustic by-product. The explosion that ensued was heard 60 miles away. A quarter of a million persons were evacuated from their homes and not allowed to return to their residences for a week.[34]

This is by no means an exhaustive review of all such accidents anymore than the earlier discussion of chemical plant incidents was a catalog of all such occurrences. The point is to demonstrate the scope of the problem and how frequently, without any terrorist action at all, we dance along the knife's edge between safety and catastrophe. In such an environment, how much would it really take to turn a major U.S. city into Bhopal?

To get a firsthand idea, I reviewed the list of the 101 most dangerous chemical plants in the country and selected one which is within an hour's drive of my house. For our purposes, I will call it the Point Plant. That's not its real name, and anyone who wants to devote about fifteen minutes to research can probably identify the facility in question, but given what I found, it will make me feel a little better not to affirmatively identify this plant in print.

I made my first visit to the Point Plant on November 14, 2008, driving up from my home near Annapolis. The plant sits just outside of Baltimore, Maryland, and in proximity to the entrance to Baltimore Harbor. That first day I drove around for a while, made a few passes by the facility, and then went home. Over the next few months I repeated the procedure on eight separate occasions, sometimes driving around the plant, sometimes walking past it, sometimes putting on my running shoes and jogging along the road in front of the plant entrance. I also took a good look at Google Earth, reviewed maps of the area, and did some standard Internet searches to compile background information. At no point in any of this did I trespass on plant property, nor did I access any information which was not freely available to the public.

What I found was chilling.

The Point Plant uses large chlorine gas in the manufacture of several different industrial products. Based on the information submitted by the plant itself in its Risk Management Plan, some 1.4 million people live within range of a chlorine gas release from the Point Plant.[35] Downtown Baltimore, home to major corporations, five-star hotels, restaurants, and shopping malls is about 5 miles away, well within the area any plume from a major release would cover. The dock areas of the Port of Baltimore, one of the nation's major port facilities, are significantly closer. This is, of course, not to mention the tens of thousands of people who also live in a host of other areas in the vicinity of the Point Plant.

In other words, if you explode this plant, and the wind is right, you kill the city of Baltimore. Forget about nuclear weapons, bubonic plague, or a terrorist group smuggling some highly sophisticated chemical dispersal device across our borders. Everything necessary to destroy a major American city is right here, and remember—this is one of at least 101 such plants in the United States.

The plant is surrounded by a wire fence about 10 feet high. This fence is not topped with razor wire, barbed wire, or any other material that would prevent it being climbed. It is fastened to standard metal poles. At no point in any of my visits to the facility did I ever see a guard anywhere. At no point did I see any security cameras. There may be a limited number at locations I did not observe, but if so, they are too few to allow any real monitoring of the plant's perimeter.

There are several gates through the fence line that allow access to the interior of the facility. These gates are chained shut with a single length of chain and a standard padlock, like something a kid might use on his gym locker. In front of those gates which are not routinely used, a handful of Jersey barriers have been set up.

The plant sits immediately adjacent to a good, paved, level two-lane road that would allow high-speed access by anyone coming to attack it. The main gate used for motor vehicle access to the interior of the plant sits next to this road. This gate, because it is used so frequently, is not blocked by Jersey barriers. It is simply chained shut.

Through this gate at a distance of about 50 meters is the rail siding on which the tanker cars filled with chlorine are parked. I will not give an exact number here. Suffice it to say that there may be a significant number of them at any given time.

As I visited the Point Plant over the months that I reviewed its status, I found it increasingly more difficult to reconcile what I saw with what I knew about the extent of the threat, and what I understood about what had already happened elsewhere in the world. To use the word again, I found it "incomprehensible" that a facility like this, posing the magnitude of danger that it did, could be sitting in this proximity to a major urban area without any meaningful security of any kind.

If I am a terrorist team leader, and I am here in the United States to stage an attack on the Point Plant, I am doing so because I want to detonate the tanks of chlorine there and release a toxic cloud that will drift into downtown Baltimore. I am not interested in seizing or holding the plant. I am not interested in stealth or escape. I have no intention of sneaking in, emplacing a device, and then trying to creep away. I am not looking for the cleanest way to carry out the attack, or the one that will require the least force. I do not care about niceties or procedure or minimizing collateral damage. What sort of response may come later from local law enforcement means nothing to me, as I will be dead—along with many thousands of others by the time anyone can organize a reaction.

I care about the plant only because it houses a large quantity of a material I can use to kill. I want to set that material free. After that, beyond that, I care about nothing at all.

So, what do I need to do? What is required to make this happen?

Well, first of all, I need to do some meteorological research and figure out wind speeds and directions for various times of year. I do not want to blow the plant and watch the cloud of chlorine drift out into the Chesapeake Bay. The wind needs to be heading in the right direction to ensure maximum casualties.

Then, I need to make the call as to the time of day and the day of the week for that attack. Do I want to kill Baltimore during a workday, when the downtown area is filled with workers? Do I want to stage the attack during the middle of rush hour, when I know that the roads are jammed and evacuation is nearly impossible? Do I want to wait until halftime of a football game, when I am assured tens of thousands will be jammed into stadium seats and there will be live television coverage of the carnage that ensues? For me, an individual who lives to cause death and suffering, these will be hard calls.

Once I have made these decisions, though, the planning of the attack itself will be straightforward. I need a large, heavy vehicle, preferably a commercial truck of some kind, such as is commonly available throughout the United States. Then, I need the materials to build a large explosive device inside of that vehicle. For the job in question, we are probably talking about something on a par with Oklahoma City. If there are ten railcars sitting on the tracks when I attack, I want to rupture them all.

Assuming I secure the vehicle, assuming I can build the device, and assuming I can produce a driver who is not afraid to die, I am now virtually guaranteed success. My driver brings the vehicle down the high-speed road to the plant and, in this large, heavy vehicle, he simply goes straight through the wire gate, the single length of chain and the padlock. The vehicle's paint job will suffer. The windshield may be cracked by debris. I doubt the speed of the vehicle will even diminish significantly. Unless someone happens to be staring at the gate at the time of impact, I doubt anyone will even know an attack is under way before the truck traverses the distance to the rail siding and detonates.

Fences and chains and padlocks do not stop trucks jammed with explosives. You might as well have left the gate wide open for all the good it is going to do.

For that matter, Jersey barriers do not stop large, heavy vehicles either. Jersey barriers are designed for highway use and engineered to divide lanes and redirect vehicles traveling at speed back onto the road surface. They were never designed for use as security barriers against VBIEDs. If you have nothing else and you are in a hurry, fine, use them. Then move as fast as you can to put in place something permanent that will actually stop a serious suicide bomber.

In 2008, a tractor-trailer crossing the Chesapeake Bay Bridge in Maryland went into the Jersey barriers lining the side of the bridge at about 45 mph. The truck went straight through the barriers and plummeted into the water below. In commenting on the incident, a Maryland state engineer noted that Jersey barriers were not meant to contain large trucks, and noted that the size of the vehicle, the speed at which it was traveling, and the angle at which it hit the barriers were key factors in the accident.[36]

And, just in case there is any predictability about the use of a heavy vehicle as a VBIED in such attack, I will quote here at some length from a document entitled "Potential Threat to Homeland Using Heavy Transport Vehicles." This report was put out in 2004 as a joint product of the Department of Homeland Security and the Federal Bureau of Investigation. It says in part:

> *This information bulletin is provided to sensitize state and local authorities and the private sector responsible for security of critical infrastructure and key resources to the potential for terrorists to use heavy transport vehicles as vehicle-borne improvised explosive devices (VBIEDs) against a range of attractive targets in the United States.*
>
> *~ Terrorists have repeatedly used heavy vehicles to conduct VBIED attacks in other countries as well as the United States.*
>
> *~ Some terrorist planners consider trucks to be one of the best tools to breach security measures and carry explosives since the U.S. airline industry significantly increased security procedures.*
>
> *~ Terrorist planners have considered how heavy vehicle drivers acquire training and Commercial Driver's Licenses (CDLs) with hazardous material (HAZMAT) endorsement.*
>
> *~ There have been multiple suspicious incidents over the last six months that heighten concern over the potential terrorist acquisition of large trucks and commercial buses.*

~ VBIEDs can be used against symbolic icons and monuments or economic and infrastructure targets.[37]

One might think that it would be very difficult for a bulletin from the Department of Homeland Security to be any clearer. In short, for those people who somehow missed things like the bombings in Beirut twenty-plus years ago, or any of the innumerable attacks since, be advised: It is likely that terrorists will jam as many explosives as they can into a large commercial vehicle, come crashing through your perimeter defenses, and then detonate the explosives contained in the vehicle.

In April 2007, almost six years after 9/11, the Department of Homeland Security (DHS) finally issued its Chemical Facility Anti-Terrorism Standards (CFATS). According to these standards, DHS will require designated high-risk chemical facilities to conduct security vulnerability assessments (SVAs) and then put together site security plans (SSPs), implementing security measures that meet the risk-based performance standards (RBPS) set by the Department.

On October 27, 2008, the DHS issued its draft Risk-Based Performance Standards Guidance, developed to assist covered facilities in complying with the RBPS established under the Chemical Facility Anti-Terrorism Standards. According to DHS, high-risk chemical facilities can use the Guidance to help them get a sense of what types and combinations of security measures and processes are likely to satisfy a given RBPS for a facility, and to help them identify, select, and implement these measures to secure their facility. Also per DHS, the Guidance does not require any covered facility to adopt any specific measure or practice; a covered facility is free to adopt and implement any security measures or practices appropriate to its circumstances, so long as DHS determines that those measures are adequate.[38]

The DHS draft Guidance alone runs almost 200 pages in length, and, as noted above, is not really prescriptive of any specific security or defensive measures. That said, a quick review of its terms shows pretty clearly and quickly that what exists currently at the Point Plant is not even close to satisfactory.

For example, for those facilities considered Tier 1 targets—which would certainly include plants using chlorine in sufficient quantities to threaten the lives of over 1 million people—the Guidance establishes this metric in regard to acceptable perimeter security: "The facility has an extremely vigorous perimeter security and monitoring system that enables the facility to thwart most adversary penetrations and channel personnel and vehicles to access control points, including a perimeter intrusion detection and reporting system with multiple additive detection techniques that can demonstrate an extremely low probability that perimeter penetration would be undetected."[39]

More specifically, in regard to vehicle barriers, the guidance provides this acceptable standard: "Vehicles would have a very low likelihood of accessing the target by force anywhere along the entire perimeter where vehicle attack is a possible mode of attack. To achieve this, a facility could, for example, use aggregate barriers with a minimum of a Department of State (DOS) K8 vehicle barrier rating or equivalent (desired barrier rating can vary based on maximum attainable vehicle speed at the barrier). Examples include: Vehicle deterrence measures such as bollards, landscaping, berms, ditches, drainage, swale, or buried concrete anchors retaining anti-vehicle cable wherever the perimeter is accessible to a vehicle. Entrances equipped with traffic control systems to slow incoming traffic, such as serpentine barriers outside the gate."[40]

Note that Jersey barriers do not appear on the list of acceptable mechanisms for barring vehicle access.

The Guidance goes on. In regard to specific areas of a chemical facility wherein actual chemicals of interest are located, it establishes this metric: "The facility has additional vigorous barriers and systems to secure each restricted area and critical target, including a highly reliable system that continuously monitors each restricted area and critical target, and can demonstrate an extremely high probability that unauthorized adversary actions would be detected and access would be denied to restricted areas or critical targets, such as those containing chemicals of interest."[41]

Nothing at the Point Plant meets this standard. Nothing at the Point Plant meets any of the standards outlined above. A kid looking to sneak into the plant and vandalize something would probably have a hard time of it. Locals looking to wander in and steal tools would also probably be deterred. A team of committed terrorists with the mission of blowing up the plant in an attempt to cause mass casualties in the Baltimore Metro Area would probably not consider any of the measures on-site to pose significant obstacles.

Baltimore also continues to have water treatment plants which use chlorine gas for purification. During my trips to the Point Plant, I took the time to visit a couple of these. I will not identify them here because their lack of any security whatsoever made the Point Plant look like a fortress. I would not consider them safe against even an amateur sabotage attempt. There were no perimeter fences. There were no guards. Any group of individuals prepared to kill the unarmed workers on-site and to cut a padlock or two would have unfettered access to the chlorine tanks, and would be able to do anything they wanted to with them. There is literally nothing to prevent an attack on these facilities, resulting in the release of toxic clouds of chlorine gas inside Baltimore itself.

Over 101,000 people live within the area that would be impacted by a chlorine gas release from the first site I visited.[42] Its proximity to surrounding neighborhoods is so great that there would be no warning time of any kind between a release and the onset of exposure. By that I mean that there is literally less than a couple of hundred meters between the water purification facility and the nearest homes. The first anyone would likely know of an attack would be when people started dying.

The second site was even worse in that it actually threatens the lives of more individuals—130,000 people live within the area that would be impacted by a toxic gas release here. Across America, there are 17 million people who are in danger everyday from sites like this. In Tampa, Florida, there is a single water treatment plant which threatens 1 million lives.[43]

In between trips to the Point Plant and water treatment plants in the Baltimore area, I took time to wander the rail yards in Baltimore to make my own examination of what kinds of security measures were present. It did not take long to determine that, in fact, eight years after 9/11, nothing had been done.

I found literally dozens of rail tankers filled with hydrochloric acid, sulfuric acid, and phosphoric acid sitting on rail sidings every time I visited the port areas of Baltimore. Less frequently, but still commonly, I found railcars filled with chlorine. I stood next to them, walked around them, photographed them, and did pretty much anything I wanted to without interference. Over the course of several months, I was never challenged or questioned. I encountered no fences, and never saw any security presence of any kind.

We have already discussed chlorine at some length, so I will not dwell on its effects again here. It bears considering for a moment, however, just how dangerous some of these other substances are.

Hydrochloric acid is a highly corrosive substance, so much so, in fact, that it has a tendency to literally eat its way through tanks in which it is kept. Small quantities will cause burning and irritation if breathed. Larger quantities can kill. It can also combine with other chemicals and form chlorine gas.[44] A train derailment in Louisiana on May 17, 2008, resulted in a hydrochloric acid leak that necessitated the evacuation of 3,500 persons from their homes for a period of forty-eight hours.[45]

The health effects of sulfuric acid are so horrific that I think it best here to simply quote directly from the Material Safety Data Sheet for the substance:

Inhalation: Inhalation produces damaging effects on the mucous membranes and upper respiratory tract. Symptoms may include irritation of the nose and throat, and labored breathing. May cause lung edema, a medical emergency.

Ingestion: Corrosive. Swallowing can cause severe burns of the mouth, throat, and stomach, leading to death. Can cause sore throat, vomiting, diarrhea. Circulatory collapse with clammy skin, weak and rapid pulse, shallow respirations, and scanty urine may follow ingestion or skin contact. Circulatory shock is often the immediate cause of death.

Skin Contact: Corrosive. Symptoms of redness, pain, and severe burn can occur. Circulatory collapse with clammy skin, weak and rapid pulse, shallow respirations, and scanty urine may follow skin contact or ingestion. Circulatory shock is often the immediate cause of death.

Eye Contact: Corrosive. Contact can cause blurred vision, redness, pain, and severe tissue burns. Can cause blindness.[46]

The release of a relatively small quantity of sulfuric acid fumes from a plant in Pennsylvania caused the evacuation of thousands from their homes in 2008. A former official of the plant from which the leak occurred described sulfuric acid as being "about as dangerous as you can get," stressing its propensity to vaporize, and noting that a "quarter bottle of the stuff would fill a house with fumes in two seconds."[47] A rail tank car contains 90 tons of this "stuff."

Phosphoric acid is another nasty substance. It too can cause irritation, burns, and death. It is not normally a vapor hazard, but can be if heated. One would assume that a terrorist attack accompanied by explosions and resulting large fires might well produce the necessary increase in temperature.[48]

Unfortunately, these kinds of observations are completely consistent with what has been reported across the nation for many years.

In 2006, the *New York Times* reported on a near total lack of any security at a rail yard located 3 miles from downtown Newark and 7 miles from Manhattan. Ninety-ton railcars of deadly chemicals were routinely stored at this location. Gates to the facility were found unlocked and unguarded. Switches were unlocked and accessible to anyone without control of any kind. During a visit to the site, the reporter writing the piece drove alongside a line of railcars holding toxic chemicals for ten minutes without ever being challenged or approached by any railroad employees.[49]

In 2007, the *Pittsburgh Tribune-Review* reported on a massive, nationwide review of chemical plant and chemical railcar security undertaken by Carl Prine, one of its investigative reporters. During his survey, Mr. Prine penetrated a total of forty-eight chemical plants and freight lines in areas of the nation as diverse as Seattle, Tacoma, Atlanta, Pittsburgh, Las Vegas, San Francisco, and New Jersey. Security on twelve separate railroads was penetrated, and Mr. Prine was never challenged by anyone at any location. In Atlanta, he climbed unguarded stores of deadly pesticides and flammable petroleum products. In Las Vegas, he photographed tankers of chlorine gas sitting unattended on tracks near the heart of the city. In Tacoma, Prine found tight security surrounding a bleach plant but tanker cars of chlorine sitting abandoned on tracks outside the security perimeter.[50]

Data provided by the Teamsters Union and obtained from their members working on the nation's freight lines makes it crystal clear that these kinds of observations are accurate and reflect the norm rather than some sort of aberration:

- 59 percent of Teamsters surveyed stated that trains carrying hazardous materials passed through their work areas in the course of a day;

- 86 percent said that their work areas were in proximity to schools, government buildings, densely populated areas, and other likely terrorist targets;

- 94 percent said the rail yards in which they worked were not secure;

- 96 percent said there was no visible rail police presence; and

- 88 percent said they had not received any terrorism prevention training in the last twelve months.

Having made all of the observations detailed above, I thought it proper to conclude my fieldwork for this part of the book by taking a visit to what can only be described as ground zero in any discussion of the danger posed by chemical plants in the United States: the Kuehne Chemical Company in South Kearny, New Jersey. I have avoided providing the true names of many potential targets in this book out of concern for offering unintentional assistance to the enemies of this nation. I have departed from this practice in regard to the Kuehne plant only because it is literally impossible to do research on terrorism and chemical plants for more than a few minutes without coming across the name of this facility, along with the exact location of the plant and detailed descriptions of exactly what substances are stored there. In short, anything and everything a potential terrorist might want to know about this site is readily available to anybody with a computer and an Internet location.

This focus on the Kuehne plant has been ongoing for years. Greenpeace and other groups began to talk about this facility in the immediate aftermath of 9/11. Back in 2003, a couple of environmental activists, Frank and Rosa Ferreira, made a number of visits to the facility. They videotaped the shocking lack of security at the location and posted the video on their Web site. The video includes images of the gates, the fences, and the storage tanks inside the plant. No security personnel were ever sighted by the Ferreiras during their visits to the plant.

Frank Ferreira summed up his motivation for his visits to the plant and his reactions as follows. "A few days before we went down there, we saw an article in our local paper that Greenpeace was looking at the safety of the chemical industry," Ferreira recalls. "They focused on the Kuehne plant. The article talked about documents filed with the Environmental Protection Agency showing that a chemical release could threaten the lives of 12 million people in a 16-mile radius. We went down there expecting to see something like Fort Knox—something you couldn't penetrate." He was wrong. "It was like a ghost town. . . . Once we finished taping, I turned to my wife and said, 'There is something terribly wrong here.' "[51]

This kind of attention has been unrelenting for years. CBS featured the Kuehne plant in 2003 in a story it aired on chemical plant security.[52] In 2006, when both U.S. senators from New Jersey introduced legislation into the U.S. Congress to toughen security at chemical plants across the country, they specifically cited the Kuehne plant as an example of the kind of danger they were trying to address.[53] That legislation was supported by a number of other legislators, including senators Obama and Biden, two individuals now uniquely poised to affect national policy on homeland security.

The Kuehne plant is located on the banks of the Hackensack River in New Jersey. The facility manufactures sodium hypochlorite, a substance used to disinfect water. To make this compound, Kuehne uses huge quantities of liquefied chlorine. This material is brought to the site in 90-ton railcars. Based on its location and the surrounding population density, EPA data indicates that the Kuehne plant is the single most dangerous chemical plant in the country.[54] A chlorine release from this site has the potential to kill more people than a release from any other plant in the nation.

In sum, if there is any chemical plant in the country which should be secure eight years after 9/11, it ought to be this facility, sitting only a few miles from the site where the Twin Towers used to stand.

I traveled to the Kuehne plant by rail and on foot. I took the PATH train from Manhattan to Journal Square, and then I walked the remaining distance through Jersey City and over the bridge to the area along the Hackensack River where the facility is located. It was a beautiful day in July 2009 when I made the trip, and I wanted to stretch my legs. I also wanted to see the area surrounding the plant so as to get a feel for the locale and the danger posed by the presence of so much chlorine.

I had never been to Jersey City before. It turned out to be a truly vibrant place, filled with new immigrants from around the world. The parks were full. I passed several baseball games in progress and maybe a dozen basketball games. Families were walking with small children. The markets were overflowing with fresh fruit and vegetables, and there were signs on storefronts in a half-dozen different languages. It was the kind of place that gave you hope for America, and reminded you that people still come here to make their futures.

Across the river I found the Kuehne plant, sitting at the end of a road lined with lots filled with tractor-trailers and storage tanks. It was a Sunday morning. The road outside the plant was empty, as were the sidewalks on either side. I was literally the only person in sight as I walked toward the plant.

Relative to what I had seen elsewhere, the Kuehne plant was good news. There were lots of signs telling truckers to slow down and be prepared to present identification. There was another sign saying something about a marine security area. There were Jersey barriers tossed about to add to the security of the perimeter surrounding the facility, and the whole site was encircled with what appeared to be a brand-new steel fence and sliding steel gates. Inside the perimeter there were buildings that appeared to be dedicated to security and probably inhabited by guards of some type.

It was not enough.

If I am a rank amateur, then the security in place at the Kuehne plant is probably the equivalent of Fort Knox. If I am a homegrown jihadist filled with the fervent desire to sacrifice myself, but not well trained in any of the skills necessary to take on a target of this type, then I am probably going to have a very bad day if I try to penetrate this plant.

This, however, is not just any plant. This is the single most dangerous chemical facility in America. Across the river is Lincoln Park, filled with picnickers, baseball games, and families out for a walk. Beyond is Jersey City. A few miles further, clearly visible, is the skyline of New York, marking the location of downtown Manhattan. It is, therefore, more than theoretically possible that an attack on this site would be executed by a team of individuals who know exactly what they are doing and are well prepared to take on the defenses in place at this location.

Whatever guards there were at the site, I saw none. There was no one outside walking a perimeter. There was no one standing on the street observing what was going on outside. I stood. I walked back and forth. I counted the number of rail tank cars sitting on the siding inside the fenced perimeter. I looked at the type of padlock on the length of chain holding shut one of the gates. Eventually, I walked away and started back toward the PATH station. On my way out, a Kearny Port Security truck drove by. The driver waved.

The keys to any defense against terrorist attack are understanding the psychology and capabilities of the attackers, and thereby anticipating their actions. In this case, making those calculations starts with a focus on the location of this plant, an understanding of its proximity to major population centers of vast significance, and recognition of the immense quantity of highly dangerous chlorine on-site at any point in time.

If I am here to attack this plant as the leader of a serious terrorist team, I am here to unleash all of the chlorine present in an effort to cause the maximum number of casualties in the surrounding communities. I will come with a team of individuals who not only are willing to die, but actually want to sacrifice themselves in the course of the operation. I will use automatic weapons, improvised explosive devices, and any other tools available to me. I do not care about signs, restricted areas, or any other security measure not backed by sufficient force to make me respect it.

A fenced perimeter which is not supported by armed force is useless against such an armed and fanatical foe. Would it be possible to ram the gates at the Kuehne plant and secure entry? Maybe. Why would I need to? There is immediate, direct, and uncontrolled access to the gates. Anybody with minimal training in breaching and some basic equipment can go through those gates in moments. After that, it is all over. There is no way on earth that any guards inside are going to react, repel a team of armed assailants, and prevent the inevitable. Every tank in the facility is going to be ruptured, either by satchel charges or vehicle-borne explosive devices, and what happens in the surrounding area is then going to be purely a function of meteorological conditions.

How is this possible? How can a facility be so dangerous that it has caught the attention of both the serving president and vice president of the United States and still be left in this posture? How is it possible that eight years after 9/11, we can have a chemical facility like the Point Plant sitting immediately adjacent to a major metropolitan area and effectively undefended against any serious terrorist attack? The standard anticipated response would probably be something about limited resources and the practical impossibility of guarding all potential targets. Is that really a valid answer?

In 2005, under the State Homeland Security Grant Program, the Department of Homeland Security gave $202,000 to the town of Dillingham, Alaska, so that it could install a total of seventy surveillance cameras in its downtown area. Dillingham has a population of 2,400. It is 300 miles from Anchorage. There are no roads to Dillingham, which is primarily a fishing port.[55] This $202,000 would go a long way toward paying for some basic defensive security measures at the Point Plant.

The same year, Homeland Security gave Montgomery County, Maryland, the amount of $160,000 to purchase eight plasma-screen television monitors.[56] Leaving aside the fact that these must have been some pretty amazing TVs if they ran $20,000 a piece, one cannot help but wonder how exactly the security of the citizens of Montgomery County was enhanced by this acquisition. In the scheme of things, was it really a bigger priority for the people of Maryland to buy some cool new television monitors than it was to make sure terrorists could not blow up the Point Plant and kill the city of Baltimore?

In May 2007, in the city of Augusta, Georgia, $3 million in homeland security funding was authorized for the protection of fire hydrants, which someone had decided constituted a top vulnerability.[57] I have no idea whether or not we need to take steps to prevent tampering with fire hydrants in this country. Maybe we do. I bet any roomful of sane citizens would say we ought to keep the chemical plants from being used against us and killing thousands of people first, though. This $3 million would pay the salaries of a significant number of guards at the Kuehne plant.

In September 2005, Homeland Security contracted with Carnival Cruise Lines to provide housing for individuals displaced by Hurricane Katrina. The cost of this contract was $236 million, because the U.S. government agreed to compensate Carnival fully for all of the profits it would have made if these individuals had, in fact, been taking a vacation cruise. Broken out per person, Carnival was paid $300 per individual, per night, for every day these persons were housed.[58]

In 2008, the Customs and Border Protection Division (CBP) of the Department of Homeland Security paid $8 million to sponsor a NASCAR racing team. The CBP defended the use of the taxpayers' funds on the grounds that it was good for CBP's image. One cannot help but wonder how many of the ticking chemical-plant time bombs in our midst could be secured with the funds squandered on this venture.[59]

A few years ago, *Forbes* magazine did a review of federal homeland security spending. According to their findings, between 9/11 and 2006, the federal government awarded at least $130 billion in contracts to private companies for projects connected to homeland security. In 1999, a grand total of nine companies received federal funding for homeland security work. In 2003, that number was 3,512. In 2005, it was 33,890. Half of those contracts went to one of the top ten defense firms in the country—companies like GE, IBM, and Honeywell. [60]

A lot of people are making a lot of money off of homeland security, but at the end of the day, we still have a lock and a length of chain separating the City of Baltimore from disaster. We still have tank cars of chlorine sitting on the doorstep of Manhattan, separated from would-be intruders by a metal fence and a gate.

It is impossible to look at the situation on the ground and the way in which vast quantities of public funds are being distributed and escape the conclusion that we have now combined complacency with greed and politics, and come up with a very deadly combination. The threat is abstract, distant, and easily disregarded. We are not focused on it sufficiently to do difficult things like actually erecting defenses and preparing for attacks. We are more than happy, however, to trot out the bogeyman of terrorism and the need for "homeland security" when it helps us to secure funding for projects of dubious utility that will please the folks back home. We are just as happy to steer massive contracts to huge corporations. Whether what they produce will ever save lives is highly debatable, but in the meantime, there is a lot of money to be made.

During the winter of 2002–2003, I was in command of a CIA base in the mountains of Kurdistan inside Iraq. We were running flat out, preparing for the invasion, gathering intelligence, and establishing covert action programs. We had to do all of this on a shoestring budget, without many critical supplies due to interference from the Turks, who continuously refused to allow us to resupply and systematically attempted to hamstring our efforts.

One of the things our effort required was the acquisition of safe sites from which to operate and at which to debrief sources and detainees. We could rent or buy buildings or pieces of property for this purpose, but we were then faced with the prospect of having to defend them both from agents of Saddam's intelligence service and from members of radical Islamic terrorist groups like Ansar al-Islam and Al-Qaeda, who wished to see us dead.

As noted, we did not have unlimited resources. Nor did we have unlimited time. We were face-to-face with daily threats. The enemies against whom we were working were skilled in a variety of tactics, including the use of massive vehicle-borne explosive devices. We had to defend ourselves. We needed to move right away.

Typically, we resolved this problem with the application of direct, practical, cheap measures. We closed off an area around a building to traffic for some distance. We sank steel pipes filled with concrete several feet in the ground and then set them in concrete as well. These pipes we placed a few feet apart across streets, sidewalks, flat grassy areas—any likely avenue of approach. We stationed armed guards around the target buildings. When possible, depending on the type of site in question, we set up signs to warn away the general public and limit the number of casual passersby.

None of it was sexy. All of it was very effective. Inside Iraq, operating with very limited capabilities, we never lost a man to a terrorist attack.

What we did not do was padlock a gate shut, dump a few marginally effective Jersey barriers in the street, and then call it a day. We did not take the limited funds we had and decide it would be more fun to buy televisions or new cars with them. It was not a game to us. We were not going through the motions in some administrative process and then going home for the day. We understood exactly whom we were dealing with, the ferocity of which they were capable, and acted accordingly.

There are many, many things which we could be doing to limit the threat of terrorist attack on chemical plants and chemical tank cars. Some of them are expensive and would require great effort.

Many others would not; they would just require us to take this issue seriously and start doing something other than penning articles, holding meetings, and commissioning studies.

Let's hope we do that. Soon. Before one or more great American cities die from the consequences of our inaction.

CHAPTER FIVE

From the Frying Pan into the Fire—LNG

SOMETIME AROUND 2:30 IN THE AFTERNOON ON OCTOBER 20, 1944, an aboveground storage tank containing liquid natural gas (LNG) in Cleveland, Ohio, began to leak. The tank was located on the property of the East Ohio Gas Company and had been built to store reserve gas for use in the war effort. As the gas leaked from the tank, it began to spread through the surrounding area, flowing down into underground sewers and, as it warmed, mixing with oxygen and forming a combustible mix. Roughly ten minutes after the leak began, the now highly volatile mixture of oxygen and gas exploded.

Underground, where much of the gas had initially collected, the force of the explosion was fantastic. Underground utilities were destroyed, pavement on the streets above ripped up, and manhole covers fired into the air like projectiles. At least one of these was subsequently found several miles away.

Aboveground the fireball and the resulting sympathetic fires totally destroyed 1 square mile of Cleveland. Fortunately, the population of this area was not high, and many of those who lived in the area were at work or school when the explosion happened. Still, at least 130 people were burned alive and a considerably larger number seriously injured. Also falling victim to the blaze were 79 homes, 2 factories, 217 automobiles, 7 trailers, and a tractor.[1]

Sixty-plus years later, this remains the single worst accident in the history of the use of LNG. Despite the fact that LNG is now used and shipped all over the world, the industry's safety record is remarkably good. In contrast to the chemical industry, for example, which, as we have seen, regularly subjects thousands to all sort of health risks in the normal course of business, LNG has been strikingly incident-free. None of this necessarily suggests that attacks on LNG facilities and the deliberate ignition of their contents are not serious threats.

LNG is an extremely dangerous material; it is shipped and used in massive quantities, and the scale of its use is expanding exponentially as we speak. The fact that the industry surrounding it is generally accident-free does not change the fact that if deliberately vaporized and ignited, LNG can be fantastically destructive. What happened in Cleveland in 1944 may only be a small foretaste of what terrorist attacks may bring us in the future.

Natural gas is colorless, odorless, and nontoxic, but is a highly flammable substance. It is generally close to 90 percent methane by volume, with a sprinkling of other compounds such as butane, propane, ethane, and nitrogen. By the time the gas reaches homes in the United States, it has been refined and is almost pure methane, with a small quantity of odorant added for safety. The other materials, such as propane, have been stripped off and are sold separately.[2]

Natural gas condenses from a vapor into a liquid, which is what we call LNG when it is cooled to a temperature below negative 260 degrees Fahrenheit. As a liquid, natural gas occupies a much smaller space than it does as a gas. In fact, its volume is only about 1/600 of what it was before it was liquefied. It is for this reason that the gas is liquefied before being shipped. Upon arrival at its destination, the LNG is then warmed, and returns to a gaseous state for transmission and use.

Historically, the bulk of the natural gas used in the United States has come from domestic producers and has moved inside the country via pipelines. As a consequence of declining supply and rising demand, however, there has been a significant increase in recent years in the amount of gas being brought into the country as LNG from abroad. This transport occurs in giant tankers specially designed to carry LNG. These ships vary in size, but the three which most frequently service the Cove Point terminal near my home in Maryland all have capacities in the neighborhood of 140,000 cubic meters.[3] The current level of consumption of LNG from abroad is so high that it is equivalent to the contents of two such tankers every three days.[4] Samsung Corporation is in the process of building eleven new tankers, each of which will have a capacity in excess of 266,000 cubic meters.[5]

There are currently seven active onshore import terminals and two active offshore import terminals in the United States. These facilities are scattered around the country in locations in Massachusetts, Maryland, Georgia, Texas, Puerto Rico, and Louisiana. There is also a single export terminal located in Alaska.[6] More than thirty additional such facilities are planned.[7]

The tankers which carry LNG to the United States are, for all intents and purposes, giant coolers. The LNG is not pressurized, but is stored inside the tankers in huge insulated tanks.[8] The tankers are also double-hulled to provide additional security to the contents.

That said, LNG tankers are not armored. Mines and/or explosives planted on board would be more than sufficient to breach the tanks and the hull and to release the contents. The double-hulled French tanker *Limburg* was attacked by a suicide vessel off of Yemen in 2002, and both its hulls were breached by the explosion.[9] Equally vulnerable are the exposed pipes that are used to pump the contents of the ship out when it docks, and the storage tanks into which the LNG is pumped ashore.[10] Typical storage tanks ashore can hold almost a full tanker's worth of LNG each, and a shore facility may house several such tanks.

The quantity of gas involved and the energy it can release is hard to fathom. A single LNG storage tank ashore may, for instance, hold a quantity of gas with a heat content equivalent to 40 Hiroshima bombs.[11] An average-sized LNG tanker will hold a quantity of gas with an energy content equivalent to fifty-five such atomic weapons.[12]

Even if ignited, LNG does not generate an atomic explosion, of course, but I think it's instructive anyway to ponder the enormity of the quantities of gas that are being moved and of the energy they contain. This is very dangerous, powerful stuff, and in the wrong hands it can do a lot of harm.

A ruptured LNG tanker will spew gas out onto the surface of the water around it. It does not matter how cold that water is; it will be a lot warmer than the natural gas which has been cooled to minus-260 degrees Fahrenheit. The spilled LNG will then, effectively, begin to "boil," converting from cubic meters of liquid to cubic meters of gas at the rate of 600 to 1. As it does so, it will also begin to mix with the surrounding air. Once that mixture reaches a level of 5 to 15 percent natural gas to surrounding air, it will be flammable. Allowing for the increase in volume caused by vaporization, and the above mixture percentage means that the contents of a single LNG tanker can produce up to 50 billion cubic feet of flammable gas-air mixture.[13]

As the gas leaves the tanker, vaporizes, and mixes with the air, if it is not ignited immediately, it will begin to drift away from the vessel in accordance with the prevailing wind. Because the vapor produced will still be cooler than the surrounding ambient temperature, it will hug the surface of the water, forming a plume. A 2006 Sandia Laboratories study of a possible LNG tanker breach found that such a plume could extend for 7.3 miles.[14] If breathed, this mixture would be deadly. If ignited, it would immediately produce a fireball of monstrous proportions. Its heat would cause third-degree burns and set structures ablaze up to 2 miles away.[15] No existing firefighting technology is capable of combating such a fire.

If the gas is ignited as it is released from the tanker, it will form a giant pool fire surrounding the ship rather than flashing into a fireball. This fire will grow and expand as the LNG is released, vaporizes, and combines with the surrounding oxygen. Regardless of the exact physical sequence of events, what results is the same: an immense conflagration that will burn until it consumes all the fuel on which it is feeding.

In a study of the risks posed by a proposed LNG facility in Providence, Rhode Island, former Clinton counterterrorism official, Richard Clarke, examined the consequences of a terrorist attack on an LNG tanker while docked at the site under review. For the purposes of the study, he assumed that terrorists would have successfully managed to breach two tanks inside of the tanker, and that a third would have been breached as the result of cryogenic damage. LNG is so cold that if released from containment and allowed to come into direct contact with normal steel, it may cause it to crack and rupture. Clarke also assumed that the devices used to blow open the tanks provided an ignition source and set the contents of the tanks on fire.

Based on these assumptions and a study of the surrounding area, Clarke found that such an attack would:

- Produce 3,000 immediate deaths as the result of the fire, and another 10,000 serious injuries. These numbers were predicted to rise substantially as the sympathetic fires created by the fireball spread. It was also expected that significant numbers of individuals not killed immediately would die as the result of untreated burns.

- Destroy 3,000 homes and damage hundreds more.

- Likely lead to sympathetic detonations of chlorine tanks, propane tanks, oil tanks, etc., in the surrounding area. As one would expect, if chemicals such as chlorine were released as a result, the death toll would be expected to rise significantly.

- Destroy the surrounding port facilities.

- Shut down nearby roads and bridges.

- Destroy surrounding power and telecommunications infrastructure.[16]

LNG may not produce a mushroom cloud, but when you look at those numbers and contemplate the scale of that damage, it does sound almost like something a nuclear weapon would produce.

In a separate study done in 2003, Professor James Fay of the Massachusetts Institute of Technology took a look at what would happen if there was an LNG spill at the Fall River facility in Massachusetts, and the released LNG was ignited. What he found was equally as frightening.

Fay noted that humans exposed to a level of thermal radiation measured as 5 kilowatts per square meter will experience unbearable pain after thirteen seconds and second-degree burns after forty seconds. Twice that level, 10 kilowatts per hour, kills. Fay also noted that wood ignites after forty seconds' exposure to 5 kilowatts per square meter.

Based on these effects, he selected an exposure level of 5 kilowatts per hour as being the criteria for severe damage to both humans and combustible materials. He then measured the amount of heat that would be produced from the LNG fire, and measured the distance from the blaze at which this level of heat would be experienced. What he found was that everyone and everything within 1,100 meters of the fire would be subjected to this level of exposure.

In short, within an area of thermal radiation surrounding the fire that would encompass 944 acres, all exposed humans would be killed or severely injured almost instantly, and all combustible materials set alight. Most frightening of all, Fay based his calculations on a spill of only 14,300 cubic meters of LNG. This is only one-tenth of the cargo of the tankers currently plying the Chesapeake Bay near my home.[17] Theoretically then, a well-planned and -executed terrorist attack on a modern LNG tanker could produce a fire ten times the size of what Fay envisioned. In fact, calculations done by the Sparrows Point LNG Opposition Team in Maryland, using charts prepared by the U.S. Department of Urban Development, show that the fireball resulting from an attack on a single average-sized LNG tanker could have a diameter of as much as 2.17 miles.[18]

There is one existing LNG import facility near my home in Maryland. A second such facility is set to be built about forty-five minutes away in Baltimore. I decided to take a look both at the existing installation and the site of the planned facility, and to begin with the one already in operation at Cove Point in Calvert County, Maryland.

Over the course of several visits to the vicinity of Cove Point, I acquired a pretty good appreciation for the security in place and the seriousness with which protection of the site was approached. I have to say that, after visits to chemical facilities which were virtually unprotected, I was pleasantly surprised by what I found at Cove Point. It may or may not be in a posture that would allow it to survive a serious attack by a team of trained and dedicated operators, but it is a pretty formidable target nonetheless. There are no high-speed avenues of attack, and people have paid attention to putting in place barriers that would require some pretty serious effort to penetrate.

That said, the best thing about Cove Point from a security standpoint has nothing to do with fences, gates, or guards. It has nothing to do with space-age technology or massive contracts for the development of new technology, either. It is something very simple and very practical.

It is location.

Cove Point sits in rural Calvert County, Maryland. There are homes near the facility, but they are relatively few in number. Population density is low. A successful attack on Cove Point, even one which is wildly successful and ignites all of the LNG stored there at any one point in time, is essentially going to start a real big fire in the woods. People will die, and I do not want to trivialize that, but there will be no massive, catastrophic danger.

Maybe some group of homegrown terrorists would be happy with such a level of accomplishment. Maybe some group of militia types who think the gas company is the root of all evil will make an attempt to destroy Cove Point as part of a plan to bankrupt Dominion Gas, which owns the facility. Al-Qaeda is not going to waste time with such a project, and neither is any other truly serious group. It would require massive resources, and the payback would not justify the investment.

There is a lesson here, and one that AES Corporation, which is behind a proposed Sparrows Point Project, should heed.

If Cove Point is the poster child for where to put an LNG facility, then Sparrows Point is exactly the opposite. It is a graphic example of a corporation disregarding all caution and prudence in the interest of profit. It may yet, if we allow it to proceed, be the death of thousands of Americans.

The proposed LNG facility at Sparrows Point will be built in an abandoned section of the Sparrows Point Shipyard in Baltimore, Maryland. The site is largely vacant right now, although it was previously part of the massive Bethlehem Steel facility at this location. It was used then for the manufacture of steel and shipbuilding.[19]

At this location, AES intends to construct a marine terminal which will include a pier for the simultaneous docking of two LNG tankers, unloading equipment, and three 160,000 cubic meter storage tanks. There will also be support buildings and the necessary pipes and transfer equipment to move the natural gas from the storage tanks into a pipeline distribution system.[20] AES anticipates that LNG tankers serviced at this facility will range in size from 127,500 to 217,000 cubic meters in capacity, and may be as much as 1,000 feet long. The storage tanks into which the gas will be pumped will be 259 feet in diameter and 170 feet tall.

AES says that maintaining the safety and security of this facility is of "the utmost importance." According to AES, "every effort will be made to ensure that the people and property around the facility and the ships transporting the LNG are protected from accident and harm."[21] The security report for their project, prepared by Good Harbor Consulting, describes the site of the proposed plant as being an "unlikely terrorist target." In reaching this judgment, Good Harbor relied upon its determination that Sparrows Point was remote and "an industrial zone." In Good Harbor's opinion, an attack on an LNG facility at Sparrows Point would produce few fatalities, minimal damage to other key facilities, and limited socioeconomic disruption.[22]

I have nothing but respect for Richard A. Clarke, who wrote the Good Harbor assessment, and, to his credit, he has weighed in against other LNG projects in the past. That said, I find it very hard to understand how a terrorist attack on an LNG facility at Sparrows Point, if built as envisioned, could be considered unlikely. The scale of what would ensue if such an attack were carried out with a reasonable degree of professionalism and thoroughness would have to be described as apocalyptic.

We talked before about Professor Fay's projections for the size and intensity of an LNG fire and the area which would be affected. That assessment was based on a spill of 14,300 cubic meters of LNG. AES, by their own admission, intends to construct a facility which will have on hand, just in the shore storage tanks, well over thirty times as much LNG.

The closest neighborhood to the Sparrows Point site is roughly 1 mile away. Sitting right next to the site is a huge steel mill, which naturally enough ought to be viewed in this context as one gigantic source of ignition. Hundreds of thousands of cubic meters of liquefied natural gas jammed together on a narrow peninsula with a blast furnace cannot help but be a bad combination. Thousands of employees work in this plant, and the company that owns it is in the process of planning for a massive expansion, and will employ thousands more. Every one of these individuals would effectively be working right next door to the planned LNG terminal and the massive storage tanks. Right on the other side of the channel into Baltimore Harbor is the Point Plant, discussed in the last chapter. That plant, and its accompanying 90-ton tank cars of chlorine gas, are less than 2 miles from the site chosen by AES for construction of its new LNG import terminal.

In 2004 at Skikda, Algeria, there was an accident in an LNG production plant. A leak in a pipe allowed the formation of a giant vapor cloud of natural gas above the plant. A malfunction in a boiler at the plant then provided the necessary ignition, and the vapor cloud detonated. The damage caused by the detonation and the resulting fire was massive. At least twenty-seven people died, and seventy-four more were injured. Material losses ran to $800 million.[23]

Three of the six LNG production units at the plant were completely destroyed. A nearby power plant was damaged, as was one of the berths in the nearby harbor and several adjacent homes and other buildings. The shock wave from the detonation leveled the maintenance, security, and administrative buildings in the plant complex. Vehicles were overturned and their metal frames melted.[24]

The size of the vapor cloud that formed and the amount of LNG that leaked remains unknown, and will probably be a permanent matter of conjecture. This much is clear: What happened in Algeria involved a small fraction of the quantity of LNG that was on-site at that location, and that would be stored at Sparrows Point. It was but a small taste of what the ignition of a vapor cloud at a large LNG terminal could produce.

If we start mapping out the area that a vapor cloud from an LNG release might cover, and use the 7.3-mile radius provided by Sandia, we discover that leaking gas from Sparrows Point might, in fact, reach as far as the center of Baltimore and the heart of the financial district. Just as easily, depending on the wind, such a vapor cloud might extend northward into densely populated areas of Dundalk and Essex. That is an area populated by literally hundreds of thousands of individuals.

All of these calculations are based, of course, on measurements from the location of the shore facility at which the LNG tankers will dock in Baltimore. They only apply, therefore, to attacks on the storage tanks on land or attacks on LNG tankers, which are actually tied up at the pier. If we envision an attack on a tanker as it is in transit through the channel to the LNG facility, for example, we might find that it is less than a mile from the Point Plant. While being turned into its slip at the terminal by tugs, a tanker, holding perhaps 200,000 cubic meters of LNG, might actually be within several hundred meters of the closest homes.

Herein, of course, lies the real rub.

We have been talking up to now about possible terrorist attacks on LNG targets and assuming, without any real justification, that those attacks must happen at the fixed sites where importation occurs. Sparrows Point will be where the tankers filled with LNG dock; therefore, that is where terrorists must attack them.

There is no logical support for such a conclusion. In fact, if we look around the world, we will see that merchant vessels are attacked at sea all the time. Sometimes, this is piracy and motivated by profit. Sometimes it is terrorism and driven by ideology. Either way, the tactics and methodology not only for the attack but for the seizure of large oceangoing vessels by small groups of armed men is well established and widely known.

On March 14, 2005, pirates in Indonesia attacked and seized control of a tanker carrying methane gas between two islands in that nation. They then released the vessel and escaped with the captain and the first engineer, holding them as hostages.[25]

On September 15, 2008, the chemical tanker *Stolt Valor* was hijacked by pirates off the coast of Somalia. Roughly two months later, just as the *Stolt Valor* was released after payment of a $1.1 million ransom, another chemical tanker, the *Chemstar Venus,* en route from Indonesia to the Ukraine, was seized.[26]

On November 15, 2008, pirates seized the largest vessel ever captured, the Saudi supertanker *Sirius Star.* This vessel, 332 meters in length, was held until a ransom was paid and not released to the control of its crew until January 10, 2009.[27] This vessel is roughly equal in size to the largest LNG tanker expected to service either Cove Point or Sparrows Point.

On November 28, 2008, five pirates in a single boat seized the Liberian-flagged chemical tanker *Biscaglia* in the Gulf of Aden.[28]

On January 29, 2009, pirates operating from Somalia seized control of a German liquefied petroleum gas (LPG) tanker and held it for ransom. The vessel was transporting LPG from Europe to the Far East.[29]

This is just a very small sampling of the total number of attacks occurring worldwide. In fact, statistics show that piracy is a growth industry, and that 2008 was a record year for attacks. According to the International Maritime Bureau, in 2008 there were a total of 293 incidents of piracy worldwide, an 11 percent increase over 2007. In all, 49 vessels were hijacked, 899 crew taken hostage, and 11 crewmen killed.[30]

All of these vessels have been captured by relatively small numbers of pirates in open boats, armed with automatic weapons and grenade launchers. Boarding of the vessels has been carried out with ropes and ladders. There is nothing particularly sophisticated about any element of these operations. The individuals who seized these craft were not members of Seal Team Six or Delta Force. They were largely former Somali fishermen who had decided that piracy was a significantly more lucrative occupation. Merchant vessels are unarmed and incapable of offering much in the way of resistance.

Most important, there is nothing that has been used by pirates in these attacks that could not readily be procured inside the United States by any group with the desire to do so.[31]

Somalia is a failed state wracked by years of internal strife and now dominated by radical Islamic groups. Links between these Islamic groups, many of which have connections to Al-Qaeda, and the pirates are strong and well known.[32] During an interview on February 7, 2009, the prominent radical Islamist Dr. Hani Al-Siba'i stated unequivocally that an alliance between Al-Qaeda and the leading radical Islamic group in Somalia, Al-Shabaab, already existed, and then recommended careful planning of joint operations by the two organizations.[33] Islamists in Somalia have already used the pirates to bring in arms shipments and foreign fighters, providing weapons and training in return. In some cases, Islamic groups even take a share of the pirates' profits. Pirates are providing training directly to Islamic groups so they can undertake their own maritime operations.

This is particularly worrisome in that, while still relatively straightforward operations, pirate attacks do show clear signs of evolution and an increase in technical capability. The *Sirius Star* was taken almost 450 miles off the coast of Somalia. This was not a chance capture. Clearly, the pirates who seized this vessel had a mechanism for acquiring data on its location, course, and speed. Just as clearly, they themselves had significant navigational ability in order to plan an intercept. Perhaps most ominously, after they seized the ship, the pirates were able to successfully navigate her back to the coast of Somalia and then to safely anchor her 3 miles offshore without running aground or encountering other difficulties. This shows an ability to control and operate large, complex vessels.[34]

It is also worth noting that recent evidence shows that Somali extremist groups have extended their reach into the United States itself. As of July 2009, at least twenty Americans of Somali extraction were under investigation by the FBI for involvement in Islamic extremist activity. Several of these individuals traveled to Somalia and underwent training by Al-Shabaab. One of them, Shirwa Ahmed, blew himself up in Somalia in October of 2008, becoming the first known American suicide bomber.[35] Given such developments, a team bent on attacking an LNG tanker might find they already had a ready-made group of support assets awaiting their arrival in the United States.

Given these realities, let's take another look at Sparrows Point in light of the possibility of an LNG vessel being seized and used as a floating bomb. In other words, given that the ability of terrorists to seize an undefended merchant vessel cannot possibly be disputed, let's at least entertain the possibility that eight years after 9/11, the same guys who came up with the idea to use commercial aircraft in suicide attacks might actually be smart enough to apply the same principle to commercial ships.[36]

From Sparrows Point it is roughly 8 or 9 miles by water to the Inner Harbor of Baltimore. This area is immediately adjacent to the downtown business district, and to several densely populated residential areas. An LNG vessel, no matter how large, draws no more than 40 feet of water. There is a 50-foot shipping channel all the way from Sparrows Point to the Inner Harbor.

Would a group of terrorists, operating without the benefit of an experienced pilot and tugboat assistance, really be able to get an LNG tanker all the way through the channel and run it up against Harborplace Mall before they detonated their prize? Maybe not. It would be little comfort to contemplate, however, that they would have to detonate it some distance short of their intended target. A vessel which goes aground and then is breached and set alight near Federal Hill, a neighborhood south of the Inner Harbor, is still going to do massive damage.

A vessel moving at the completely reasonable speed of ten knots is going to cover the distance from Sparrows Point to the Inner Harbor in well under an hour. There is no existing commando or assault force within the United States that would be able to organize an assault and the retaking of a pirated LNG tanker within that period of time. It is equally as impossible that anyone would be able to orchestrate any kind of evacuation of the city of Baltimore within that time frame. In fact, if we contemplate the confusion that is likely to surround the seizure of a tanker, the amount of time it would take for messages to be relayed, responsible parties briefed, and decisions made, it is entirely likely that no evacuation would be ordered at all until after the tanker had been set ablaze. The first warning the tens of thousands of people downtown would have of the catastrophe would be when everything around them bursts into flame.

Stephen Flynn, a respected expert in homeland security, considered a similar scenario concerning the LNG facility near Boston in his book, *The Edge of Disaster.* He concluded that an attack on an LNG tanker there by a suicide boat bomb, similar to that used against the USS *Cole,* could cause 10,000 casualties, melt roadways, and set off sympathetic detonations of fuel tanks nearby.[37] The detonation of the contents of a tanker that had been seized and then rigged properly for maximum effect could create much greater damage.

To his credit, in his report regarding the proposed Sparrows Point facility, Mr. Clarke spelled out a number of security measures he would expect to see put in place if and when the terminal was constructed. None of these, however, had anything to do with the protection of the tanker in transit. All of them were oriented toward the prevention of an attack on the terminal itself, and on tankers while at dock.

Similarly, after poring over literally hundreds of pages of reports and testimony concerning the Sparrows Point LNG terminal, I could not find any discussion anywhere of what specific security arrangements were to be taken to prevent the seizure of a tanker on its way to the facility. The most that I could find were numerous references to the Coast Guard and vague assurances that this organization would be responsible for the security of LNG tankers on the waters of the Chesapeake Bay. In one of its PowerPoint presentations used as part of its road show, for instance, AES Corporation makes statements such as: "The U.S. Coast Guard is responsible for the safety of the LNG tankers" and "U.S. Coast Guard escorts minimize external threats."[38]

I have a lot of respect for the men and women of the Coast Guard. My older brother was in the Coast Guard, and I know very well that he risked his life on many occasions to rescue mariners in distress. I also understand, however, that the responsibilities of the Coast Guard are vast, and that this organization, even in these days of huge budgets, is often shortchanged on resources. I cannot help but wonder, therefore, if the Coast Guard is really capable of providing the kind of airtight security that would be required to ensure that what amounts to giant floating bombs are not commandeered and used for evil purposes.

That concern was only heightened by the discovery that other, significant voices were already wondering the same thing.

Testifying before a committee of the House of Representatives, Maryland senator Barbara Mikulski stated,

> *I pushed the Coast Guard to review how they will keep Cove Point secure. Believe it or not, it was the very first of its kind for [an] LNG terminal. In their report, the Coast Guard assured me they had sufficient resources to control and secure LNG tanker shipping. The Coast Guard promised to provide waterside security during gas transfer, scrutinize crew lists, board and inspect tankers, escort the tankers up the Bay, and enforce exclusion zones.*
>
> *The Coast Guard stood up and took the lead, and they have done their job effectively. But guess what? They are overstretched. Now the Coast Guard is turning over some of its security responsibilities to Dominion Power. The Coast Guard has bailed out. Now security for Cove Point is shared between the Coast Guard, Dominion Power, and local law enforcement. So the safety and security of the people of Calvert County and all who live or work on the Bay is provided by an uncertain mix of private security guards, local law enforcement and the overstretched Coast Guard. What will this mean? I've tried to find out—all I get is platitudes and abstractions—and a lot of paper. If there is a problem, do you call the Sheriff of Calvert County? Do you call the rent-a-cops from a private security firm? We must have these answers![39]*

Mikulski's is not a lone voice. In fact, concerns about the safety of LNG tankers and facilities in the Chesapeake are such that the entire Maryland congressional delegation has been on record for some time as opposing the building of the new terminal at Sparrows Point. Mikulski's partner in the Senate, Senator Benjamin Cardin, has stated,

> *To service the Sparrows Point LNG facility, LNG tankers would have to travel through the narrowest portions of the Chesapeake*

Bay, under the Bay Bridge, through heavily used commercial fishing and recreational boating areas, to the mouth of the Port of Baltimore. This is a densely populated area that is less than 2 miles away from the residential neighborhoods of Dundalk, Turners Station, and Edgemere, home to 65,000 Marylanders.

Based upon its review of AES's waterway suitability assessment for the Chesapeake Bay, the U.S. Coast Guard found in 2008 that the Bay is not currently suitable, but could be made suitable for the type and frequency of LNG marine traffic associated with the proposed Sparrows Point Terminal. The Coast Guard found the waterway unsuitable because the measures proposed by AES to mitigate the risks associated with LNG transits in the Bay were inadequate, because the port community "currently does not have sufficient resources available to implement the safety and security measures necessary to responsibly manage the maritime safety and security risks," and because AES did not explain how it would ensure that adequate resources would be made available.

Further, the Coast Guard indicated that AES must develop a formal Transit Management Plan that details those measures that would be implemented to mitigate the risks associated with LNG tanker transits through the Bay. To date, a final Transit Management Plan has not been developed, and there is no formal indication from the Coast Guard either that AES has proposed measures adequate to mitigate the risks associated with LNG tanker transits in the Bay, or that adequate resources necessary to implement these risk mitigation measures have been put in place in the Bay.[40]

Interestingly, even the Coast Guard, which is generally referred to as being responsible for the security of LNG tankers in the Chesapeake Bay, has expressed its own very significant concerns about its level of resources and its capacity to guard vessels under way. In its Waterway Suitability Report, prepared in connection with the proposal to build the Sparrows Point terminal, the Coast Guard stated, "An armed, multi-vessel escort will be required to enforce the federal safety/security zones around any loaded LNG vessel navigating with specified areas of the Chesapeake Bay. The escort may be comprised of vessels provided by the Coast Guard; other Federal, State, or local agencies; and/or private entities. The escort required will range from one to four vessels. . . . The availability of Coast Guard vessels for escorts will be subject to the Coast Guard's daily mission prioritization and resource allocation that is based on many variables outside of AES's control. Should Coast Guard vessels not be available, any assisting agency must have the required ACCCP (authorities, capabilities, competencies, capacities and partnerships) to enforce a federal safety/security zone . . ."[41]

This does not sound like an agency saying that it would assume all responsibility for the protection of vessels from attack. To the contrary, it sounds very much like the Coast Guard was echoing exactly what Mikulski was saying—that it did not have the resources to make any guarantees, and that it was going to take a mix of some unspecified other resources to handle the task at hand.

The Waterway Suitability Assessment for Cove Point contains exactly the same kind of language. It talks about multi-ship escorts and enforcing security zones around vessels, but it does not say explicitly that the Coast Guard will take responsibility for all of this. In fact, by virtue of frequent references to patrol boats from state and local law enforcement agencies, this report clearly contemplates that the Coast Guard will not have the resources to enforce these measures on its own.[42]

All of which left me with the same fuzzy, uncomfortable feeling: It did not seem clear who, if anyone, was actually responsible for making sure that LNG tankers could not be seized and used by terrorists for nefarious purposes. Sparrows Point was not yet built, so that mystery might just have to be unresolved for the time being.

Cove Point was up and running, however, and there was one sure way to find out what was and was not being done at that location.

I went back. Not to look at the storage facility this time, but to watch what was and was not being done to secure the tankers themselves.

The first step, of course, was to figure out when the tankers arrived and departed. Initially, I assumed that was going to be a matter of shoe leather and time on target. To my surprise, I discovered that it was a lot simpler than that. With a little persistence and some time spent wandering the Internet, I discovered that I could actually track the tankers in question online. I won't go into the details here (because we don't need to make this easier than it already is), but suffice it to say that I was quickly able to get to the point where I knew the exact arrival dates and times for LNG tankers coming into Cove Point, and to have that information well in advance of the ship's approach to the terminal. It made my life a lot easier. It was also very, very frightening.

Armed with that information, it was a simple matter to then identify locations from which I could observe the arrival, docking, and unloading of the LNG tankers at Cove Point. This let me set up unmolested and take my time examining and evaluating what was and was not being done to protect these incredibly sensitive vessels. At no point in any of my many visits to the vicinity of the facility was I ever questioned or approached. At no point did I see any indication that there was any countersurveillance presence focused on individuals doing exactly what I was doing—making book on the security procedures in place. Over a period of months, I developed three conclusions:

First, it is absurd that information regarding the movements of these vessels is available as widely as it is. It may well be that individuals involved in the merchant shipping industry need this information. The general public does not. I am not suggesting that this data be classified; I am merely suggesting that access to it be restricted to those who really need it.

Second, security for a facility like Cove Point can't begin with a patrol boat doing donuts in the water around a tanker. That's good, but it's not sufficient. Security needs to extend well beyond that, and should include measures designed to determine who is casing the facility and planning an attack. The Coast Guard assessment I referenced states explicitly: "State, local and private LE agencies will provide landside security patrols for surveillance along the facility's waterfront and portions of the transit route prior to and during an LNG vessel's transit and during the LNG off-load operations."[43] In line with my methodology throughout this project, I broke no laws; I never trespassed, and I never employed any of the hundreds of methods I could have used to conceal myself or my purpose from observation. I sat, and I watched. I wiggled my toes in the sand, watched the blue herons fly by, and tossed stones in the water. If I was ever asked about my purpose, my plan was the same as it was throughout this project: to tell the truth, the whole truth, and nothing but the truth. I was never noticed. I was never approached. This is unacceptable.

According to the Department of Homeland Security, their number-one "Core Priority" is to "Protect our nation from dangerous people."[44] I have known, worked with, and worked against a lot of "dangerous people." If you start the game by letting them sit unmolested and make book on your procedures and your available resources, you are done. I do not mean you are at a disadvantage. I mean you are done. Game over. You lose before you even know you are playing.

Third, there is no security presence at Cove Point that would stop a determined attempt to seize an LNG tanker there. There are security personnel. There are limited patrols. They do not begin to have sufficient manpower or firepower to resist a concerted effort to take a ship. I do not mean by this that a battalion of Marines could accomplish this objective. I mean that half a dozen guys in a Zodiac with the kinds of weapons available at gun shows all over this country could do this job. The most that security on-site would succeed in doing would be sounding an alert to the Coast Guard that someone had just stolen a tanker filled with liquid natural gas. This, too, is unacceptable.

This is not intended as a commentary on the dedication or commitment of the security personnel at Cove Point. I am sure they are good people who would do their best in an emergency to save the lives of their countrymen. It is a reflection of the reality of the resources dedicated to this issue. There are simply not enough men, weapons, and other equipment available at the likely point of attack.

All of this notwithstanding, on January 15, 2009, the Federal Energy Regulatory Commission (FERC) approved, with conditions, the proposed Sparrows Point LNG terminal. This new liquefied natural gas (LNG) import terminal and connecting interstate pipeline will bring in 1.5 billion feet per day (Bcf/d) of natural gas. Storage capacity at this facility will be 480,000 cubic meters of LNG, or the equivalent of four average LNG tankers.

According to the FERC chairman, "When FERC reviews a proposed LNG import project, our primary concern is assuring public safety." Keller added that he believed FERC had done so in this case, and that "The AES Sparrows Point LNG Project will provide service in a safe and secure manner and provide fuel to generate electricity and heat homes. I realize this is not a popular decision, but it is the correct decision, rooted in a voluminous record and based on sound science."[45]

How, eight years after 9/11, in the middle of a worldwide war against a dangerous and determined foe, building what amounts to a giant bomb in the heart of a major American city qualifies as being safe and secure is beyond me. In my opinion, all it says is that while we spend a lot of time talking about homeland security, and hold a lot of hearings, when push comes to shove, and dollars are on the line, security takes a backseat to profit. If I were bin Laden, I would have a big smile on my face, and I would be taking a very hard look at what the expansion of the use of LNG in America means to me.

CHAPTER SIX
Noah Knew

ON MAY 31, 1889, THE CITY OF JOHNSTOWN, PENNSYLVANIA, WAS essentially obliterated by a flood that swept down the valley of the Little Conemaugh River, killing 2,209 people. Trees "snapped like pipe stems" and houses were "crushed like eggshells." Railroad locomotives at several locations were tossed around like toys by the force of the rushing water. Above Johnstown, in the path of the onrushing water, several smaller towns simply vanished. One, the town of Mineral Point, was erased from the face of the earth so completely that only bare rock remained where it had stood.

The floodwaters formed a wall of water sometimes as high as 75 feet,[1] rushing downhill at 40 miles an hour and driving everything in front of it. Many of those fortunate enough to survive reported later that they could not even see the water itself, but, instead, heard a roaring noise and then saw what appeared to be a moving wall of houses and debris churning toward them.[2] Above it all hung a dark cloud of mist, which many would forever after refer to as the "death-mist."[3]

Many of the homes washed away in downtown Johnstown were crumpled and washed up against the pillars of the old stone railway bridge below town. There this mountain of wreckage collected and piled up, forming a dam soaked in oil from lamps and businesses. Trapped inside many of the wrecked homes remained hundreds of terrified residents of the doomed city.

Then, sometime during the night following the flood, this horrible tangle of wreckage, bodies, and stranded survivors caught fire. Rescuers tried valiantly to reach all those trapped inside, but in many cases it proved physically impossible. At least eighty people died at the bridge, many of them burned alive in their own homes.

What remained the next day was a scene of devastation that had never been witnessed before in the United States. In many places, entire blocks of buildings had ceased to exist. In others, streets were buried under rubble and debris two stories high. Hundreds of bodies were never found. Many more could never be identified. Within days typhoid began to break out due to the lack of clean water and sanitation.

All of this horror was the result of one single event: the failure of the South Fork Dam, a privately owned earthen structure located 14 miles from Johnstown.

The South Fork Dam was originally built to supply water for the Pennsylvania Mainline Canal. The Pennsylvania Railroad bought the dam four years later. Eventually, the railroad abandoned the dam, and in 1879 it was purchased by the South Fork Club, a fishing and hunting club for wealthy Pittsburgh industrialists. They maintained the dam simply to provide a lake on which their club members could boat and fish. The dam was 72 feet tall and created a lake 2 miles long, 1 mile wide, and up to 60 feet deep. That worked out to be approximately 20 million tons of water.

The dam was 450 feet higher in elevation than the city of Johnstown and had been poorly maintained over the years since its acquisition by the South Fork Club. When, after a night of heavy rain, it failed on May 31, 1889, the waters of the lake behind the dam followed their natural course downhill. The entire reservoir emptied in less than forty-five minutes.[4] It took a total of fifty-seven minutes for the contents of the reservoir to reach Johnstown. Calculations by engineers have demonstrated that the power of the onslaught was equivalent to having turned the full force of Niagara Falls onto the city of Johnstown, Pennsylvania.[5]

In the United States, there are 79,500 dams that are used to control flooding and to provide power and water. A significant number of these structures are many times the size of the South Fork Dam. Many of these would pose a significant hazard if destroyed. In fact, as of 2003, the American Society of Civil Engineers listed 10,049 dams in the United States as being "high hazard," meaning that there was a city less than 1 mile downstream from the structure.[6] Some of these structures literally hold back millions of gallons of water, which, if unleashed, would destroy property and kill huge numbers of people.[7]

Across the country, the federal government alone has built hundreds of water projects—primarily dams and reservoirs for irrigation development and flood control—with municipal and industrial water use as an incidental, self-financed, project purpose. Out west, Bureau of Reclamation projects supply water to millions of people and irrigate farmland in seventeen separate states. Around the country, the Army Corps of Engineers alone operates 609 dams and 166 reservoirs.

The scope of some of the larger projects is sometimes difficult to comprehend. If the Glen Canyon Dam upstream from the Hoover Dam were to fail, the resulting flood might destroy Hoover Dam itself. Assuming that Hoover Dam held, it would still take eleven days for the resulting 500-foot-tall wall of water to diminish and overtopping of the dam to cease. Lake Mead, the reservoir formed by Hoover Dam, is the largest such body of water in the United States. It holds almost 35 million cubic meters of water and supplies water to 30 million persons. The destruction of this structure alone would cripple the cities of Las Vegas, Phoenix, and Los Angeles, and it might take a decade for recovery to be complete.

Still, despite its critical involvement in such projects, especially in the West, the federal government is responsible for only about 5 percent of the dams whose failure could result in loss of life or significant property damage. The remaining dams belong to state or local governments, utilities, and corporate or private owners.[8] These structures are scattered around the nation, and there is no single entity of any kind responsible for their safety or security.

Even absent terrorist attack or sabotage, these structures fail with some frequency. Beyond the two examples cited above, there have been a host of other significant dam disasters around the globe, many of them in the United States:

- 2006, Kauai, Hawaii: 7 killed

- 1985, Trento, Italy: 268 killed, 62 buildings and 8 bridges destroyed

- 1982, Lawn Lake and Cascade dams, Rocky Mountain National Park: 3 killed, $31 million in damages

- 1979, Morvi Dam, India: 15,000 killed

- 1977, Kelly Barnes Dam, Georgia: 39 killed

- 1976, Teton Dam: 11 killed, several towns destroyed, $300 million in damages

- 1975, Banqiao and Shimantan dams, China: 85,000 killed.

- 1963 Baldwin Hills Reservoir, Los Angeles, California: 5 killed, 277 homes destroyed

- 1963, Vajont, Italy: 2,000 killed

- 1959, Côte d'Azur, France: 421 killed, $68 million in damages

- 1928, Los Angeles, California: 450 killed, one power plant destroyed

- 1911, Potter County, Pennsylvania: 78 killed, $10 million in damages

The failure of the Teton Dam in 1976 is instructive not only in the danger posed by dams, but also in how surprisingly fragile they can be. The Teton Dam failed as it was being filled for the very first time. It was a large earthen structure, and construction had just been completed. The failure was catastrophic. The leak began in the morning, and by nightfall the entire reservoir had emptied. The wall of water resulting was 30 feet high. Eleven people were killed and several small communities were entirely destroyed. Other damage included 100,000 acres of farmland inundated and 427,000 acres of land left without irrigation.[9]

As I write this, there is significant concern about the possible catastrophic failure of two large dams in Kentucky and Tennessee: the Wolf Creek and Center Hill dams, both of which are decades old and located on top of geological formations, which are steadily eroding. The Army Corps of Engineers has huge projects ongoing at both locations to attempt to rectify the situation and remove the danger.[10,11] In the meantime, they are steadily dropping reservoir levels, and the city of Nashville, 100 miles from Wolf Creek, is making preparations for managing the flooding caused by a dam failure.[12]

In West Virginia, the Corps of Engineers is focused on the safety of yet another large structure, the Bluestone Dam. As with Wolf Creek and Center Hill, they have drawn down the reservoir level behind the dam to decrease the pressure and are undertaking stabilization projects. In discussing the possibility of a dam failure, Colonel Dana R. Hurst of the Army Corps of Engineers noted that such an eventuality would cause not only flooding in communities close to the dam, but also as far away as the state capital of Charleston. "I was talking with Governor Manchin in his office; I told him there would be 15 feet of water in the governor's office if this dam fails at full flood control pool," Hurst said. He also noted the concentration of major chemical plants along the banks of the Kanawha River in Charleston, and the obvious impact on them of a flood of such magnitude.[13]

These are not isolated cases. Nationwide, according to the American Society of Civil Engineers, there are over 4,000 "unsafe" dams.[14]

As suggested by the example of the Johnstown Flood, large government-owned dams are not the only structures about which we need be concerned. On February 26, 1972, a tailing mine owned by the Buffalo Mining Company in Buffalo Creek, West Virginia, failed, destroying an entire valley inhabited by in excess of 6,000 persons, killing 125 people, injuring 1,110, and leaving at least 3,000 homeless. The flood destroyed 502 homes and 44 mobile homes.[15]

In discussing dam safety and trying to understand how these kinds of accidents happen, it helps to understand a little bit about dam construction. There are actually several different types of dams, classified by the material from which they are constructed and their design. These differences define how dams fail.[16] The different types of dams include embankment dams, gravity dams, arch dams, and buttress dams. Embankment dams are generally made of semipermeable natural materials such as earth and rock, while the others are usually constructed of concrete.

The function of a dam is to hold back the flow of water and form a reservoir. Obviously, it must be strong enough to hold back the force of the water it is containing. It must also be able to pass floodwaters through the structure in times of high water. This means it must have spillways, which allow it to release water.

If the spillways become blocked or if the spillway gates malfunction, there is a danger the water level will rise higher than the dam. This is called "overtopping." One-third of all dam failures are caused by overtopping. The erosion that results as the water pours over the top and around the sides of a dam that has been overtopped will begin to eat away at the integrity of the dam and destroy its support. If the dam is made of earth, the overtopping will begin to chew away at the structure of the dam itself. In fact, an earthen dam, no matter how large, is essentially mortally wounded if overtopped. Its destruction is virtually assured.

How catastrophic this failure can be, and how rapidly it can occur, was graphically demonstrated in 2005 by the disintegration of the Taum Sauk Dam in Missouri.

Unlike most dams, the Taum Sauk did not hold back the flow of a natural watercourse. Instead, it contained a large man-made reservoir which was part of a storage system to allow generation of electricity at times of peak demand. During evening hours, when there was excess capacity on the grid, water was pumped up into the reservoir on top of a mountain in the Ozarks. Then, during the day, when demand was highest, water was released into a hydroelectric plant, turning turbines and generating electricity.

On December 14, 2005, during the final pumping cycle for the day, the dam was overtopped. Apparently this was the result of an error in the installation of equipment and computer programming problems. Together, these combined to prevent the automatic cutoff system from shutting down the inflow of water once the reservoir was filled. Instead, the pumps continued to run, and sometime around 5:00 a.m., water began to spill over the top of the dam.

It took approximately twenty-five minutes from the time this spillage caused the initial breach in the dam wall until the entire 4,350-acre reservoir was empty.[17] The outgoing floodwaters, in total something in the neighborhood of 1 billion gallons, cut a 700-foot-wide breach in the dam wall.[18] Fortunately, the reservoir was located in a relatively remote area; a second dam at a lower reservoir held and contained much of the flooding, and a campground in the path of the floodwaters was closed for the season. Had the same kind of event occurred with a dam near an inhabited area, the loss of life could have been catastrophic.

A dam's foundation is also critical to its safety. If the foundation fails, so will the dam. Another third of dam failures are due to this cause. No matter how large, a dam will not continue to stand if its foundation has been sufficiently damaged.

One-third of all dam failures are caused by piping and seepage. Once seepage begins inside of a dam, it will steadily erode the structure of the dam until it has weakened it to the point of collapse. Detecting this seepage and then figuring out a way to repair the problem inside a standing structure the size of a major dam can be extremely challenging.

Not all of these issues pertain directly to the topic of a terrorist threat, of course. What they do bring home, however, is that our habit of looking at dams holding back massive reservoirs as somehow part of the landscape, immovable and rock-solid, is flawed. In fact, when we look at a major dam, what we ought to understand is that there are massive physical forces at work, and that the power of the entrapped water is enormous. Should that power be turned loose at the wrong time, and in the wrong place, the resulting loss of life could be staggering.

Fortunately, to date, we have not seen any terrorist attacks on dams. There have been, however, quite a number of military operations against dams, several of which have produced catastrophic results and may provide terrorist groups with examples of how such actions can be carried out.

On May 16, 1943, British Lancaster bombers belonging to Squadron 617 attacked several dams in Germany's Ruhr valley. Utilizing 6,000-pound bombs specially designed for the task, the British airmen brought down two of the three dams they attacked, producing widespread flooding and damaging or destroying a large number of German industrial facilities. Each of the dams destroyed was struck by two of the bombs in question, which were constructed so as to strike the side of the dam and then sink to a depth of 60 feet before detonating.[19] That may seem like a lot of explosive, but it is worth remembering that the device built by Timothy McVeigh weighed 7,000 pounds, and he built that by himself in the back of a rented truck. Presumably, operatives sent by Al-Qaeda, the most dangerous terrorist organization the world has ever seen, would be at least as capable.[20]

In 1937 soldiers from General Franco's Fascist forces in Spain attacked and damaged two gravity dams: the 298-foot-tall Burguillo Dam near Avila, Spain, and the 184-foot-high Ordunte Dam near Bilbao, Spain. Fortunately, although both structures were damaged, they survived the attack.[21]

In 1941, Soviet troops, retreating before the advancing German forces, detonated explosives in a tunnel inside the Dnjeprostroj Dam on the Dnieper River. The upper portion of the dam was obliterated, and the flood that resulted reached a rate of 1.2 million cubic feet of water per second at one point.[22]

More recently, in 1993 Serbian forces made an attempt to destroy the Peruca Dam and flood a valley with a predominantly Croatian population of between 20,000 and 30,000 people. The dam was severely damaged and weakened, but, fortunately, Croatian forces were able to retake the structure, open the sluice gates, and relieve the pressure from the reservoir in time to save the structure. It has since undergone significant repair.[23]

The vulnerability of dams in this country has been recognized by the Department of Homeland Security, and a great deal of discussion has taken place regarding the threat they pose. In fact, the danger is judged so great and the whole subject so sensitive, that the Sector-Specific Plan for protection of dams in the United States is classified and, unlike most other Sector-Specific Plans, is not available to the public. According to a study funded by the Department of Homeland Security, one of the cities in the United States judged most vulnerable to terrorist attack is Boise, Idaho. Boise, population 200,000, was ranked tenth behind cities such as New York City–Newark; New Orleans, Louisiana; Baton Rouge, Louisiana; Norfolk, Virginia; and Charleston, South Carolina—all port cities. Boise was, in fact, evaluated as the most vulnerable city in the entire western United States.

This determination was based largely on the proximity to Boise of the Lucky Peak Dam, which is located 17 miles away. Lucky Peak Dam is 2,340 feet long and 340 feet high. It forms a reservoir 12 miles in length, which stores 300,000 acre feet of water.[24]

In Summit County, Colorado, in July 2008, the huge earthen Dillon Dam was closed completely to visitors and traffic after receipt of undisclosed threat information. This dam holds back a reservoir of 83 billion gallons of water and is poised 231 feet above a nearby community. Evaluation of the dam indicated that any explosion that caused enough damage to allow overtopping to occur would destroy the structure by virtue of the resulting erosion. The level of reservoir when full is only 6 feet below the top of the dam, so any blast which created a crater deeper than that would doom the dam. The Oklahoma City bomb left a crater 8 feet deep and 30 feet in diameter.[25]

As I noted earlier, to date terrorists have not staged any successful attacks on dams, but that is not the same as saying that they have not exhibited any interest in undertaking such an operation, or even that they have not tried. In March 2009, Indian authorities reported that Islamic terrorists associated with Lashkar-e-Taiba (LeT) were planning an operation against the Bhakra Dam in the Punjab. LeT has carried out a large number of high-profile attacks and was the organization behind the bloody fedayeen-style attack on several targets in Mumbai, so, understandably, Indian authorities took the intelligence seriously and surged significant security forces to protect the dam.[26] Other reports out of India have suggested that the threat extended to a total of six dams, and that terrorists planned to seize control of the structures and then open the floodgates, thereby avoiding the necessity to acquire sufficient explosives to demolish the structures.[27] The connections between LeT and Al-Qaeda are long-standing and intimate. Methodologies and capabilities available to LeT may well find their way into Al-Qaeda's repertoire as well.

In 2008 the Afghan Ministries of Defense and Interior reported that they had information regarding Taliban threats to the Naghlu Dam in that country. A spokesman described the Taliban effort as part of a plan to destroy infrastructure targets in Afghanistan, and noted that the government had taken steps to prevent such attacks.[28]

In 2007 there was heavy fighting in the area surrounding the Kajaki Dam in Afghanistan when Taliban forces numbering in the hundreds attempted to attack and destroy that massive structure.[29]

It required the involvement of significant numbers of British and Dutch troops to keep the dam intact.

While in custody at Guantanamo Bay, Al-Qaeda member Abdullah Al-Matrafi, who was involved in providing significant high-level logistical support to the organization, admitted that he was aware of Al-Qaeda planning for attacks on dams and nuclear power plants. Al-Matrafi has since been released into the custody of the authorities of Saudi Arabia, his home nation. Al-Matrafi had direct contact with a number of senior Al-Qaeda officials, including Osama bin Ladin.[30]

In January of 2002 in Afghanistan, U.S. forces found a computer inside of an Al-Qaeda office in the capital city of Kabul. On the computer were models of a dam, made with specialized architectural and engineering software. This software allowed the users of the computer to simulate the catastrophic failure of the dam and to analyze complex steel and concrete structures. The computer also contained software designed for use in identifying and classifying different types of soil. Such software would have been extremely useful to someone trying to predict the path of floodwaters resulting from a dam breach.[31]

This discovery was so alarming that it prompted the FBI to send a bulletin out to security experts around the country, warning that Al-Qaeda terrorists had been studying U.S. dams in preparation for new attacks. The bulletin was not made public, but was sent by the FBI's National Infrastructure Protection Center to members of the InfraGard program, an information-sharing partnership between the FBI and private industry.[32]

When I decided to begin my personal examination of security at potential target dams, I chose not to visit the handful of dams like Hoover Dam, which are typically discussed in the literature. It seemed to me that there were, in fact, strong indications that the top tier of targets had been secured to some extent, and, in addition, I had some real questions as to the practicality of constructing an improvised explosive device of the size that would be required to take out such a target. Dams may not be as impregnable as many people think they are, but still, something like the Hoover Dam is going to require a truly massive bomb to bring down.

So, instead, I chose to look at some of what I considered to be much more likely targets—the many fairly large dams surrounding big cities in the United States. Typically, these dams were built to create reservoirs of freshwater for municipal water supplies. Usually, they were also built some distance outside the urban area initially, but, in most cases, the spread of development had since engulfed these dams. Now, they often sit poised overtop heavily populated subdivisions, schools, hospitals, and nursing homes.

The first dam I looked at was in rural Montgomery County, just north of Washington, D.C. I had no trouble finding this dam, because the main state road ran directly over the top of it. On the far side I found a pleasant place to park and a lovely expanse of flower gardens. There were no physical barriers of any kind to prevent me from putting as large of a vehicle-borne explosive device as I could build directly onto the structure.

This dam stood about 15 meters high and was holding back a reservoir of 800 acres, averaging 52 feet in depth. That's roughly double the amount of water that was in South Fork Reservoir and effectively killed a small American city when it was released.

The only good news here is that downstream from this dam are several miles of state park and forest before the river valley begins to be heavily populated. Is that enough distance? The answer is unclear, even to the experts. In my calculus, though, what it says is that while this is a very easy target and an ideal location to hit with a large vehicle-borne explosive device, the resulting damage is probably not going to be sufficient to justify the magnitude of the operation that would be required to carry it out.

Next, I drove about an hour north to take a look at another large dam, this one on the outskirts of Baltimore instead of Washington,

D.C. The dam in question sat in a picturesque location beside a public road. I pulled up and parked my car directly across the street from the dam, then got out and walked around for a while. There was a fence to prevent direct access to the structure, and the mandatory hardware-store padlock on a length of chain holding it shut. There was also some razor wire along the top of the fence, and at some other points on the structure to discourage climbers; a handful of signs; and a bar that could be raised and lowered, put in place to keep people from pulling into a small access road right next to the dam.

This is the kind of stuff you use to keep teenagers from spraying graffiti on the dam or diving off it on a dare. None of this has anything to do with preventing a serious effort by capable terrorist organizations to attack this structure. Maybe it constitutes a target worth hitting to a serious group. Maybe it does not; but as it stands, it is open for the taking.

Below the dam the streambed runs hard to left, around a small ridge, and then directly into a heavily populated upscale residential area. Not too far down that valley is an elementary school. After I was done, I drove around the area for a while. There were people out mowing their lawns, kids riding their bikes, and people out jogging.

The dam in question is 240 feet tall. It is fed by a river that flows down from the north. The reservoir that is formed covers 2,400 acres and has a capacity of 23 billion gallons of water. The shoreline extends for a total of 39 miles. That is an awful lot of water poised 300-plus feet over the heads of a thriving suburban community.

The last dam I examined sat on the line between Howard and Prince George's counties. The first road I tried to take to the dam had a gate chained shut across it and a sign saying no trespassing. I could have walked around the gate, because there was no fence, but, in keeping with my methodology throughout this book, I chose not to. That would have been trespassing, and I had vowed to break no laws. I could also have cut the chain and driven any vehicle I wanted down the road to the dam, but, again, that would have put me out of bounds. I moved on.

The second gate I found was in a wire-mesh fence, but it still took only a little bit of poking around to get myself to a location from which I could see the dam and the access road. The dam was also visible from another major highway a short distance away.

Other than the padlocked gates, there were no other security measures in place. I saw no cameras. There were no guards. Neither were there any barriers that would have posed a significant obstacle to the movement of a large vehicle out onto the dam. I could have cut the lock and chain with bolt cutters, or I could have just rammed the gate and broken it open. In any event, for someone bent on mass murder, there was nothing there that would have been a real issue or would have required more than a few moments to deal with.

Behind this dam was a reservoir 9.5 miles long, encompassing more than 800 acres of water and 120 feet deep. That is several times as much water as was unleashed on Johnstown. The dam itself was 840 feet long and 134 feet high. As of 2008, it was officially classified as being "unsafe." Less than 1 mile downstream sat a small city with a population in excess of 20,000 individuals.

After I visited the dam and finished my observations there, I drove down into the city in question, parked my truck, and wandered around downtown for a while. It was a nice place. There was a pleasant elementary school, a surprising number of well-maintained houses right in town, and a park along the banks of the river below the dam.

There was no indication here of any sense of the danger hanging over the heads of everyone living in the community. No warning sirens on poles. No signs. No marking that I saw of evacuation routes. Maybe just as well, I finally decided, because if that dam were to go suddenly, there would be no time for anyone to do anything. There would be the terrifying roaring noise the people in Johnstown heard, then the onslaught of the grinding, churning mountain of trees, houses, and bodies, and, then, ultimately, silence.

The last dam I wanted to take a look at was the Kensico Dam near New York City. I name it here, in contrast to most of the other structures I examined, because it is one of those targets that have been discussed so widely. A minute on the Internet would be sufficient to identify it and to appreciate its significance. Anyone who thinks that our enemies are not sufficiently aware to have assimilated this information is dangerously delusional.

The Kensico Dam is part of the vast system of dams, reservoirs, and aqueducts that supplies drinking water to New York City. It sits north of the city at the head of the narrow canyon of the Bronx River. Below it is one of the most heavily populated areas in North America.

The water level in the reservoir behind the Kensico Dam is 355 feet above sea level and 168 feet above the level of the ground below it. On either side of the dam are two hills over 400 feet in height. A breach of this structure would be catastrophic. There is no place for the water to go. There is no possibility for the water to spread out, for the force of the flood to dissipate. If the dam goes, a wall of water at least 100 feet high is going to explode into the dense, urban area below it.

In the path of these floodwaters will be expressways, train stations, schools, hospitals, churches, apartment houses, and homes. It will follow a path through a narrow river valley that twists from side to side and drops steadily toward the sea. This will ensure that not only does the wall of water keep moving, but that it accelerates as it goes. It may at points, in fact, reach a speed of 300 miles an hour—a wall of wreckage, eerily reminiscent of Johnstown, but exponentially more destructive. By the time the flood begins to slow and spread out through the streets of the South Bronx, there will likely be tens of thousands dead.[33]

For anyone charged with homeland security, Kensico is a true nightmare. For those enemies of ours who dream of killing on a massive scale, it is a dream come true.

I asked an associate of mine, the same individual who helped me with much of my research on the New York Subway system, to take a hard look at Kensico and report the results. Over a period of two weeks, my associate made two separate lengthy visits to the site, taking notes, wandering around, and snapping a significant number of photographs.

On the negative side, nothing that my associate did attracted any attention at all. As with all aspects of this book, all "casing" was done in the open without the employment of any techniques for disguising what was being done. The plan in the event of challenge by security was also the same as I employed at all times: to tell the whole truth and nothing but the truth. This was not necessary. No questions were asked. Even when my associate used a flash on a camera to take some pictures of security barriers as the sun was setting, this did not appear to attract attention.

On the plus side, however, there appeared to have been a significant amount of work done to secure the site and to prevent the possibility of anyone getting a vehicle-borne explosive device out onto the dam itself. On the east side of the dam the road that runs atop the dam was blocked by concrete Jersey barriers, and the road was clearly marked as closed. At this location there were also cameras and floodlights. Beyond these barriers there was a military vehicle parked in front of additional hydraulic barriers, which could be raised or lowered. The number of security personnel present was unclear, but it was obvious that there were guards on-site.

The west side of the dam appeared to have similar security in place. There was a police vehicle on location and barriers here as well. Past these outer barriers there were, again, hydraulic barriers in line with a guard shack.

The plaza below the dam was open for recreation but also subject to significant security. The east parking lot was closed with a metal bar barrier. The west parking lot was open, and from there you can walk into the plaza below the dam. Inside the plaza, however, was a uniformed security officer. Close to the foot of the dam on the east side was a 9/11 memorial with a security camera positioned on it.

There were two staircases on either end of the dam, both of which are cordoned off with orange mesh and labeled with CLOSED FOR CONSTRUCTION signs.

There were floodlights positioned around the plaza and several on top of the dam, but no visible personnel above the dam.

Whether all of this security was sufficient to defeat a determined attack by a large terrorist team employing a combination of vehicle-borne explosive devices and assault forces is open to debate. Relative to what I had seen at every site I examined, however, what my associate found was an impregnable fortress. Once again, in New York City, where perhaps the pain of 9/11 is most intense, there was clear evidence that officials charged with homeland security and counterterrorism were taking the threat seriously and paying attention.

In 1941, then FBI director J. Edgar Hoover wrote: "It has long been recognized that among public utilities, water supply facilities offer a particularly vulnerable point of attack to the foreign agent."[34] It is nice to see that at least in New York City, there are people who understand that, and who have absorbed the significance of this vulnerability. Now, if we could only spread some of that same focus and determination elsewhere in the nation.

CHAPTER SEVEN
Remembering Caffa
BIO LABS

I say, then, that the sum of thirteen hundred and forty-eight years had elapsed since the fruitful Incarnation of the Son of God, when the noble city of Florence, which for its great beauty excels all others in Italy, was visited by the deadly pestilence. Some say that it descended upon the human race through the influence of the heavenly bodies, others that it was a punishment signifying God's righteous anger at our iniquitous way of life. But whatever its cause, it had originated some years earlier in the East, where it had claimed countless lives before it unhappily spread westward, growing in strength as it swept relentlessly on from one place to the next. . . .

Against these maladies, it seemed that all the advice of physicians and all the power of medicine were profitless and unavailing. Perhaps the nature of the illness was such that it allowed no remedy; or perhaps those people who were treating the illness . . . being ignorant of its causes, were not prescribing the appropriate cure. At all events, few of those who caught it ever recovered, and in most cases death occurred within three days from the appearance of the symptoms we have described, some people dying more rapidly than others, the majority without any fever or other complications.[1]

SO DID GIOVANNI BOCCACCIO BEGIN WHAT IS PERHAPS THE MOST famous account of the spread of the Black Death through Europe in the fourteenth century. Famously, and perhaps inaccurately, the Black Death, more properly known as "the plague," began when Muslim forces besieging the town of Caffa in the Crimean catapulted the infected bodies of victims of the plague over the city walls and into the midst of the Christian defenders. The plague is still with us, and is, in fact, a common disease among wild rodents in the Southwestern United States. If we are not careful, we may yet find it turned loose against us once again by Muslim forces engaged in jihad.

As I was writing this book, there was a big scare in the United States regarding the swine flu. Upwards of a hundred people died throughout the country, and in Mexico the disease was widespread enough to disrupt the pattern of life in the capital city. You could hardly turn on a television for weeks in the United States without hearing dire predictions regarding a pandemic and the disruption of life as we knew it.

Yet, the swine flu so pales in significance in comparison to the plague as to seem almost trivial. If we are to comprehend the enormity of the danger that hangs over our heads in regard to diseases like the plague, we may have to recalibrate our minds and accept the possibility of something altogether qualitatively different. We may, in fact, have to think about something that approaches the end of days.

In England in the fourteenth century, all available evidence indicates that something like 48 percent of the population perished from the plague. Nearly half of the people in the country died, and this happened in a period spanning eighteen months from beginning to end. Stop and think about that for a moment. Imagine an occurrence of that magnitude in our time.

Even if you are one of the lucky ones who survives, you will be living in a United States of America in which something like 150 million people have died in the last eighteen months. One-half of your family members will be dead. Cities will be emptied. Services will be disrupted. People will be traumatized by the spread of the disease into fearing contact with outsiders and retreating into their own enclaves. It may take decades or longer before anything approaching normality returns.

This is the kind of disaster that a disease like the plague can unleash.

Since 9/11 there has been a great deal of focus in this nation on the possibility of a terrorist group acquiring biological weapons and using them against us. In fact, two of the Homeland Security planning scenarios deal with biological attacks:

Scenario 2: Anthrax-making laboratories have been found in Al-Qaeda training camps in Afghanistan. Intelligence reporting indicates that terrorists continue to be interested in weaponizing the virus, and, of course, the mystery of the anthrax attacks in the United States remains unresolved to this day. Against that scary real-world backdrop, another scenario is that terrorists spray an aerosolized form of anthrax from a van into three cities, and then two more cities shortly afterwards. Thirteen thousand people would die, and, again, the economic impact would number in the billions.

Scenario 3: Terrorists release pneumonic plague into an airport bathroom, a sports arena, and a train station in a major city and the contagion spreads rapidly. Some 2,500 people would die, and 7,000 people would be injured. The economic impact is estimated to be in the billions.[2]

I agree with this emphasis. I was head of the CIA's weapons of mass destruction unit before I retired in May of 2008. We focused on all terrorist programs worldwide that were looking to acquire nuclear, radiological, chemical, or biological capability. One of our biggest concerns regarding a true mass casualty event centered on biological weapons.

That said, to date much of our homeland security effort regarding biological weapons seems to have focused on spending a lot of money and building a lot of facilities without necessarily focusing on why we were doing it, and whether we were improving the situation or making it worse. We have a lot more labs now and a lot more people in them, but that may have made us much less safe than we were before. While we worry about germs and the possibility of someone setting them loose against us, we are rapidly growing the pathogens ourselves and placing them in facilities all over this country, including major population centers.

Since 2001 over $20 billion has been spent on biodefense programs.[3] The budget for biodefense research at the National Institutes of Health alone in 2008 was $1.6 billion. The number of laboratories working with dangerous pathogens has exploded. By the time current construction is complete, there will be ten times as much lab space dedicated to this work as there was in 2001.

In 2001, there were a total of five Biosafety Level 4 (BSL 4) labs in the United States. Those are the labs approved to handle the most dangerous pathogens on earth. There are now, or soon will be when construction is complete, fifteen. No one, including the U.S. government, has any clear idea how many Biosafety Level 3 (BSL 3) labs there are, but the number is in the thousands. At least 15,000 technicians in the United States are working in BSL 4 and BSL 3 labs today. Since most of this growth in labs has happened in the last few years, we have the additional factor to contend with that a huge percentage of these lab technicians are recently hired and relatively inexperienced.

While the growth in this area has been fueled by homeland security concerns, this does not translate into the Department of Homeland Security having control over what is happening. There are at least twelve different federal agencies with jurisdiction in this area. No single one of them is in charge of safety or security standards.[4]

To understand the full import of what this all means, it helps to take a moment and look closely at exactly what BSL 4 and BSL 3 labs are, and what kind of pathogens they handle.

According to the National Institutes of Health, BSL 4 labs are used to study agents that pose a high risk of life-threatening disease for which no vaccine or therapy is available. That means we cannot cure them. If you contract such a disease, you are effectively already dead.

Lab personnel in these facilities are required to wear full-body, air-supplied suits and to shower when exiting the facility. The labs incorporate all BSL 3 features and are supposed to occupy safe, isolated zones within a larger building. When you think of the popular image of a biological research facility as portrayed on television or in the movies, with people walking around in what look like spacesuits, it is a BSL 4 facility you are visualizing.

BSL 4 labs study diseases like the Ebola virus, the Marburg virus, hemorrhagic fever, and Lassa fever. These are the most lethal killers on the planet. People infected with Ebola virus, as an example, have sudden fever, weakness, muscle pain, headache, and sore throat, followed by vomiting, diarrhea, rash, limited kidney and liver functions, and both internal and external bleeding. Death rates for populations infected with Ebola are close to 90 percent.

Given the lethality of the agents studied at BSL 4 labs, you could probably be excused for thinking that such facilities would be hidden away in remote locations in the mountains, surrounded by impenetrable defenses and far from any significant human populations. You would, of course, be mistaken. Of the original five BSL 4 labs, one was in Atlanta, another in San Antonio, and one in Frederick, Maryland, only about an hour from D.C. The distribution of the additional BSL 4 labs under construction is similar. One of the most controversial is in downtown Boston.[5] That one is completed and waiting to open.

BSL 3 labs are used to study agents that can be transmitted through the air and cause potentially lethal infection. Researchers perform lab work in a gas-tight enclosure. Other safety features include clothing decontamination, sealed windows, and specialized ventilation systems. These are much less secure facilities than BSL 4 labs. As noted above, there are by this point thousands of them in the United States, many of them located inside major hospitals in urban areas.

Surprisingly, though, many of the diseases which the public knows best and fears the most are actually allowed to be studied in BSL 3 labs. Anthrax, for example, is held, studied, and grown in

BSL 3 labs all over the country. Other pathogens that are worked with in BSL facilities include West Nile virus, encephalitis, SARS, salmonella, and yellow fever.

The irony of all this, of course, is that our obsession with the possibility of biological terrorism is based largely on one incident—the 2002 anthrax attacks in the United States. Those attacks, assuming that we can trust the conclusions of the Federal Bureau of Investigation (FBI), were perpetrated not by a foreign terrorist organization but by a researcher working in a BSL 4 facility inside the United States. The anthrax used in those attacks came not from a secret terrorist lab hidden in the mountains of Pakistan, but out of a known sample of the bacteria grown as part of our own research programs.

In other words, in response to attacks that originated inside one of our own bio labs, we have decided to dramatically increase both the numbers of such labs and the numbers of individuals working inside of them. We have not, however, significantly changed anything regarding the security of those labs.

The anthrax attacks took place in two waves. The first wave is believed to have consisted of a total of five letters, all mailed from Trenton, New Jersey, on September 18, 2001. These letters were sent to ABC News, CBS News, NBC News, the *New York Post,* and American Media, Inc. The second set of letters, also sent from Trenton, New Jersey, was mailed on October 9, 2001. These went to the offices of senators Tom Daschle and Patrick Leahy. Ultimately, five people died of anthrax contracted from exposure to the substance in these envelopes. Seventeen other individuals were also infected but recovered.

Eventually, after years of frustration, the FBI's investigation centered on a researcher at Fort Detrick, Maryland, named Bruce Edward Ivins. Ivins was employed in probably the nation's premier biodefense facility and had direct access to anthrax spores. With the FBI apparently closing in and about to formally charge him, Ivins chose to opt out. He committed suicide on July 27, 2008, by taking an overdose of a common painkiller.

There has been a lot of controversy about the FBI's case against Ivins. That is understandable. It took seven years to solve the case, and, in the end, Ivins killed himself, thereby preventing a full public display of the evidence against him. That said, I have read the bulk of the documents that have been unsealed by court order regarding the case, and I have to say that the case against Ivins is pretty compelling. A detailed review of the evidence is well beyond the scope of this work, but the summary provided by the FBI in its applications for search warrants in the case gives a good flavor of the facts stacked up against Ivins:

The Federal Bureau of Investigation and the U.S. Postal Inspection Service (hereinafter "Task Force") investigation of the anthrax attacks has led to the identification of Dr. Bruce Edward Ivins, an anthrax researcher at the U.S. Army Medical Research Institute for Infectious Diseases, Fort Detrick, MD, as a person necessitating further investigation for several reasons: (1) At the time of the attacks, he was the custodian of a large flask of highly purified anthrax spores that possess certain genetic mutations identical to the anthrax used in the attacks; (2) Ivins has been unable to give investigators an adequate explanation for his late-night laboratory work hours around the time of both anthrax mailings; (3) Ivins has claimed that he was suffering serious mental health issues in the months preceding the attacks, and told a coworker that he had "incredible paranoid, delusional thoughts at times" and feared that he might not be able to control his behavior; (4) Ivins is believed to have submitted false samples of anthrax from his lab to the FBI for forensic analysis in order to mislead investigators; (5) at the time of the attacks, Ivins was under pressure at work to assist a private company that had lost its FDA approval to produce an anthrax vaccine the Army needed for U.S. troops, and which Ivins believed was essential for the anthrax program at USAMRIID; and (6) Ivins sent an e-mail to [name excised from record] a few days before the anthrax attacks, warning that "bin Laden terrorists for sure have anthrax and sarin gas" and have "just decreed death to all Jews and all Americans," language similar to the anthrax letters warning "WE HAVE THIS ANTHRAX . . . DEATH TO AMERICA . . . DEATH TO ISRAEL."[6]

Unfortunately, the very strength of the FBI's case against Ivins also serves to point out just how dangerous the profusion of biodefense labs is to our security. Ivins was not a grad student somewhere making anthrax in his basement. He was an anthrax researcher working in the heart of the nation's premier biodefense lab. He remained in that position despite what were apparently severe mental and emotional issues, and he had the obvious ability to access, cultivate, and remove anthrax spores without any effective supervision.

Since producing anthrax spore preparations was one of Dr. Ivins's principal responsibilities at USAMRIID, he had multiple and unfettered opportunities to produce or divert Ames strain spores for illegitimate purposes. His access to Suite B3 and USAMRIID afforded all of the equipment and containment facilities which would have been needed to prepare the anthrax and letters used in the Fall 2001 attacks.[7]

In fact, some of the most compelling evidence against Ivins was the FBI's analysis of his work habits and the time that he spent in his lab. While Ivins was allowed to come and go from the lab where the anthrax was stored and cultivated as he chose, and without supervision, access to the lab required that he swipe a security badge through a card reader. The same procedure was required to exit the lab when he was done. All of the times and dates pertaining to Ivins's lab time were, therefore, retrievable electronically and accessible to the FBI.

Analysis of the data obtained from the card reader showed a very clear and disturbing pattern. Immediately prior to the mailings of both sets of anthrax letters, Ivins logged several long late-night sessions in the lab. He was alone and unsupervised on all of these occasions. These late-night sessions were out of character and do not show up at any other time in his tenure at Fort Detrick. No one else working at the facility demonstrated any such pattern.[8]

When questioned by the FBI about the work he was doing during these late-night lab sessions, Ivins could provide no coherent explanation for his activities. He admitted that there was no real work requirement that he be there, and did not deny that his own actual legitimate role in the ongoing anthrax work at the lab at that point in time was relatively minimal.

All of this activity was transpiring in a very sensitive facility, inside a lab housing some of the most dangerous pathogens on earth, and at a time when Ivins was apparently going through some very serious mental and emotional problems:

The investigation has shown that in 2000 and through the mailings in 2001, Dr. Ivins had mental health issues. Dr. Ivins's mental health issues came to the attention of investigators while reviewing e-mails of USAMRIID researchers. Through the e-mails it was determined that Dr. Ivins was undergoing significant stress in both his home and work life. The mental health issues and stress were significant to the extent that Dr. Ivins sought professional help from a psychiatrist and was immediately prescribed medication that started in February 2000.

The following are excerpts from e-mails dated April 2000 through December 2001, from Dr. Ivins to a friend regarding work, home, state of mental health, and use of medication (emphases are as they appeared in the e-mails):

April 3, 2000, "Occasionally I get this tingling that goes down both arms. At the same time I get a bit dizzy and get this unidentifiable 'metallic' taste in my mouth. (I'm not trying to be funny. It actually scares me a bit.) Other times it's like I'm not only sitting at my desk doing work, I'm also a few feet away watching me do it. There's nothing like living in both the first person singular AND the third person singular!"

June 27, 2000, "Even with the Celexa and the counseling, the depression episodes still come and go. That's unpleasant enough. What is REALLY scary is the paranoia. . . . Remember when I told you about the 'metallic' taste in my mouth that I got periodically? It's when I get these 'paranoid' episodes. Of course I regret them thoroughly when they are over, but when I'm going through them, it's as if I'm a passenger on a ride. . . . Ominously, a lot of the feelings of isolation—and desolation—that I went through before college are returning. I don't want to relive those years again. . . . I've been seeing the counselor once a week. . . ."

July 4, 2000, "The thinking now by the psychiatrist and counselor is that my symptoms may not be those of a depression or bipolar disorder; they may be that of a "Paranoid Personality Disorder. . . ."

July 7, 2000, in an e-mail, Dr. Ivins offered to be interviewed as a case study, as long as it remained anonymous. Dr. Ivins indicated that he did not want to see a headline in the National Enquirer *that read, "PARANOID MAN WORKS WITH DEADLY ANTHRAX!!!"*

July 23, 2000, "It's been a really stressful week, from all standpoints. Home, work, and it's not going well with the counselor I'm going to. (She said she thinks I'm going to have to ask to get put with another counselor or into a group session. . . . Sometimes I think that it's all just too much.)"

August 12, 2000, "Last Saturday, as you probably guessed from my e-mail, was one of my worst days in months. I wish I could control the thoughts in my mind. It's hard enough some-times controlling my behavior. When I'm being eaten alive inside, I always try to put on a good front here at work and at home, so I don't spread the pestilence. . . . I get incredible paranoid, delu-sional thoughts at times, and there's nothing I can do until they go away, either by themselves or with drugs."

March 4, 2001, "The people in my group just don't pick up on what I try to say. They are not into the kinds of problems I bring up, so it's hard for them to deal with them. The psychiatrist is helpful only because he prescribes the Celexa. He's not that easy to talk to, and he doesn't really pick up on my problems. The woman I saw before I went into group wanted to get me put in jail. That wasn't very helpful either. I'm down to a point where there are some things that are eating away that I feel I can't tell ANYONE . . ."

September 15, 2001, "I am incredibly sad and angry at what happened, now that it has sunk in. Sad for all of the vic-tims, their families, their friends. And angry. Very angry. Angry at those who did this, who support them, who coddle them, and who excuse them."

September 26, 2001, "Of the people in my 'group,' every-one but me is in the depression/sadness/flight mode for stress. I'm really the only scary one in the group. Others are talking about how sad they are or scared they are, but my reaction to the WTC/ Pentagon events is far different. Of course, I don't talk about how I really feel with them—it would just make them worse. Seeing how differently I reacted than they did to the recent events makes me really think about myself a lot. I just heard tonight that bin Laden terrorists for sure have anthrax and sarin gas.

December 15, 2001, "I made up some poems about having two people in one (me + the person in my dreams) . . .

I'm a little dream-self, short and stout.

I'm the other half of Bruce—when he lets me out.

When I get all steamed up, I don't pout.
I push Bruce aside, then I'm free to run about!
Hickory dickory Doc—Doc Bruce ran up the clock. But
something then happened in very strange rhythm. His other self
went and exchanged places with him. So now, please guess who
is conversing with you. Hickory dickory Doc!
Bruce and this other guy, sitting by some trees, exchang-
ing personalities. It's like having two in one. Actually it's rather
fun!"

What I have cited above is only a portion of the information acquired by the FBI concerning Ivins's behavior, but I think it is more than enough to get the point across. This was an individual who was coming apart at the seams. He was seriously mentally ill and screaming for help. And, yet, as his problems and his paranoia grew ever more severe, he remained in a position which allowed him to have unrestricted, unsupervised access to dangerous pathogens and a laboratory in which to work with them.

It would be one thing, of course, if the Ivins case were a complete aberration occurring against the backdrop of a biodefense industry which otherwise appears to be well run and thoroughly secure. Unfortunately, that is not the case, and the list of incidents that have already happened is lengthy.

Following the revelations regarding Ivins and his connection to the anthrax attacks, Fort Detrick undertook a series of actions to attempt to get a handle on activities at the facility concerning dangerous pathogens. One of the actions taken was a comprehensive review of what bio-agents existed at the facility. It is, after all, hard to figure out what is missing or being misused if you do not first have an idea of what you are supposed to have.

You might expect that such a process at what is the nation's most sensitive biodefense facility would be relatively straightforward. You would probably anticipate that dangerous microorganisms would be tightly controlled and that accounting for containers in which they were stored would be rigorous.

Again, you would be wrong.

The inventory of items on hand at the U.S. Army Medical Research Institute of Infectious Diseases identified 9,220 samples that hadn't been included in the master database. These included dangerous pathogens such as the Ebola virus, anthrax bacteria, and botulinum toxin. There were also a number of less-lethal agents like Venezuelan equine encephalitis virus and the bacterium that causes tularemia. Some of these samples dated back as far as the Korean War.

The fact that there were 9,200 samples sitting around but not on any existing inventory is already hard enough to accept. Maybe even more troubling, however, is where they were found. They weren't located in some hidden storage room or inside an underground bunker that had remained sealed for years. They were found all over the lab, often in storage areas in common use, mixed in with other samples that were on the inventory.

In fact, the probe was ordered after a spot check found twenty samples of the equine encephalitis virus in a box of vials instead of the sixteen listed in the institute's database. That resulted in an order directing that all research at the institute would be halted until a thorough inventory of viruses and bacteria could be conducted.

The reality is that, as demonstrated by this inventory, no one really had any idea of how many containers of dangerous pathogens existed at the lab, or what those pathogens were. Many of the materials found were things that had been worked with in the past by researchers who had either retired or left to work elsewhere. No one had any idea of their existence, meaning that no one really had any idea of what had happened to any of this material. There was no control over these samples, and, until the inventory, there was no awareness at all that they were even there.

In such a situation, it is, of course, ludicrous to claim that you have any control at all over what pathogens are in the lab, what is being brought in, and, most importantly, what is being taken out. There is nothing at all to stop someone working with dangerous microbes in the lab from simply carrying out vials of the material whenever he chooses. You are completely at the mercy of the individual researchers working in the facility, and, should they, like Ivins, have bad intentions, you are in deep trouble.[9]

This is not an aberration. This kind of situation is the norm.

In 2003, a professor at Texas Tech University was found guilty of forty-seven out of sixty-nine charges filed against him by federal prosecutors. This case began as the result of the disappearance of thirty vials of plague bacteria from the lab in which the professor was working. While the researcher in question, Thomas C. Butler, chief of the infectious diseases division at the Texas Tech Health Sciences Center, was acquitted of some of the most serious charges against him, the exact disposition of these thirty containers of plague bacteria was never conclusively determined. In the best case, they were destroyed, and the lab's records were never updated. In the worst case, they were taken out of the lab and remain unaccounted for. In the course of this investigation and trial, it was, in fact, determined that Dr. Butler had shipped samples of the plague out of the country to Africa. Dr. Butler indicated that these shipments were sent to research associates, but there was apparently no question that he mailed the samples without the appropriate approvals, and that he labeled the Federal Express packages merely as laboratory materials.

Dr. Butler was an expert on plague and had been conducting research on which antibiotics should be stockpiled in case of a plague outbreak. Studies conducted in Tanzania in 2002 focused on the use of two antibiotics, doxycycline and gentamicin, for this purpose, and both were found to be effective. It is, therefore, likely that Butler was sending materials to Tanzania for legitimate research purposes. That does not change the fact, however, that he was able to do so in direct circumvention of established procedures, without detection by anyone.

Butler also brought blood samples from Tanzanian patients to his Texas Tech laboratory in April 2002 to identify the specific strains of plague. These were carried by Butler in his checked luggage on regular commercial airline flights. Butler also took samples in his personal automobile to the Centers for Disease Control and Prevention facility in Fort Collins, Colorado, and the Army's Medical Research Institute of Infectious Diseases in Fort Detrick, Maryland. He was not charged with any offense for this activity, and the investigation apparently showed that this was a relatively common practice among researchers.[10]

In April 2009, three vials of equine encephalitis were reported missing from Fort Detrick. An investigation was initiated, but the state of recordkeeping at the lab made it unlikely that the fate of the vials would ever be determined. It was possible that they had been destroyed and records not updated. It was also possible that they had been carried out of the lab. An Army official commenting on the incident said, "We'll probably never know exactly what happened. It could be the freezer malfunction. It could be they never existed."[11]

In February 2009, a Newark, New Jersey, lab reported that it lost two dead mice infected with the plague. Apparently, the loss had been discovered three months earlier, but the lab did not immediately report the incident.[12]

In August 2007, a lab worker at St. Louis University was stuck with a needle contaminated with monkeypox, a disease similar to smallpox.

In June 2007, an hour-long power outage at the CDC's newest top-security lab outside of Atlanta raised serious questions about the safety of the agents inside the facility after the backup generator failed to deploy. A lab of this type relies on maintaining negative pressure within the research spaces to ensure that microorganisms do not escape through air ventilation systems. When the electric power is out, the systems that maintain negative pressure do not work, and that means that one of the primary mechanisms for preventing the escape of dangerous pathogens is off-line.

In May 2007, a lab employee at the University of Kentucky was exposed to plague bacteria after a protective bag leaked.

At the University of Texas at Austin in April 2007, a researcher mistakenly came into contact with a cross between the bird flu and human flu. The researcher was put on drugs and the lab was shut down for decontamination.

In 2006, a lab worker at Texas A&M University was infected with Brucella, and later that year, several researchers were exposed to Q fever. A&M failed to report the incidents at the time. After the news broke in 2007, at least a dozen other violations surfaced. A&M had its biodefense research suspended while an investigation was conducted.

In Newark, New Jersey, in 2005, mice infected with the plague escaped into the city from a lab. They were never recovered. This was the same facility from which mice again disappeared in 2009.[13]

At the University of Wisconsin in 2005 and 2006, researchers conducted work on the Ebola virus without authorization from appropriate authorities.

At the University of Chicago in 2005, a lab worker stabbed himself with a needle contaminated with anthrax.

A Russian researcher died in 2004 after being exposed to Ebola in a lab.

In 2004, a researcher at the Medical University of Ohio was infected with Valley fever. The following summer other workers were exposed to the same agent.

Three lab workers were infected with tularemia at Boston University in 2004, but the infections weren't immediately reported to authorities.

Several Chinese researchers working with SARS in Asia in 2003 and 2004 were infected with the disease. One individual died.[14]

In 2004, live anthrax was accidentally sent to Children's Hospital & Research Center in Oakland, California.[15]

In August of 2007, contamination of foot-and-mouth disease was discovered at several farms near Pirbright, a top-security lab in the

United Kingdom working with the live virus that causes the disease. When investigators began to dig into the case, they found that the animals in question were infected with precisely the same strain of the disease that was being worked with at Pirbright. Subsequently, they were able to identify leaking pipes and poor drainage at the lab and determine that it was likely the contaminants got into the farm soil through this route. Six hundred cattle had to be slaughtered to prevent further dissemination of the disease.[16] The lab in question was a private facility that worked with the virus in order to create vaccines, exactly the same type of work done by many of the BSL 3 labs in the United States.[17]

During the 1990s, lab specimens of anthrax spores, Ebola virus, and other pathogens disappeared from Army labs at Fort Detrick and were never recovered. An inquiry into the issue found that an unidentified individual was entering a lab late at night and conducting unauthorized research, apparently on anthrax. In commenting on the subject, a former commander of the installation noted that it was impossible to determine what happened to the materials, and said that it was likely some of them were simply thrown out with the trash.[18]

None of this appears to have resulted in significantly tighter security or control. Commenting on the situation in late 2007, Keith Rhodes, an investigator with the U.S. Government Accountability Office, said, "The labs are pretty much overseeing themselves at this point. I would have to say we are at a greater risk today of an infectious disease outbreak."[19]

As bad as internal procedures have been, and as chaotic as oversight appears to be, the physical security of the labs springing up all around the country does not appear to be much better. In fact, considerable concern has already been expressed regarding this topic.

In September 2008, the Government Accountability Office (GAO) issued a report on physical security at the nation's existing Biosafety Level 4 laboratories. Two of the five labs then existing and in operation were found to be seriously deficient. These were the Georgia State University's Viral Immunology Center and the Southwest Foundation for Biomedical Research in San Antonio, Texas.[20]

The Viral Immunology Center, which is located right in the heart of downtown Atlanta, and which is one of two facilities on the planet where smallpox is known to be stored, was found to lack the following:

- an outer perimeter boundary
- blast standoff
- barriers to prevent vehicles from approaching the lab
- loading docks located outside the footprint of the main building
- a command and control center
- CCTV monitored in a command and control center
- an active intrusion-detection system
- camera coverage of the full exterior of the building
- a visible armed-guard presence
- X-ray machines in operation at entrances
- vehicle screening
- visitor screening

In short, at this facility—one of the five most sensitive laboratories in the country, approved to work with the most virulent diseases known to man—there was no meaningful physical security of any kind. This was not thirty years ago. This was late 2008 in the middle of a major American city.

The situation at the Southwest Foundation for Biomedical Research was, if anything, worse. There was no armed-guard presence. There were no roving patrols. The GAO even found that it was possible to gain direct access to the lab by simply climbing in an outside window. One off-site portion of the lab was not even monitored by the laboratory's security force at all. Responsibility for that location had been turned over to a private alarm-monitoring company.

In the summer of 2009, having done my background research, I decided to go and have a look myself at the level of security in place at U.S. bio labs. Since they were more numerous, I thought I would begin with some of the BSL 3 labs in the vicinity of my home. As I have noted earlier, these are relatively common, and not difficult to locate with a few minutes' research on the Internet.

The first lab I decided to visit was a private, commercial facility in suburban Maryland. The biotechnology company that operates the lab in question claims significant expertise in infectious disease. A large portion of its business, in fact, consists of propagating select human infectious diseases and then supplying these organisms to other labs for research purposes. In other words, this company grows microorganisms that prey on human beings. For this purpose, it operates a 28,000-square-foot facility, inside of which are two separate BSL 3 laboratories for the large-scale production of viruses.

I found the facility in a quiet suburban office park about forty-five minutes from my home. Next door was the headquarters for a bank. Across the parking lot was a company specializing in property management. It was a beautiful, sunny day. There were squirrels on the lawn out front, and some employees from the biotechnology firm were having lunch at a picnic table under some spreading oak trees, to one side of the company's building. It was a very pleasant place, and indistinguishable in every aspect from the dozens of similar, tree-shaded buildings in this part of suburban Howard County.

There were no fences. There were no gates. There were no guards. The front door to the facility was made of glass and unsecured. I walked down the sidewalk along the front of the building, glancing through the windows as I went at rows of company offices, printers, fax machines, and the other standard paraphernalia of modern business. In one room I could see employees sitting around a table having a meeting. In another I could see some guys who looked like they were on break, shooting the breeze.

I wandered around the back of the building, past the picnic tables and a guy asleep in the front seat of his pickup truck, and strolled past the loading docks at the rear of the building. There were no security cameras. There were no barriers or fences at the rear of the building either. There were no guards. Behind the building was a wooded area, and beyond that I could see another, virtually indistinguishable office park.

Having completed my circumnavigation of the building, out of curiosity I walked over to the bank headquarters next door. I strolled along the front of this large building for several minutes before heading back to my car. It did not escape my notice that there were security cameras all over the exterior of the bank building, and signs regarding access at its main entrance. It appeared that you had to declare yourself to a receptionist as soon as you entered, and be buzzed in to proceed any further into the building. Evidently, it was significantly more important to protect money than viruses capable of killing human beings.

A few days later I visited the new laboratory facility constructed by the University of Maryland at its College Park campus. This building was opened in the fall of 2007. The 134,000-square-foot building contains thirty-five separate labs, and two of those are BSL 3. The entire top floor of the structure is occupied by the Maryland Pathogen Research Institute (MPRI), whose express purpose is to conduct research on dangerous microorganisms that cause disease.

Again, what I found was no physical security of any kind. The building in question sits in the middle of a university campus. Behind it is a baseball field. Next door is the student union. The doors are wide open, and there is no control over visitors. I walked in, roamed the halls. I rode the elevators. I checked out the flyers on the bulletin board offering on-campus part-time work and advertising an upcoming student social event.

I noted that the new building was actually constructed to connect directly to another apparently older building sitting next to it. In other words, you didn't even have to enter the lab building directly from the outside. You could wander in on a variety of levels from the hallways of the other structure. I did not physically make entry into the labs themselves, but, realistically, there was no measure of any kind in place that would have prevented me from doing so. Whatever agents or organisms are present and under cultivation or examination are accessible to anyone willing to exert even a modest amount of force.

I wandered outside and took a walk around this building as well. There was no indication of security anywhere. There were some kids playing Frisbee on the lawn next to the building. There were some guys that looked more like laborers than students loafing by the loading dock at the rear of the building. Beyond that I saw no one and noticed nothing of significance. There were no cameras or barriers or guards.

I wondered what it would take to actually attract attention or raise suspicion in this environment. If I walked down the sidewalk in front of the building with half a dozen suitably dressed associates carrying gym bags and backpacks, I could be inside and upstairs in moments, and no one would ever even think twice about what they had seen. We could bring guns, explosives, electronic devices— virtually anything we wanted inside—and until we were right outside the lab doors and opening up the bags we were carrying, there would be no possibility of detection. I tried for some time to think of any security measure at all that was visible, of anything I could see that was meant to prevent bad people from gaining entry to this facility. I failed. It wasn't a matter of evaluating the security. There was nothing to evaluate.

Next I visited George Mason University's new Biomedical Research Laboratory. This facility is brand-new and still not officially open. It sits just outside of Washington, D.C., and is one of several regional labs specifically intended to work on pathogens believed to be of potential utility to terrorist groups. In short, what this lab is going to do is grow and propagate precisely those diseases that we believe pose the greatest bioterror danger to the population of the United States.

In fact, George Mason's own literature on the labs says, "The university is building a BSL 3 laboratory, named the Biomedical Research Laboratory (BRL). Research will focus on diseases considered by the U.S. government to be potential bioterror threats, such as anthrax, tularemia and plague, as well as emerging infectious diseases, such as SARS, West Nile virus and influenza."[21]

In other words, this lab is not just intended to grow organisms that prey on human beings. It is also intended to grow those specific organisms judged to be of the most potential utility to terrorist organizations bent on our destruction.

The BRL sits in a lovely setting. It is located on a 10-acre plot of land adjacent to George Mason's Prince William campus. Nearby is the city of Manassas, Virginia. About 20 miles to the east is Washington, D.C.

I drove out to BRL from my home on a sunny summer afternoon with an associate who had helped me with other aspects of the research for this book. We toured the campus first, noted the locations of the local police station and the regional FBI office, and then went over and parked in front of the new lab building for a while. It was a Sunday. There was no one around. The facility appeared essentially complete, but there was still clearly construction work going on at the site.

As I noted above, to the best of my knowledge at the time of my visit, this lab was not yet actively conducting research, nor was all work on the structure absolutely finished. So, I wasn't really focused on the presence or absence of security personnel. What I was keying in on was the construction of the place and the presence or absence of security measures incorporated into the design. I was looking for indicators that someone involved with the building of this facility had considered the question of physical security, and safeguarding the materials that would be kept inside from theft and misuse.

What I found, unfortunately, was all too predictable. The lab sat adjacent to the Prince William campus of George Mason, as I had expected. It was at the end of a short drive and situated immediately adjacent to another building. There was no fence. There were no guard booths. There were no barriers to control vehicle access. There was no indication at all that there would be any real serious physical barrier to vehicles or personnel attempting to force entry in the facility.

On the drive back to my home from George Mason, I tried to make sense of the totality of what I had seen in my visits to the several BSL 3 labs. I turned the situation over in my mind, trying as hard as I could to come up with a rationale that would explain in some acceptable fashion what I had seen. In the end, of course, I failed.

Based on fears that we would be attacked by terrorists using biological agents, we had, at huge expense, opened vast numbers of new laboratories dedicated to the propagation of exactly those deadly microorganisms about which we were so concerned. We had located these laboratories throughout the nation, including, as I had seen, in immediate proximity to our nation's capital. And then, having built the labs and grown the bugs, we had chosen to simply neglect imposing any kind of meaningful requirements regarding physical security.

I thought about George Mason. I envisioned a lone armed security guard at the entrance, while admittedly I was not sure there would even be that much muscle on-site. I knew it would not take nineteen armed men to breach that level of security. A handful with weapons and the requisite knowledge to know what they were looking for would be enough. In minutes the operation would be concluded. The attackers would be leaving the site. What would they have? The plague? Anthrax? Something else, lesser-known but equally horrible?

I hoped that security at the BSL 4 labs might somehow be better, although everything I had read made me fear otherwise. I knew there was only one way to find out.

A few weeks after my trip to George Mason, I drove up to Fort Detrick in Frederick, Maryland. This is the home of the nation's premier bioterror research facilities and also the place where Dr. Ivins acquired the anthrax he used in his mailings. As noted in the literature that I have already cited, it was also the BSL 4 laboratory judged most secure by the GAO.

First, the good news.

I was actually denied access to Fort Detrick. For the first and only time in a year of research, casing, and investigation, I was required to speak with a security officer, and he told me, politely but firmly, to go away.

I drove up to the entrance to the installation and responded to the inquiry of one of the guards at the gate by indicating that I wanted to go look at one of the original biowarfare research chambers, a large metal sphere known commonly as the "eight ball." After some discussion among the several guards at the gate, it was decided that this was not allowed. I was told to leave and was supervised closely as I turned my car around and left the area. Relative to what I had seen elsewhere, this was a major security victory, and it was with some difficulty that I resisted the urge to get out of my vehicle, shake hands, and thank the security personnel for doing their jobs.

Now for the not-so-good news.

Fort Detrick sits about an hour from our nation's capital. It also sits right in the middle of the small city of Frederick, Maryland.

When I say that, I mean it literally. There are neighborhoods which directly adjoin the installation. In many places, there are homes with backyards that end directly at the chain-link fence that encircles the base. On the other side of that fence, there is typically an expanse of neatly mowed grass several hundred meters wide, and then the research buildings in which work is done on some of the most dangerous organisms on earth. I watched children in a playground swinging and playing on a merry-go-round in one park, while less than a quarter-mile away, I could see the buildings where some of the nation's most sensitive bioterror research is ongoing.

How this is possible I don't know. We are right now in the midst of a massive realignment of U.S. military bases, which involves the consolidation of many functions and the movement of entire armored and infantry divisions thousands of miles from one base to another. All of this is being done in the name of "rationalizing" our defense posture and financial efficiency.

One would think that particularly now, this would have been a great time to relocate this entire bioterror research complex away from major U.S. population centers. A location in New Mexico or Nevada, surrounded by desert and open space, would be a much more logical location for Fort Detrick than downtown Frederick. In looking at it, I kept having the same feeling that I experienced while examining the Sparrows Point LNG site. There was no margin for error. Even the slightest hiccup or problem might have devastating consequences.

The entire perimeter-security situation at Fort Detrick was problematic as well. While the guards at the gate were on top of things and the construction of the entrance was well designed to deter forced entry, the rest of the boundary of the base was encircled by nothing more than the stereotypical chain-link fence. I spent hours driving and walking the perimeter of the base. I never saw a guard. I saw many places where, if I breached the fence, I could then drive a vehicle directly to the vicinity of buildings I knew from my research had labs inside. Again, what I was seeing was security that seemed sufficient to keep out the public and deter petty thieves, but not in any way designed to block the attack of a determined adversary.

Would an attack on Fort Detrick by a team of terrorists be guaranteed of success? Probably not. It would not be out of the question either. If someone wanted what was inside bad enough, and was willing to devote resources on a par with what was used on 9/11, I think the guard force would be hard-pressed to react quickly enough to prevent catastrophe.

I suppose that all of this bad news is made that much worse by the established level of terrorist interest in biological warfare. That interest is historical, but it is also current.

In the summer of 2008, a woman named Aafia Siddiqui was arrested in Afghanistan. She is now on trial in New York City. Until her capture, Siddiqui, a senior Al-Qaeda operative, was the FBI's most wanted woman in the world. When I was still serving in the CIA and running operations against terrorist WMD programs, Siddiqui's name was commonly heard and discussed.

Siddiqui has degrees in biology and neuroscience from the Massachusetts Institute of Technology (MIT) and Brandeis University. She is an extremely bright and talented individual. At the time of her arrest, she was carrying documents concerning a whole range of Al-Qaeda targets inside the United States. Among these was the Plum Island Animal Disease Research Center. Plum Island, which is located several miles off the coast of Connecticut in Long Island Sound, is a research facility focused on a range of diseases transmitted by animals to humans. These include polio, hog cholera, African swine fever, and foot-and-mouth disease.

Prior to its current incarnation, Plum Island was a biowarfare lab. Plum Island has been the subject of much discussion in the press due to the nature of the work done there, and the proximity of the facility to major population centers. The fact that an operative like

Siddiqui, with her scientific background, had Plum Island on a list of targets she was carrying in the summer of 2008 should answer pretty much any question about the level of Al-Qaeda's interest in biological warfare and our research laboratories.[22] It tells us that not only is Al-Qaeda still working on plans for bio attacks, but also that it has recognized the shortcut to staging such attacks is to obtain the necessary pathogens right here on our soil.

That Al-Qaeda has had an interest for some time in the development of biological weapons is well documented. Prior to the U.S. invasion of Afghanistan, Al-Qaeda had actually started two separate programs for the weaponization of anthrax. The first involved a Pakistani veterinarian by the name of Rauf Ahmad. The second involved a Malaysian named Yazid Sufaat who had studied biology at the California State University. How far those programs would have progressed had we not physically entered Afghanistan remains a matter of conjecture.[23]

The British are so worried about the danger posed by bioresearch facilities on their soil that they are carefully screening all scientists who handle dangerous microorganisms in labs in that country. MI-5 has explicitly cautioned labs in the UK that Islamic terrorists may try to steal deadly viruses from research facilities. MI-5 and the National Counter Terrorism Security Office have also begun examinations of the physical security of facilities working with pathogens.[24] We might do well to pay attention and to consider that we need to undertake similar efforts here.

Putting myself in the shoes of a terrorist leader bent on staging a biological attack inside the United States, it seems obvious that the profusion of biological research facilities dedicated to working with organisms of known bioterror utility is like a gift from heaven. I am no longer faced with the task of acquiring and cultivating the organisms abroad and then attempting to move them secretly into the United States. I now have the ability to acquire those agents inside the United States, in immediate proximity to the targets against which they will be employed. My job is much easier than it would be otherwise.[25]

Labs are, of course, ripe for exploitation by terrorist organizations using insiders employed in the facilities. I am not normally fixated on "insider threat" when it comes to terrorism. I think it is usually much more difficult to get someone into a position of trust inside a target than it may seem, and I have seen very few examples of terrorists actually managing to acquire the necessary degree of access to facilitate an attack.

A biological research laboratory in the United States, I think, is a clear exception to this rule. Especially those that are in any way affiliated with U.S. educational institutions and are likely to have large numbers of foreign undergraduate and graduate students employed in them. While the overwhelming majority of these individuals are going to be diligent, honest, and beyond reproach, a certain number are likely to be from backgrounds that make them susceptible to recruitment by extremist groups. Even if they are not sent here from abroad with the goal of penetrating a lab, the odds that at least a handful of them might come to the attention of a group like Al-Qaeda and be pulled into extremism seem good.

We have seen that security and control inside even the most sensitive BSL 4 facility in the country, Fort Detrick, has repeatedly been shown to be virtually nonexistent. Security elsewhere in the country at the myriad other BSL 4 and BSL 3 labs is even worse. The difficulty in having a graduate student researcher, then acquire a sample of anthrax or the plague, therefore, seems rather minimal. Assuming that individual is reasonably careful and patient and comes prepared with the necessary items to allow transport, there is little to stand in his way.

Even if all this proves impossible, however, I, as the terrorist team leader, still have other options. Assuming I cannot find a way to surreptitiously acquire the pathogens I want, I can still take them by force. Maybe on balance I will decide that an assault on a facility like Fort Detrick is simply too great an undertaking to justify what is, after all, a preliminary stage of a much-larger operation. In that event, I will simply shift my focus to the plethora of BSL 3 labs, many of which work with organisms like anthrax and the plague.

Nowhere is there any indication of the existence of security at any of the potential target BSL 3 labs that would stand up to even a handful of armed fanatics bent on penetrating a lab and stealing the organisms necessary to stage an attack. Postulating that I have among the personnel on my team at least one individual who can locate and identify the containers holding the agents we want, and assuming I have the necessary materials to allow for "safe" transport of the microorganisms, this operation is going to be relatively easy. I will be in and out of the facility without meeting significant resistance, and well before any force arrives on-site which is capable of presenting serious resistance.

Having acquired the organisms I want by either of the two methods described, I need only then propagate them in sufficient quantity to allow for their use as a weapon. This can be done using common laboratory items available on the Internet and through supply stores, and needs only about as much space as is found in the average apartment. The law enforcement agencies faced with the task of identifying where stolen pathogens were taken and are being cultivated are going to have their work cut out for them. Time will be limited. A terrorist cell in northern Virginia which has gotten its hands on the plague is going to use it as a weapon the moment the cell leader believes he has a sufficient quantity of the disease to carry out an attack on the intended scale. It will not take years. It may only take weeks.

Ironically, as we continue to spend huge sums of money to grow vast numbers of deadly microorganisms on our own soil, we are devoting millions of dollars, not to securing all the new bio labs, but to fielding equipment to tell us when the diseases we have propagated are set loose against us. Since 2003, the Homeland Security Department has been putting sensors in thirty major American cities in an effort to develop a capability to detect a bio attack. Starting back in 2007, the Department added to this effort, called Biowatch, by rolling out a new generation of sensors, which were claimed to dramatically enhance the ability to detect dangerous microorganisms.

Unfortunately, as with so many things the Department has attempted, this effort fell short. In 2009 the Department announced it was stepping back from this new program and pulling a network of "improved" sensors from service.[26] These sensors, previously billed as a tremendous leap forward in capability, turned out to have been a complete technological failure.

In October 2003, shortly after the launch of Biowatch, detectors in Houston detected evidence of the bacteria that causes tularemia. This is one of the pathogens of greatest concern as a possible bioweapon for terrorist use. Analysis later showed that this result stemmed from a naturally occurring bacteria found in the environment, and ruled out any malicious intent. Since then there have been at least fifteen other such false alarms.[27]

Since its inception in 2003, the Department has spent $500 million on this program. Perhaps first we should have directed that money into efforts to ensure that the pathogens about which we are concerned do not escape in the first place.

The Commission on the Prevention of WMD Proliferation and Terrorism began its 2008 report as follows: "The Commission believes that unless the world community acts decisively and with great urgency, it is more likely than not that a weapon of mass destruction will be used in a terrorist attack somewhere in the world by the end of 2013. The Commission further believes that terrorists are more likely to be able to obtain and use a biological weapon than a nuclear weapon. The Commission believes that the U.S. government needs to move more aggressively to limit the proliferation of biological weapons and reduce the prospect of a bioterror attack."[28]

We are not talking about fantasy. This is not the plot for the next summer blockbuster. This is the reality in which we live in the twenty-first century. The potential consequences of a properly executed terrorist biological weapons attack are almost unimaginable. We simply cannot afford to continue to allow facilities that create these lethal pathogens to continue to mushroom all around us while simultaneously neglecting to address security. It is imperative that we act now, before we find that we ourselves are experiencing the return of the Black Death.

CHAPTER EIGHT
We Have Been Warned

AT 4:00 A.M. ON MARCH 28, 1979, THERE WAS A MECHANICAL malfunction within the Three Mile Island Nuclear Power Plant near Harrisburg, Pennsylvania. The main-feed water pumps that provided the critical cooling water to TMI-2, one of the plant's nuclear reactors, failed. Without the continuous circulation of water, the cooling system for this reactor was crippled. Safety systems kicked in immediately as they were intended to do. The reactor shut down.

Despite the reactor's shutdown, however, the temperature inside the primary cooling-water system in the nuclear portion of the plant began to increase. This caused a corresponding dramatic increase in pressure in this part of the system. To compensate, a valve on the top of the plant opened and bled off sufficient steam to stabilize the pressure at a safe level. Again the system functioned exactly as designed.

Then two more very bad things happened: First, the valve stuck open. Instead of the pressure stabilizing, it continued to drop. Precious coolant continued to be vented. Before this malfunction was finally detected many hours later, more than a quarter of a million gallons of cooling water would have been lost.

Second, a design defect in the system and in the instruments in the control room prevented the men running the plant from detecting this problem. In fact, instruments in the control room continued to show that the pressure in the system was high. As coolant continued to flow out of the system, the men working the problem continued to believe that they had too much pressure, and took a series of steps that not only did not rectify the situation but made it dramatically worse.[1]

The heart of any nuclear power plant is the reactor. This is the furnace, if you will, which creates the heat that turns water to steam, because in principle, despite harnessing the power of the atom, a nuclear power plant is not a lot different from one fired by coal. The plant creates steam. This steam in turn spins giant turbines and generates electricity. The reactor in question at Three Mile Island, TMI-2, stood 12 feet high and weighed 100 tons.

Reactors are controlled by aptly named control rods. Control rods are pushed into the reactor or withdrawn from it to moderate the pace of the reaction inside. Pushing the rods in means they absorb more particles and slow the reaction. Pulling out the rods increases the speed with which the reaction occurs.

Regardless of the pace at which the reactor is running, however, it needs to be cooled. The primary mechanism for accomplishing this cooling is through the circulation of water through the system. At heart, this system functions a lot like the radiator in your car. Water circulates, and heat is carried away.

Due to the radioactive nature of the "engine" in question, however, there are actually two systems of circulating water involved in a nuclear power station. Water in a primary loop circulates around the nuclear core inside the reactor. This water is radioactive, and during normal operation does not leave the primary loop. Heat is transferred indirectly from this primary loop to a secondary loop, which then circulates outside of the reactor area. The water in this secondary loop is allowed to turn to steam and drive the turbines.[2]

The amount of heat generated by the reactor core is almost impossible to comprehend. Even after it was shut down on March 28, 1979, TMI-2 was still producing enough heat to generate electricity for 18,000 homes. Roughly two hours into the accident, the loss of coolant from the primary system reached the point where the top of the core, the radioactive fuel itself, became uncovered. Superheated steam filled the reactor. The control rods themselves began to react with the steam to produce a number of dangerous gases, including hydrogen. Three hours into the incident, one-half of the radioactive core was uncovered.

Nine hours into the incident, hydrogen—created by the reaction between the steam and the control rods—had collected inside the containment structure (the concrete shell that surrounds the reactor), and it exploded. There was an audible thud throughout the facility and a noticeable shudder. Fortunately, despite the explosion, the containment structure held.

Finally, roughly fifteen hours into the incident, as the result of a series of incremental changes by control room personnel and some considerable luck, the core's temperature finally began to come under control. It would be several more days before the emergency was officially declared over, and 140,000 people would flee their homes in the surrounding area by then, but the crisis had passed. The containment had held. Although there had been a considerable release of radioactive steam from the plant, the worst had not happened.

A full meltdown had not occurred.

A nuclear power plant is not an atomic bomb. They both utilize nuclear material, but beyond that, they are dramatically different. An atomic bomb does not produce electrical power. A nuclear power plant, no matter what transpires, does not produce a mushroom cloud.

That does not mean that a nuclear power plant is not dangerous. It will not explode in the way a bomb will, but it may melt down, and the results of such an event may be as catastrophic as those produced from any weapon of war.

"The China Syndrome" is an expression often used to refer to the result of the meltdown of a nuclear reactor. It is based upon the premise that once the nuclear fuel melts completely, it will burn through the containment and into the ground below. Then, according to this theory, it will continue to melt its way entirely through the planet and come out in China.

For a whole bunch of reasons, that is a pretty silly notion, but it does serve to highlight the extreme temperatures with which we are dealing. In reality, assuming that events unfolded in such a way that the fuel did melt through the floor of the containment building, it would ultimately cool sufficiently to stop its descent. No one knows how far down that would be, but it would be a long, long way short of China.

In all likelihood, the fuel would strike the groundwater table, and impact with this cooling liquid would rapidly begin to take down the temperature. This collision would also, of course, produce massive quantities of radioactive steam, which would erupt from the ground in massive geysers, sending radiation out into the atmosphere and poisoning the surrounding area and anyone in it. The impact would be horrific.

In reality, this is only one of the possible scenarios involving the meltdown of a nuclear reactor. All the term meltdown really means is that the safety systems at a power plant have failed, and the nuclear fuel itself has melted. What happens in the course of such an incident is largely a matter of conjecture, because fortunately, we have very little real-world experience with this kind of event. The fuel may burn through the containment as hypothesized in the classic "China Syndrome." The amount of hydrogen produced in the course of the reactions occurring inside the reactor and the primary coolant system may be so massive that when it detonates, it may simply shatter the concrete containment shell. Explosions inside the containment shell may actually propel the entire reactor out through the surrounding wall, like some kind of giant radioactive missile. Something entirely different and unforeseen may occur.

In any event, if a full-scale meltdown occurs, the details of exactly what happens next are probably going to be of primary concern to historians and engineers. The worst will have happened. The dragon will be loose. Massive quantities of radiation will have been released.

After the Three Mile Incident was over and everyone was satisfied that the immediate danger had passed, what exactly had transpired inside the reactor itself remained a mystery for many years. The reactor core was so hot that no one could approach it or even consider opening it. Finally, in 1984, engineers were able to actually remove the reactor head and examine what had happened inside the chamber. A specialized robot was lowered into the interior of the reactor for direct observation.

What experts found was that the nuclear fuel itself had been reduced to rubble by the extreme forces at work on it. Twenty tons of nuclear fuel had melted. The extreme thermal damage to the pressure vessel led to the inescapable conclusion that sometime on Wednesday, March 28, 1979, the plant had been within thirty minutes of a catastrophic meltdown. Thirty minutes had separated the world from a full illustration of the China Syndrome.[3]

In 1986 at Chernobyl in the Ukraine, people would not be so lucky.

On April 26, 1986, the Chernobyl power plant suffered a major accident. Prior to the shutdown of the Unit 4 reactor for routine maintenance, officials decided to conduct a test of the electrical system at the plant. As the result of a number of errors by plant personnel, compounded by design deficiencies, a power surge occurred during this test. This produced a series of cascading explosions that almost totally destroyed the reactor in question. The resulting fires only added to the damage. There was no concrete containment structure at Chernobyl as had existed at Three Mile Island, and, consequently, once the reactor exploded, there was no physical mechanism for preventing the escape of radiation from the site.[4]

There was a widespread and prolonged release of radiation and radioactive materials. These materials included gases, aerosols, and particles of the nuclear fuel material itself. This release continued for ten days, and by the time it was complete, a large portion of the nuclear fuel had vaporized. The heat from the fires served to ensure that the particles were carried to a high altitude and that dispersal was widespread. In fact, every inhabitant of the Northern Hemisphere of the planet was exposed to some level of increased radiation as a result of this incident.[5]

The number of people killed outright in the explosion and fire was relatively small. How many people will ultimately die of cancer as a result of radiation exposure remains a matter of intense debate to this day. A report prepared by an organization called the Chernobyl Forum concluded that there would be roughly 4,000 such deaths. The World Health Organization compiled a lengthy report which found that 9,000 people would perish. Greenpeace believes that both of these estimates are, for a number of reasons, far wide of the mark. Their own report, prepared in 2006, stated that there would be 93,000 cancer-related fatalities as a result of the Chernobyl disaster. Other environmental groups have come up with even higher figures.[6]

In the days following the accident, 160,000 people were evacuated. Entire small cities were emptied of their populations. This was not a temporary measure. It was a permanent relocation. There remains today an exclusion zone surrounding the plant that is in excess of 18 miles in diameter. All human habitation has been abandoned within this area, and there is no estimate of when or if it may ever be safe again. Pripyat, once a Ukrainian city of 50,000, is today a ghost town.[7]

Yet even Chernobyl was a long way from being a worst-case scenario. In the scheme of things, it was just another warning. After all, both Chernobyl and Three Mile Island were industrial accidents. They showed what could happen, despite safeguards, without any assistance from outside hostile forces. What may be coming if we are not careful is of such magnitude that it almost defies comprehension, because the great fear is not that another valve will stick open. The great fear is that terrorists will deliberately and systemically engineer a meltdown.

The Indian Point nuclear power plant provides a very good example of what kind of danger is hanging over our heads. This plant sits on 239 acres on the Hudson River in Westchester County, New York. There are two operating pressurized water reactors at the site, both of them operated by Entergy Nuclear. Indian Point is located in one of the most densely populated areas in the United States; 35 miles away as the crow flies is Manhattan. More than 300,000 persons live within a 10-mile radius of the plant; 17 million live within 50 miles.[8]

In 1982, Sandia Labs did a study of the impact of a core meltdown and a radiological release from a single reactor at Indian Point. According to that study, there would be 50,000 near-term deaths and another 14,000 long-term deaths from cancer. When these results were disclosed to the public, in an effort to downplay the results, a Nuclear Regulatory Commission (NRC) official responded by saying that such an event was about as likely as a jet crashing into a football stadium during the Super Bowl.[9]

Post–9/11, perhaps we no longer consider such an analogy quite as comforting.

In 2004, the Union of Concerned Scientists decided to take another look at the problem. They updated the study, took into account a much larger set of variables, and employed the latest in computer technology. They concluded that an attack on Indian Point which resulted in a meltdown of one of the reactors could, depending on the weather, kill 44,000 people in the short term and produce another 518,000 long-term deaths from cancer among people living within 50 miles of the plant.

In addition to the loss of life, there would be other horrific consequences. As much as $1.1 trillion in economic damages would ensue. Huge areas would be rendered unusable for human habitation for the foreseeable future. Millions of individuals would have to be relocated, not temporarily, but permanently. Vast portions of the New York City metro area would become forbidden zones, wastelands.

On September 11, 2001, we experienced the impact of a major terrorist attack, one which killed 3,000 people and radically changed our way of life. A successful attack on Indian Point, resulting in a full-scale meltdown of even one of the reactors, would be something altogether qualitatively different. On September 11th, we lost many lives and several buildings. As the result of an attack on Indian Point, we might lose New York City entirely, and never be able to recover it. Manhattan would no longer be the commercial capital of the world. It would be an eerie, haunted hulk with grass pushing up through its streets and wild animals roaming its parks.

It is important to emphasize here that injuries resulting from a catastrophic release of radiation from a nuclear power plant fall into two broad categories. A certain, relatively limited number of individuals would be exposed to levels of radiation of such magnitude that they would die almost immediately, perhaps within days or weeks. Another, much larger group of individuals, who do not receive levels of exposure of this magnitude, would still be exposed to sufficient radiation to produce genetic damage. This is what leads in many cases to cancer. How long that cancer takes to manifest itself is impossible to predict. It may take years. It may take decades.

There are 103 reactors at 64 different locations in the country. These sites are in a total of 31 different states.[10] Indian Point and New York City are not exceptions, merely examples.

Nuclear power plants are marvels of modern engineering. They are also, unfortunately, extremely dangerous and capable of being turned against us by our enemies as what amounts to giant prepositioned weapons of mass destruction. The key to doing this is to cause the reactor to melt down, and, unfortunately, that just isn't all that hard to do.

The nuclear industry tends to spend a lot of time talking about the strength of the containment structures built in this country around all functioning civilian power reactors. These are massive structures, it is true. They are giant, robust concrete structures built over and around the reactors in a plant in order to contain radiation in the event of an accident. It would, in fact, probably take a truly massive terrorist explosive device to breach one of these. The simple truth, however, is that this does not matter. The terrorists do not need to get inside the containment. Everything they need to hit to destroy the plant is located outside the containment in buildings that are not armored or protected in any way.

At Three Mile Island, as soon as the personnel running the facility knew they had a problem with the feed water pumps, they shut down the reactor. The nuclear reaction inside the plant ceased. They almost lost the reactor anyway. They came within thirty minutes of a full meltdown. This is because of the enormous heat within the reactor. This energy does not simply go away because you have shut down the reactor. It has to be dissipated, and the only way to do that effectively is through the use of the cooling system.

So, let's assume that a terrorist attack begins on a nuclear power plant and that the second it starts, the alert control room staff shuts down all reactors at the site. Let's also assume that the terrorists then: seize the control room and shut down the entire cooling system; or, that they blow the pumps that circulate the water through the cooling system with a truck bomb; or, that they simply rupture all the pipes and allow the coolant to flow out of the system.

Once any of these things happens, the plant is doomed. A nuclear reactor that has been shut down can experience a full-scale meltdown within an hour if the cooling system is shut down. The terrorists don't have to breach the containment, because the forces at work inside the reactor will do that for them. When the fuel melts through the floor of the containment building, whether the reactor explodes through the wall or a giant cloud of hydrogen shatters the concrete shell, the desired effect will have been achieved. The radiation will be loose.

A terrorist with an understanding of the control-room systems can cause a meltdown without any great degree of difficulty.[11] Finding an individual with the requisite amount of training and education is not likely to prove difficult for a major group. Contrary to popular images of bearded insurgents living in caves, Al-Qaeda and other Sunni extremist groups have large numbers of individuals who have received higher-level education, often in Western institutions.

Prior to 9/11 in Afghanistan, Al-Qaeda was receiving assistance from, or had contact with, a significant number of individuals with scientific backgrounds, including former members of the Pakistani nuclear program. These included Sultan Bashiruddin Mahmood, who, prior to his retirement, had been one of the most senior nuclear scientists in Pakistan. Mahmood met personally with Osama bin Laden on at least one occasion.[12]

In talking about bio labs earlier, I made reference to the capture of senior Al-Qaeda operative, Aafia Siddiqui. Ms. Siddiqui holds biology and neuroscience degrees from Massachusetts Institute of Technology (MIT) and Brandeis University. At the time of her arrest, Ms. Siddiqui, who is now on trial in New York, was carryings notes referring to a "mass-casualty attack," and listing locations such as Wall Street, the Brooklyn Bridge, the Statue of Liberty, and the Empire State Building. She was also carrying a computer thumb drive.[13]

An organization which can draw on the expertise of individuals of the caliber of Siddiqui and Mahmood presumably is going to be able to produce a team that will include individuals with an intimate knowledge of how nuclear reactors work and how nuclear power plants are designed.

In fact, a study of 172 Al-Qaeda terrorists conducted in 2003 by a forensic psychiatrist and former CIA case officer found that the vast majority of the individuals he looked at came from surprisingly stable, middle-class or upper-class backgrounds. Two-thirds of them went to college, and most of those went on to become engineers, physicians, architects, or scientists. Attacks in Britain have, in fact, been carried out by individuals who were practicing physicians and trained engineers. We should not, therefore, operate under any illusion that somehow our enemies are incapable of putting together attack teams that would include people with sufficient technical background to know exactly what steps to take once inside a nuclear power plant.[14]

The physical security for a nuclear power plant in the United States is based on something known as the Design Basis Threat (DBT). This means that nuclear power plant operators do not simply guess at how much security they need or should provide. They are required by the Nuclear Regulatory Commission (NRC) to have in place sufficient security to defeat a threat posed by a certain level of force. The NRC, not the nuclear power plant operators, determines the DBT, and based on that, what security must be provided.

It sounds like a very good system. A nuclear power plant operator is not simply free to imagine that he is subject to less of a threat than the NRC envisions. A plant operator in a rural area is not allowed to come up with his own analysis and conclude that no one poses a serious threat to his facility. There is a single, uniform standard, and it is enforced by an independent government agency.

This assumes at least a couple of things, however. First, it assumes that when the NRC sets the DBT, it actually bases it on reality. Just as it is not acceptable for a plant manager, trying to cut costs, to fantasize that he is not at risk, the NRC should not be allowed to "hope" that the bad guys will use less force than intelligence suggests they will. The DBT, in short, needs to reflect what is going on in the world, and take into account what tactics and capabilities terrorists are known to be employing.

Second, there needs to be integrity in the evaluation process. It is all well and good to tell plant personnel that they must meet a certain standard. For that to have any meaning, however, their performance against this standard must be measured, and it must be measured accurately and fairly. Plant operators must not be allowed to cut corners. They must not be allowed to simply claim they have put in place defenses that will hold up against the agreed-upon level of threat. It must be proven that they have met this standard.

I knew that there was only one way I was going to really explore the two factors outlined above, and that was to wade into it myself. That said, I went into the process with more than a little apprehension.

So far, in working on this book, I had not found a lot of good news. Given the magnitude of the threat posed by nuclear power plants, I was really hoping that was going to change this time around.

I should also add that I am a big proponent of energy independence. I have spent a lot of time in the Middle East. I have seen how much of the profit from oil sales ends up filtering into the hands of our enemies. I am not an economist, but even I can understand that until we stop sending billions upon billions of our dollars abroad to pay for oil and gas, it is going to be hard for us to regain our economic equilibrium.

Nuclear energy has the potential to make a huge dent in our energy dependence. Nuclear plants can generate fantastic quantities of energy, and they can do it without requiring the import of a single barrel of crude. Just to sweeten the deal, they produce no greenhouse gases. Building new nuclear power plants could free us of dependence on foreign oil, deprive extremists of a source of funding, radically improve our overall economic posture, and save the planet.

All of this is predicated, however, on the requirement that we safeguard those plants and prevent them from being used against us as engines of terror. As I was about to discover, we are not doing that.

I also knew going into this portion of the book that I was not going to be able to simply walk around the facilities in question and see for myself exactly what level of security they were employing. That was simply not an option. Nor, for reasons that I have touched on earlier in this work, was I going to consider approaching this as I would a live op, employing clandestine or covert means of collection. The security of nuclear power plants is not a game. As a private citizen, I was not about to start playing with the security systems in place to protect these vital installations.

And, so, having done my research on the Internet and having taken a firsthand look from the outside at several nuclear power plants within driving distance of my home, what I did was begin to contact a wide range of individuals across the country who have worked at nuclear power plants, or have spent years functioning as watchdogs regarding plants in their areas. I then conducted a lengthy series of interviews, some telephonic, some face-to-face. Most of the people with whom I spoke were very forthcoming, and to a man they were extremely worried about the state of security at nuclear power plants in this country. To a man they were also insistent that I not mention them by name at any point in this book, because, while the NRC does not pay much attention to their demands for greater security, it does periodically lean on them and threaten some sort of action against them for discussing sensitive topics. Collectively, they painted for me a very disturbing picture, one which really ought to trouble every American citizen at this point in our history.

The DBT is set by the NRC. That means that the NRC lays out in concrete terms the level of force against which power plant security personnel must be prepared to defend. Up until a few years ago, the NRC had instructed the nuclear industry that the maximum size of an attacking force against which they would be expected to defend was three men. I have no idea how that figure was calculated, nor did any of the numerous individuals with whom I spoke in researching this book. Even prior to 9/11, it is hard to understand how the NRC could have seriously contended that the absolute maximum force any terrorist group on earth could muster in an attack on a nuclear power plant would be three men.

The good news is that this number has now been increased. The bad news is that it has not been increased by very much. I was given this new number by numerous individuals. I will not provide it here out of deference to the sensitivity of the subject with which we are dealing. Suffice it to say that while the number of attackers contemplated by the DBT is no longer three, it is not a hell of a lot larger than that.[15] There were nineteen hijackers on 9/11. A team of that size would be several times what the DBT envisions as the maximum force that might stage an attack on a nuclear power plant.

The DBT is severely limited in other ways as well. For instance, the NRC has arbitrarily decided that the attacking force would only use certain weapons. Rocket-propelled grenades (RPGs), for example, which are commonly used by terrorists around the globe, have been declared to be unavailable to any team that might attack a nuclear power plant in the United States. Guard forces are not expected to defend against them.[16] The same goes for shoulder-fired rocket launchers and .50 caliber sniper rifles, despite the fact that these weapons are commonly available worldwide and are part of the standard armament of light infantry forces everywhere.

Similarly, guard forces are not required to defend against an attack which employs both numbers of armed assailants and a vehicle-borne explosive device. The NRC has decided, arbitrarily, that the attackers will not combine these two capabilities. The possibility that an attacking team might utilize an assault force to overwhelm guard posts and security barriers and then, having nullified these measures, drive a large car or truck bomb into the plant site has simply been dismissed. Security forces are not required to deal with this option.[17]

A whole host of critics have attacked the DBT as inadequate and unrealistic. As far back as 2004, the Project on Government Oversight (POGO) put together a very specific alternative DBT which would have required plant security forces to be prepared to defend against a force of roughly squad strength, twelve to fourteen individuals, armed with all of the commonly available light infantry weapons found around the world, including RPGs, .50 caliber sniper rifles, explosive charges, and shoulder-fired missiles.[18] This proposal was put together based on information acquired by POGO in the course of discussions with Special Forces personnel at Fort Bragg, the Department of Energy, the Defense Threat Reduction Agency, and the General Accounting Office, among others. It was ignored.

To fully understand how absurd the current DBT governing defenses in place at nuclear power plants is, let's take a look at an attack that occurred while I was in the process of writing this book.

On June 9, 2009, an attack occurred on the Pearl Continental Hotel in Pakistan. While the Pearl had been known for many years to be a favorite of Westerners and Pakistani officials, it was otherwise without military or political significance of any kind. In other words, while an attack on it would produce casualties and have a psychological impact, it was certainly not a target on par with a nuclear power plant. The resources dedicated by the local Taliban to this operation should, therefore, be fairly considered to be only a fraction of what Al-Qaeda would bring to bear in a high-profile assault on a nuclear plant inside the United States.

The attackers of the Pearl Continental employed a two-phased approach: First, they sent an assault force, armed with automatic weapons, against the security checkpoint that controlled access to the facility. This phase of the operation was accomplished quickly using overwhelming firepower. Then the attackers, having neutralized the checkpoint, drove a large vehicle-borne improvised explosive device onto the hotel compound, pulled it up beside the structure, and detonated it.[19] At least a dozen people were killed and in excess of fifty wounded.

In short, in order to overcome security measures outside of a hotel in a frontier city in Pakistan, Islamic militants utilized a tactic which the NRC in its wisdom has decided would not realistically be employed against a nuclear plant in this country. A local Taliban unit in the Northwest Frontier Province is apparently capable of a greater level of sophistication in its operations than it is reasonable to expect the perpetrators of 9/11 would employ against a high-profile target in an operation designed to kill thousands.

If you want to get a little taste of the tactics Al-Qaeda might employ on a nuclear power plant, perhaps we should look to the example of what was used against Abqaiq in Saudi Arabia. Abqaiq is a processing facility for crude oil coming out of Saudi Arabia for export to the rest of the world. Saudi Arabia is the world's largest producer of oil. Two-thirds of all its production passes through Abqaiq. If you destroy Abqaiq, you wreck the world's economy.

On the afternoon of February 24, 2006, Saudi security forces opened fire on three vehicles as they headed for the Abqaiq collection and processing facility. All three of the vehicles had been painted in the color scheme of Saudi Aramco, the national oil company. Two of the vehicles were carrying large explosive devices. The third, a four-by-four vehicle, was carrying a supporting team of armed attackers.[20] The assault team in the four-by-four attacked the checkpoint controlling access to the facility, and killed or wounded all of the guards at that location. Both of the vehicles carrying explosives then successfully entered the facility.

The guards at a second checkpoint inside the outer perimeter then either fled or laid down their arms and surrendered. Both of the car bombs which had entered the facility were successfully detonated by the attackers. Fortunately, the damage caused by the attack, probably due to ignorance of the exact location of the key elements of the mammoth plant, was relatively minor.[21] The Saudi government, terrified at how close it had come to catastrophe, lied through its teeth in reporting the incident, claiming that the attackers had never entered the facility and that the car bombs had detonated harmlessly outside.[22]

In fact, the methodologies employed at Abqaiq and against the Pearl Continental are completely consistent with the tactics seen in use by Al-Qaeda and associated groups all across the globe:

- On September 30, 2008, the Taliban attacked the Marriott Hotel in Islamabad, a facility heavily frequented by American officials and senior Pakistanis. A vehicle loaded with explosives was used to breach the outer defense and then a second, larger vehicle was rolled through the breach and detonated close to the side of the hotel.

- On September 17, 2008, the Yemeni Islamic Brigades, an Al-Qaeda affiliate, staged an attack on the U.S. Embassy in Sana'a. A car bomb was detonated against the main gate, and then assault teams opened fire on the forces defending the embassy. Six terrorists, six guards, and several civilians were killed.

- On November 10, 2005, three separate suicide-bombing teams successfully penetrated security and struck the Grand Hyatt, Radisson, and Days Inn hotels in Amman, Jordan. Fifty-six civilians were killed and ninety-seven wounded.

- On April 13, 2005, Al-Qaeda in Iraq assaulted a U.S. military base near the Syrian border. Three truck bombs were used in succession. Following this, an assault force attempted to gain entry to the compound.

- On December 6, 2004, Al-Qaeda staged an attack on the U.S. Consulate in Jeddah, Saudi Arabia. The gate was breached and a terrorist assault force succeeded in gaining entry to the facility. Six Foreign Service nationals, a security guard, and three Saudi soldiers were killed.

This list is by no means exhaustive. In Iraq alone there have been any number of other examples, in addition to the April 13, 2005, attack, of the use by Islamic terrorists of sophisticated tactics involving what amounts to combined-arms teams of suicide car bombers and infantry assault forces. Fortunately, in Iraq, such attackers were typically met by disciplined defenders, either U.S. Army or U.S. Marines, who were only too happy to take advantage of the opportunity to confront their foes head-on. Were such an attack launched against a nuclear power plant guarded by a total of twenty poorly trained, poorly equipped security guards, the outcome would be anyone's guess.

The DBT's artificial limitation on what weapons a security force must be prepared to defend against is equally specious. Across the border in Mexico, there is an all-out war going on between heavily armed drug cartels and Mexican military and police personnel. By

Mexican estimates, 86 percent of the illegal weapons in use in that country come across the border from the United States. The arsenals of the drug cartels currently include such weapons as .50 caliber machine guns and sniper rifles, antitank rockets, grenade launchers, fragmentation grenades, and mortars. The cartels often simply outgun the opposing security forces.

If drug cartels on our doorstep can acquire enough sophisticated weaponry to stand toe to toe with the Mexican Army, one suspects that Al-Qaeda could manage to acquire a handful of the same weapons for use in a high-profile operation against a target like a nuclear power plant. In any event, when we are talking about betting the future of the entire New York Metropolitan Area on the question, I would suggest we ought to err on the side of caution and assume the worst.[23]

Despite 9/11 and the ongoing war against Islamic terror, efforts to increase the DBT have had only limited success. That is because, ultimately, the discussion is not really about threats or tactical necessity. It does not take a counterterrorist expert or a rocket scientist to look at the level of force being employed around the world by terrorist teams and conclude that setting the bar at a handful of individuals armed with a very limited number of weapons makes no sense. The point is, though, that objective physical reality is not what is being discussed.

It is all about the money.

Anything required by the DBT is paid for by the operator of the nuclear power plant. If we bump the requirement to something like that suggested years ago by POGO, then the big corporations that own the power plants have to pay. They are responsible for funding all security measures required by the DBT.

Any measure beyond DBT becomes the responsibility of the taxpayer. If it gets done, you and I pay. So, semantics aside, we are not really talking about a Design Basis Threat, we are talking about a Money Basis Threat. We work the equation backwards. We decide what we are willing to make the power companies pay, and then we calculate how many guards and guns that will buy. The public gets cheap power and a false sense of security, and we tell ourselves that we have taken care of the problem. We have not.

The really sad thing about nuclear power plants and the DBT, however, is that the current security forces are not even capable of standing up to this artificially reduced threat level. Even in the face of what any objective analysis would have to describe as a small fraction of the combat power a major terrorist group would be likely to field, the guard forces fail, and they fail miserably.

Prior to 9/11, the NRC mandated five to ten security guards on post per reactor.[24] That number has now been increased. Still, as of 2005, there was a grand total of 8,000 security personnel for all of the nuclear reactors in the country. If you start breaking that down, taking into account the number of sites and the number of shifts required to provide twenty-four-hour coverage, you end up with roughly twenty security guards on duty at any one point in time at each location.[25]

These security guards are often grossly underpaid. In many plants, they make less than the janitors. They train with their weapons no more than two to three times a year.[26] Often, they are hired off the street and put through less than a week's worth of training before they begin to stand post. During their training, a large portion of time is consumed by learning administrative procedures and other routine tasks. Only a very limited amount of time is spent on handling firearms and tactics.

Morale among the guards is chronically low. I was told by current and former guards that while many of the personnel employed to protect nuclear power plants are former military and very capable, many others are simply collecting a paycheck. It is common during exercises to hear discussion among members of the guard forces regarding the individual locations in which they intend to hide if and when there is a real assault on the plant. There appears to be a common feeling at most plants that there is no way the guards will ever defeat a determined, well-armed opponent.

Evaluations of security forces in 2000 found that 60 percent of them could not successfully defend against the DBT. Remember, this was set at three attackers at this time. The entire guard force of the plant could not prevent three armed individuals from entering and taking steps that would have caused a meltdown of the reactor.[27]

The situation has improved only marginally since then. Testimony by numerous guards from a variety of locations over the years continues to show the complete inadequacy of the current force, even to handle the absurdly small number of attackers set by the DBT.

Speaking in 2002, former Seabrook Nuclear Power plant guard, John Middlemiss, described some of the results of the exercises in which he participated while working at that facility. "My first night on shift was uneventful. I met some of the other officers, but mostly I just felt my way around, getting my feet wet, so to speak. Night two was when we started the drills; this would be the first set of drills at the plant in more than six months . . . We had three drills that night, though the first two I only heard over the radio because the drill was in a different part of the plant. They killed multiple officers and blew up a number of vital components, and in at least one of the drills, they got a complete target set which would have resulted in a meltdown.

"On the third drill they came at my post. I was posted in the radiological controlled area (RCA). They came in through a door that only requires a crowbar to open it. There were only two attackers, and they were upon us in under a minute and easily killed me and another officer with grenades. The room we were guarding was one of the two ways into the reactor itself. Once we were dead, they had a clear path into the reactor—the plant would've melted down again. And while doing all this, the

adversaries did not lose a single guy. This was an eye-opener for me; I was highly alarmed by the results of the drills.

"The next night we had three more drills. I was posted outside with two other officers who had worked there for more than a year. The first drill started on the other side of the plant and finished in my area. The adversaries in this drill had hit all the target sets they needed and still had one person alive, so once again the plant was melted down. The next two drills had about the same results—all three of us died outside and they melted down the plant. . . .

"Over the last two nights we had six drills, and the drill team had succeeded in having some sort of radiological release in nearly every drill."

Kathy Davidson, a former security guard at the Pilgrim Nuclear Station south of Boston, stated in 2005 that even in tabletop exercises done inside the facility, the attacking "terrorist" teams won twenty-eight out of twenty-nine times.[28] Guards and former guards that I spoke with said that as of the present day, guard forces still lost to attacking forces roughly half the time.[29] That was despite the fact that the exercises were canned and limited to the repetition of the same, exact scenarios over and over. One former guard told me that the entire time he worked at the plant to which he was assigned, a period of several years, there were only two scenarios that were ever run against them. In short, within seconds of the beginning of the exercise, the guards would know, by virtue of endless repetition, exactly how many attackers were coming, where they were coming from, and what their objective was. The guard force at this installation was still lucky if they won half of the time against the attacking force.[30]

The evidence suggests pretty strongly that post–9/11, as there was some modest pressure to increase security, plant operators responded not so much by hiring additional personnel as by making existing personnel work longer hours. The most notorious example of the impact of this is probably the scandal surrounding Peach Bottom nuclear power plant, where guards were found to have been routinely asleep on duty. Peach Bottom is only one of several locations at which such problems have been identified, however. Throughout the period of 2004 through 2006, the NRC investigated a whole series of incidents at the Turkey Point facility near Miami, in which guards had fallen asleep, covered for each other while they slept, and, incredibly enough, actually removed the firing pins from their weapons.[31]

In 2005 the Union of Concerned Scientists and the North Carolina Waste Awareness and Reduction Network filed a complaint with the North Carolina Attorney General alleging a whole host of problems with security at the Shearon Harris nuclear plant in that state. Among the litany of allegations was one that Securitas, the company running the plant guard force, was simply handing its personnel the answers to the state certification exam required of all security personnel. In fact, according to the complaint, the guards were required to accept the answer key whether they wanted it or not. Apparently, Securitas had concluded that it could not afford to lose any personnel who might fail the exam and, so, had simply decided to game the system.

An investigation into this allegation and several others consumed the better part of two years. In the end, following admissions by Securitas personnel that the claims were true, fines were assessed against the plant operator.[32]

The NRC often responds to allegations of problems with the level of security at nuclear power plants by making reference to there being some other, governmental level of force that would be employed against attackers who had the capacity to overwhelm the existing guard forces. The implication is that somehow or another, it is the job of the guard force simply to buy time, and that a reaction force of some kind would be dispatched to confront any terrorist team larger than that set in the DBT.

The only problem is, of course, that there is no such reaction force, and that even if there were, it could not possibly arrive on-site in time to do any good. The typical protocol for a nuclear power plant calls for the security guards at the plant to report any intrusion to local law enforcement and to await the arrival of responding police officers. What that means in practice is that plant security calls in and says they have an intruder, and some time later, often thirty or forty minutes later, a police officer arrives at the scene. In some cases, it may even be two officers.[33]

I have nothing but the greatest admiration for law enforcement officers, but in the context of the kind of threat we are considering here, one or two police officers are irrelevant. In fact, any response, no matter how big, that takes half an hour to arrive is probably of no consequence. The outcome of the attack is likely to have been decided before any reinforcements can arrive. State police showing up at the scene of a major terrorist attack on a nuclear plant thirty minutes after it has started are either going to be limited to putting toe tags on dead terrorists or employed primarily in evacuating nearby residents from the area surrounding a plant which is about to experience a catastrophic meltdown.

The situation is not any better if we begin to take a look at the possibility of an attack by air. Containment buildings were not constructed to withstand strikes by commercial aircraft. Some of them might survive. Some of them might not.[34] The key, however, is that it is probably not necessary to breach the containment structure in any event. The reactor and the primary cooling system are inside the containment shell and protected by it. The control room and pumps and most of the other critical systems which ensure that the reactor remains under control are outside the containment. These can be hit and destroyed by a light aircraft much less a commercial jetliner.

In any event, the NRC imposes no requirement on power plant operators to defend against aerial attack. Proposals to build what amounts to giant steel girder and cable birdcages around the plants have gone nowhere. Likewise, arguments in favor of putting air defenses of some kind at the sites have also been rejected.[35] The standard industry response is that even building "birdcages" would be too expensive, although some estimates indicate the cost would be relatively minimal when compared to the overall cost of a nuclear power plant.[36]

All of the discussion to this point regarding an attack on a nuclear power plant has contemplated that it would be the goal of the terrorist team to cause a meltdown in the reactor. In other words, the terrorist assault force would have to gain entry to the heart of the nuclear power plant facility where the containment, the control room, and the feed water pumps are located. Unfortunately, the reality is that this may not even be necessary, because the reactor is not the only location on-site where dangerous radioactive material is located.

All nuclear reactors produce spent fuel. This is a natural by-product of the nuclear reaction within the reactor. The nation's 103 operating reactors collectively produce 2,000 metric tons of this waste annually. This waste is dangerously radioactive and remains so for literally thousands of years. Its radioactivity is such that when first removed from the reactor, it can provide a lethal dose of radiation to a person standing nearby in seconds.

Typically, when the waste is taken out of the reactor, it is then immediately placed into a storage pool inside the nuclear power plant. The water provides shielding against the radiation. The fuel, which is in the form of rods, is then kept immersed for years until its level of radioactivity declines to the point where the rods can be removed from the pool and placed into what are know as dry storage casks. These are enormous cylinders that look a lot like giant thermos bottles.

The spent fuel is essentially what is left over after the nuclear reactor has extracted all of the energy it can from the nuclear fuel. It is a collection of different isotopes, many of which remain radioactive for a very long time and are very lethal. The radioactivity of the spent fuel is such that it continues to generate considerable heat for a long time. Among the isotopes that are contained in the spent fuel are things like strontium-90, cesium-137, and iodine-131. These isotopes are deadly to most living things and are the substances that caused the most harm when the Chernobyl disaster took place.[37]

A nuclear reactor typically shuts down for refueling about every eighteen months. At that time about one-quarter to one-half of all the fuel rods inside are removed. The fuel rods are not removed individually but instead are lifted out in groups called assemblies. An assembly may contain anywhere from a few dozen to a few hundred rods, and may weigh half a ton.

As noted above, when removed from the reactor the assemblies are then placed into a large pool inside of a building adjacent to the reactor containment itself. These are typically 40 feet deep, steel-lined, concrete structures. They were intended originally for the temporary storage of spent fuel, which would eventually be moved to some sort of permanent national storage site for used nuclear fuel. No such storage site has ever been commissioned, and so, spent fuel continues to accumulate across the country at nuclear power plants.

As long as the spent fuel remains immersed and covered with a certain minimum level of water, it remains cool and can be stored essentially indefinitely. The big problem occurs when and if the fuel is uncovered. In such an eventuality, it is possible that the result will be a high-temperature fire in the fuel's zirconium cladding, followed by the release of massive amounts of deadly, radioactive material.

The building in which the spent fuel is held is adjacent to the reactor containment. It is not inside of it. Called "fuel-handling buildings," they are not fortified in any fashion. They are standard industrial structures that were never designed to resist attempts at forced entry. Typically, once attackers have succeeded in breaching the security perimeter surrounding the spent fuel pool, all that would be required would be for them to breach a single door to gain entry to the pool. At that point, they need only to blow a hole in the wall of the spent fuel pool, something that can probably be accomplished with a backpack-sized satchel charge. Once that is done, gravity is going to do the rest. The pool is going to drain, a fire is almost certainly going to start, and the result is going to be devastation.

Lest blowing a hole in a wall seem like something that would be beyond the capability of an attacking group, it bears examining just a few figures. A single U.S. Army M3–shaped charge will penetrate 60 inches of reinforced concrete. That's 5 feet. That charge weighs about thirty pounds.[38] This item has been in the U.S. Army inventory for decades, and similar devices are used all over the world. Even if a terrorist group could not obtain such a military-grade item, a competent bomb maker would be capable of manufacturing one from scratch. The principles involved are well known and have been in use widely since at least World War II.

The average spent-fuel pond contains five to ten times the amount of long-lived radioactive material as does a single reactor. Per the NRC, close to 100 percent of dangerous isotopes like cesium-137 could be released into the atmosphere in the event of a fire in the fuel in a spent fuel pond that was drained. Research indicates that an area between 75,000 and 95,000 square kilometers in size could be rendered permanently uninhabitable by a pool fire. All of New York State comprises only 127,000 square kilometers.[39]

A 1997 study done for the NRC estimated the consequences of a spent-fuel fire at a nuclear reactor, and concluded that such an accident would cause 54,000 to 143,000 cancer deaths, contaminate 2,000 to 7,000 square kilometers of agricultural land, and cause $117 to $566 billion in economic damages. A 2003 study by Dr. Robert Alvarez and several colleagues concluded that these results were just about right, and fit with their calculations as well.[40]

Spent-fuel pools all around the nation are filling up. New spent fuel is being removed from reactors continuously. There remains no movement on a national storage site. So, the industry, faced with a dilemma, has moved to a system called dry casking.

Dry-cask storage involves the sealing of spent nuclear fuel into steel and concrete canisters that provide both protection and radiation shielding. The system is referred to as dry because, rather than being immersed in water, the fuel is surrounded by helium gas. Typically, canisters are roughly 20 feet tall and 11 feet in diameter. Cask walls may be as much as 2 feet thick. When loaded, a single canister may weigh as much as 360,000 pounds. The fuel inside is cooled solely by passive means, with heat dissipating through cooling channels built into the canisters.[41] Each canister may hold as many as 24 to 40 fuel assemblies, but this system is suitable only for fuel that has been out of the reactor for a minimum of ten years, because only then will radiation and heat levels have declined to the point where dry casking can be utilized.[42]

Dry storage casks are typically located on large concrete pads on the grounds of the nuclear power plant. These storage pads provide a sound foundation for the storage of the casks, and also integrate cooling systems to prevent overheating. These pads are not, however, always located in the immediate vicinity of the containment, the control room, and the other vital areas of the plant. Often, in fact, they are set some distance away.

In such cases, the pads are typically surrounded by chain-link fences. They are not guarded in the sense of having a continuous guard presence. Guards make periodic trips to the storage site to check on its condition, but they are not posted there. These pads are, in fact, not considered part of the core or vital areas of the plant. They are controlled by the plant security, but largely this means only that they are fenced, that access to the public is denied, and that they are on plant property.[43]

The key to understanding this arrangement is recognition that plant security does not actually fully control access to the grounds of a nuclear power plant. There is no NRC requirement that access to the entire facility be denied in the sense of having a fence, gates, and guards along the entire length of the perimeter. So, the usual practice is to post signs at the edge of the plant's property and make sure the general public is aware that access is not allowed, but to only have barrier fences around certain select structures on plant property. Then, around an even smaller number of core buildings, there will actually be not only fences, but also barriers capable of stopping car bombs, guard towers, armed guards, etc.

In short, the spent-fuel casks are not judged critical enough to rate the top level of security. They get a fence and a roving patrol. They sit on a concrete pad, probably with security cameras monitoring their condition, and, at periodic intervals, a security guard drives by. That's it.

Maybe even more disturbingly, the usual guidance is that even if there are intruders detected at the location of the dry storage casks, and even if the intruders are detected breaching the fencing and gaining direct access to the casks, the security guards are not to respond. They are to monitor the situation. They are to contact the authorities. They are not to attempt to respond to the scene. Instead, they are to remain at their posts and await the arrival, maybe thirty minutes later, of the police.

So, an attacking force of terrorists that has cut its way through the chain-link fence surrounding a dry-cask storage site can literally walk around, planting charges and preparing to release all of the radioactive material contained in the casks without any interference of any kind from the guard force. They can also expect that the only police response likely to be able to arrive in any reasonable time is going to be so small and so hopelessly outgunned as to be irrelevant. By the time any jurisdiction in the United States is going to be able to organize a response by a significant SWAT-like element, it's all going to be over.

This deficiency, like so many of those surrounding nuclear power plant security, has been noted for sometime. Numerous advocates have demanded that the NRC require the strengthening of security of dry-cask storage sites. To date, no such requirement has been imposed.

There is no question about the level of terrorist interest in attacking nuclear power plants. Khalid Sheikh Mohammed, the mastermind of the 9/11 attacks, admitted during questioning by interrogators that his original plan was to have the commandeered aircraft crash into nuclear power plants. The 9/11 Commission report states that Mohamed Atta, the pilot of the first plane to hit the World Trade Center, had considered targeting a nuclear facility that he had noticed during training flights in the New York City area.[44] In an article published in several European newspapers, documentary filmmaker Yosri Fouda said Khalid Sheikh Mohammed and Ramzi Binalshibh, another Al-Qaeda operative, told him they had decided against the attack on nuclear power plants "for the moment" because of fears it could "get out of control."[45]

In the face of this level of interest and of the almost unimaginable consequences of a successful terrorist attack on a nuclear power plant, what we need are truly robust defenses and security measures. What we have now is a system that has little or nothing to do with the actual threat. It consists of a series of measures based on cost rather than effectiveness, and designed not to withstand an anticipated level of force, but simply to give the impression to the public as a whole that all is well and the plants are safe. We have, in short, made a very conscious, willful decision to stick our heads in the sand, cross our fingers, and hope we never pay the price for our neglect.

We learned the cost of that kind of behavior at the outset of World War II. We learned it again on September 11, 2001. We would do well to not tempt fate and ask for further lessons.

CHAPTER NINE
Making It Safe

I SAT DOWN TO READ THE PAPER AND HAVE A CUP OF COFFEE ONE morning as I was pulling together the final elements of this book. Inside the paper, on page three, I found an article about a Marine platoon in Afghanistan that had been ambushed by Taliban fighters and ended up fighting a pitched engagement, with the support of helicopter gunships, to break the ambush and drive the Taliban from the field. It was a gripping article, and one which suggested that the reporter writing it had likely been in the thick of the action herself. Particularly compelling were those portions of the article dealing with the actions of a machine-gun team consisting of CPL Kowalski and LCPL Faddis.

I probably would have been focused on the article in any event, given its subject matter. I have to admit, however, that my interest in the piece was significantly heightened by the fact that LCPL Faddis is my eldest son, serving in Afghanistan with 2/8 Marines. If you've never had the experience, reading an account of your son's actions in combat is the purest possible blend of intense pride and abject terror any parent can imagine.

For the purposes of this book, however, what that article brought home to me was the stark contrast between our actions in the world abroad and our security posture here at home. In Afghanistan, the Marines are heavily engaged with Taliban insurgents as part of an ongoing worldwide war against Islamic extremism. In Iraq, our intelligence operatives and special operations forces remain on the hunt for terrorists who continue to demonstrate the capacity to stage large-scale, coordinated bombing attacks and inflict mass casualties. In Pakistan, we are furiously funneling support to the Pakistani military and pressing its government to take decisive action to prevent the possible implosion of that nation and the seizing of an intact nuclear arsenal by Islamic militants.

In short, we are, outside the United States, at war, and we acknowledge that we may continue to be in a state of war for many years to come. At home, though, we are not. We go about our daily lives with only the briefest acknowledgment of the existence of any terrorist threat. Outside of the inconvenience we experience when passing through security at a major commercial airport, most of us probably could not identify any significant security measure in place in the world around us beyond what was in place eight years ago.

Nothing has changed. Life goes on. Yes, we are at war, but the war is confined to territory outside of our national boundaries. Who decided this, and how we have convinced ourselves that it is true, remains unclear, but it is a fact.

We live in a dream world.

Several weeks ago, I was contacted by a woman who works as a community activist in Prince George's County. She was aware of some of my comments concerning the proposed LNG facility at Sparrows Point, and asked if I would be willing to talk with her about an LNG installation going into her neighborhood. I agreed to do so, and made a visit to the site to see the situation.

What I found was that at this location, a local gas company planned to construct a massive LNG storage tank capable of holding 1 billion cubic feet of liquefied natural gas. That is similar in size to what is planned for Sparrows Point. The proposed location is in the middle of densely populated residential neighborhoods, and right on the line between Prince George's County and Washington, D.C. I have discussed at length elsewhere the thermal effects of LNG, and I will not repeat that discussion here. Suffice it to say that a terrorist attack on this site has the potential to incinerate an area extending to the edge of Catholic University in Washington, D.C. A vapor cloud released from this facility could potentially extend virtually to the White House itself.

In short, eight years after 9/11, a commercial entity is pushing ahead with plans to build what amounts to a massive thermal bomb on the doorstep of the nation's capital. What a massive, unexpected, and unnecessary gift to our enemies. No need to smuggle anything into the country. No necessity for slipping past border security or bypassing customs. Right here, on a silver platter, will be a mechanism by which even a marginally competent terrorist organization will be provided the ability to torch the capital of our country.

And yet, all of the ongoing proceedings regarding the necessary approvals for this project are being handled through routine state and local entities. There is no involvement by federal authorities, no coordination with Homeland Security, no discussion whatsoever of terrorism or national security. For all intents and purposes, we might be talking about building a new gas station and convenience store.

In August 2009, the FBI arrested seven men in North Carolina and charged them with planning to undertake "violent jihad." The seven individuals in question had weapons, 27,000 rounds of ammunition, $13,000 in cash, and training manuals for terrorist activity. The oldest of the seven was thirty-nine years of age and had fought against the Soviets in Afghanistan.[1] This was not in some inner-city enclave among recent immigrants from Somalia or Pakistan. This was in a largely rural Southern state in which are located some of the largest military bases in our nation.

One wonders how it is that these two disparate "realities" can coexist. How can we simultaneously be arresting and incarcerating cells of armed militants on our own soil and pushing ahead with the building of new industrial facilities with no regard whatsoever for where they are located or how they will be protected? Eight years after we lost 3,000 lives in the heart of our nation's largest city, how can we possibly have forgotten that feeling? By what logic have we decided to characterize the threat as anything less than immediate and strategic?

I don't pretend to be able to answer these questions fully. I have no illusion that somehow I have a unique capacity to map out the course we should be steering on homeland security. I do hope that the observations I have made will prove helpful as we move forward, and I do have a few brief recommendations on where we go from here.

Start Taking the Threat Seriously

In 2006 the Congress appropriated $127.8 million for mass transit security. This is a drop in the bucket relative to some other elements of the budget for homeland security, but still nothing to sneeze at. As of March 2009, only 8.2 percent of that money had actually been spent. This was, in fact, par for the course with the Department of Homeland Security, which has to date, apparently, spent only a small portion of the money that Congress has allocated for mass transit security. According to Congress, there remains a total of $1.3 billion in unspent funds for mass transit security.[2]

How this is possible is very difficult to explain. As I have demonstrated and as has been shown by many other investigators and authors, security for mass transit in this country is virtually nonexistent. The greatest hurdle I faced in trying to analyze it was in identifying any actual security measures that could be evaluated. Most of the time, I found that it was more a matter of simply accepting that anyone could largely do anything they liked. There was no security. The safety of the passengers on mass transit was wholly dependent on whether or not someone wanted to kill them. Any group with a minimum of knowledge and capability could pull off an attack anytime they wanted.

Even more alarming is the fact that all this is happening against the backdrop of a series of attacks on mass transit worldwide over a period of many years. This is not like the case of nuclear power plants, where at least there is the weak excuse for lapses in security—the fact that no one has yet tried to seize and melt down a reactor. There cannot possibly be anything theoretical or intangible about the threat to mass transit. It is real. Attacks have been launched. More will come. Of that there can be no doubt.

So, in this context, if we are allowing a billion dollars to sit around unspent, there can really only be one explanation: We have decided for some indefinable reason that there is no likelihood of attack. We are feeling fat, smug, and complacent. No one has staged a successful attack on U.S. soil for several years now. We have begun to nod off. The money will be spent eventually on something, but there is no particular hurry.

At the battle of Isandlwana during the Zulu War of 1879, a small British army was crushed and exterminated by a Zulu force. There are a lot of reasons for that disaster, but one of the key factors certainly was the fact that the British soldiers on the firing line literally ran out of ammunition and were then overrun and stabbed to death. They did not run out of ammunition because their supplies were exhausted. They ran out of ammunition because they were required to return to the supply wagons from the firing line and stand in line while quartermasters methodically opened one box of cartridges at a time, issued a certain designated number of rounds to each soldier, and completed the requisite paperwork.While men were fighting for their lives a few hundred meters away, the men in control of the ammunition were still living in a peacetime world of forms, regulations, and property accountability.

The men at Isandlwana paid with their lives for the complacency and detachment from reality of their support troops. We may yet pay the same price for our own complacency and inability to adjust our thinking. If we are at war, and if we are faced with a threat so massive that we believe we need to appropriate a billion dollars to deal with it, then we need to move with dispatch and purpose. The key to winning this war is not putting in place massive new programs to defend against the attack that already happened. It is getting one step ahead and putting a robust, effective defense in place before the enemy has the opportunity to exploit our weakness.

Stop Using Homeland Security as an Excuse to Dispense Pork and Engage in Corporate Welfare

As of 2008 the Homeland Security Department had spent $63 million on programs to teach commercial truckers to look for terrorists on the road and at highway rest stops. Now, I don't have any problem whatsoever with the idea of getting people involved in domestic security. Even if I am not always clear on exactly what kind of behavior we expect the average citizen to notice that will be indicative of impending terrorist activity, it seems only a matter of common sense that the more eyes and ears we have at work, the better our chances of catching someone before he has a chance to act.

How on earth, though, does it cost $63 million to encourage commercial truckers to call in and report suspicious behavior? Every state in the Union has a 911 system. Every state in the Union has not one but many different police forces and law enforcement agencies. We don't need to create a new command center, establish a hotline, or employ a whole building full of new bureaucrats. About all we have to do, if we even have to do that much, is put the word out, preferably on the radio so that it will be heard by truckers on the road, as to what they should be looking for. The men and women at the wheel will do the rest.

Common sense, though, seems to be in very short supply when it comes to homeland security. In 2003 we spent $182,080 on streetlights for the town of Port Royal, South Carolina, population 3,950. I have been to Port Royal. It is a nice little town, and the music festival I attended there was great. I have no idea, however, what target of terrorist significance exists there, or how streetlights are going to keep Al-Qaeda at bay.

In 2005 we spent $48,600 on security cameras for a water tower in Arizona.

In 2004 we spent $48,550 on a tractor to pull airplanes in Wisconsin.

In 2006 we spent $2,789 on a "terrorism prevention" printer for a small town in North Dakota.

In 2004 we spent $22,335 on fitness equipment for the fire department in a small town in Massachusetts.[3]

Every time I open any of the many magazines devoted to homeland security in our country, I find a sea of ads for new products that will make us "safer" and more "secure." Every time I turn around I see the award of another new major contract to some massive corporation for the development and testing of another yet more exotic piece of gear. Everyone, from the local municipality looking for a new printer to the biggest defense contractor searching for a way to siphon off another billion dollars of the taxpayers' money, has figured out that pitching something as being related to "counterterrorism" or "homeland security" means big bucks.

Meanwhile, huge, gaping holes in our defenses continue to exist. Long lines of railcars packed with the most dangerous substances on earth sit unattended all over our nation. Nuclear power plants continue to be guarded by relative handfuls of poorly trained and poorly paid private security guards. Bio labs containing the most dangerous organisms on the planet are being built, literally in our backyards, in many cases without physical security measures of any kind.

We have turned our national defense into an excuse to feed at the public trough. It should not and cannot be so trivialized. Our focus needs to be not on making money but on staying alive.

Recognize that Paperwork and Bureaucracy Are Not What Stop Bad People from Doing Bad Things

On June 13, 1942, a German submarine landed four Nazi saboteurs on the beach near the Long Island town of Amagansett. The four men, all dressed in German military uniforms, came ashore with explosives, demolitions equipment, and over $175,000. Their mission was to sabotage aluminum and magnesium plants, canals, waterways, locks, and other key infrastructure targets. German planning called for the team to carry out attacks over a period of two years.

Unfortunately for the Germans, their operation went off the rails almost immediately. While the team was still on the beach, burying its equipment and changing into civilian attire, they were discovered by a Coast Guardsman named John Cullen. Cullen was on beach patrol, part of a World War II security effort aimed at preventing enemy saboteurs from doing exactly what this German team was attempting.

After a confused conversation between Cullen and the Germans, who attempted to claim they were shipwrecked fishermen, Cullen ran to the local Coast Guard station and raised the alarm. The Germans fled and were temporarily able to evade pursuit, but, within days, their leader, sensing the end was near, turned himself in and went over to the Allies. All of the gear the team had brought with it was recovered. No attacks took place. Information obtained from the team leader led to the subsequent detection and arrest of another German team that had landed undetected in Florida. The German intelligence apparatus was so shaken by the failure that they canceled all plans for the dispatch of further teams of saboteurs.

The most audacious German attempt to stage terrorist attacks on U.S. soil was an abject failure because of a guy with a flashlight walking a beach.[4]

Earlier, in discussing the proliferation of bio labs in this country, I mentioned a study the Government Accountability Office (GAO) made of the external security measures in place at the five BSL 4 labs then existing in the country. I will not rehash that discussion here, but, in brief, what was found was shocking, and two of the labs were judged horribly deficient and lacking in meaningful perimeter security.

In 2009, the GAO revisited the same topic with the express purpose of determining what action had been taken by the Center for Disease Control (CDC) to correct the noted deficiencies. Because the BSL 4 labs in question work with organisms that pose a threat to humans, it is the CDC which has this oversight responsibility.

As the first step in this process, the GAO asked the CDC for a list of what steps it had taken. In response, the CDC stated that:

- It had established a task force on biosafety and biocontainment oversight which, at the time GAO asked, had held a single public consultation meeting and at some future date was to communicate recommendations to CDC on how to proceed.

- Hosted a workshop series for all its registered parties and entities at which physical security was discussed.

- Convened a working group to review regulations and laws.

Beyond this, the CDC had done nothing. In fact, not only had it not yet taken any action, it had not yet even formulated a plan as to how to proceed. GAO found some indication that the individual labs had, on their own initiative, begun to take some limited steps toward addressing the problems found, but this was done in the absence of any formal decision by CDC as to how to proceed.[5]

If you were looking to create a perfect example of the contrast between the practicality with which we confronted the Nazi threat and the complete lack of realism that characterizes so many of our alleged homeland security measures, you could not do better than this. In the midst of World War II, we were concerned with good reason about the possibility of saboteurs landing on our shores. So, in response, we paid personnel to patrol likely landing spots and raise the alarm if they spotted anything. In much the same way, we even recruited groups of unpaid volunteer boaters and yachtsmen to watch for U-boats. Ernest Hemingway was a member of such a group and used his experiences therein as inspiration for his novel, *Islands in the Stream*.

Now, in the midst of another war with another fanatical foe, when confronted with evidence that some of our most sensitive biological laboratories are wide open and severely lacking in security, how do we respond? Do we fire the managers of the facilities and replace them with individuals charged to clean up the mess? Do we issue a short list of straightforward, commonsense physical security rules, something which a decent security specialist could probably draft in an hour or so off the top of his head? Do we take any kind of immediate, direct, and effective action to eliminate the threat?

No; we convene working groups and task forces. We give presentations and schedule workshops. We think deep thoughts. We write a lot of papers. And, of course, we spend a lot of money on meetings and travel and communication and luncheons.

Al-Qaeda uses no such methodology. While we are busily drawing new lines on wiring diagrams and formulating plans to convene task forces that will propose further study by a commission of some sort, Al-Qaeda is moving forward with concrete, tangible plans. We need to confront those plans with defensive measures that are no less concrete. We don't need a new committee or a board to tell us how to secure our chemical plants. We need to hire guards, put in place physical barriers to prevent the use of vehicle-borne explosive devices, and move those facilities that are particularly dangerous away from major population centers. We don't need a board or a new agency to protect our nuclear power plants. We need to hire more guards, equip them better, and give them significantly enhanced training. We need action, not equivocation.

Start Thinking Like the People Who Are Trying to Kill Us and Design Our Defenses to Respond to the Threat

Throughout this book I have pointed out countless examples of situations in which the "security" measures in place at an installation have nothing whatsoever to do with the threat of terrorist attack. Perhaps my "favorite" was the decision to require trash cans in train stations to be transparent so that it would be more difficult to hide explosive devices in them. This was done in response to the Madrid train bombings—attacks in which no bombs were placed in trash cans, and the devices used were carried onto the trains in backpacks.

Similarly, at locations all around this country, we employ security personnel who take actions that have absolutely nothing to do with the likely threat. Sensitive installations are "protected" from terrorist attack by signs saying that visitors must provide a photo ID, and by guards who ask to look inside purses or peer inside your car. None of this has the slightest thing to do with preventing an attack by a group of Al-Qaeda operatives carrying AK-47s and driving a truck jammed with thousands of pounds of explosives.

In looking at these measures around the country and across a wide range of targets, I could not help but get the impression that these kinds of measures had been developed and implemented in a vacuum. They had nothing to do with the threat. If they were based on anything, it was on the idea that it would make the public feel safer and provide the illusion that terrorist attacks were being deterred.

There is only one way in which to design defensive measures that makes any sense. You need to look at the likely threat and you need to then put in place a defense which will defeat it. If you see, as we have with Al-Qaeda, a clear ability to field large teams of well-trained operatives armed with automatic weapons, and to couple these teams with large vehicle-borne explosive devices, then you need to put in place physical security barriers and guard forces at likely targets that will be capable of withstanding an attack using these capabilities. That means you need to be able to physically close the road into the facility, not just wave people to a stop. That means you need to have standing by and ready to act a force of individuals armed with heavy weapons and trained in their use, not a lone sentry with a handgun. It means that you need to be prepared to confront raw, naked brutality, kill all the attackers, and emerge victorious. If you are doing anything less, you are simply preparing for defeat.

Stop Wasting Time

In February of 2009, the Arabic television network Al Jazeera aired a video of a speech by a Kuwaiti cleric named Abdullah al-Nafisi. Speaking before a crowd in the nation of Bahrain in the Persian Gulf, al-Nafisi discussed plans by Al-Qaeda for an anthrax attack on the United States: "Four pounds of anthrax—in a suitcase this big—carried by a fighter through tunnels from Mexico into the U.S. are guaranteed to kill 330,000 Americans within a single hour if it is properly spread in population centers there. What a horrifying idea; 9/11 will be small change in comparison. Am I right? There is no need for airplanes, conspiracies, timings and so on. One person, with the courage to carry four pounds of anthrax, will go to the White House lawn, and will spread this 'confetti' all over them, and then we'll do these cries of joy. It will turn into a real celebration."[6]

Al-Nafisi is a Kuwaiti dissident, a recruiter for Al-Qaeda, and someone known to have had communication directly with senior Al-Qaeda and Taliban personnel. His speech may or may not represent an insight into current operational planning, but at a minimum, it was intended to encourage his followers and members of Al-Qaeda to undertake new attacks of even larger proportions than those we have seen to date.

We as a nation have passed through the frantic years of hysteria and panic that followed 9/11, and we have now drifted off into some kind of deep, complacent slumber. We have wrapped ourselves in an imaginary world of security, and turned homeland security, the most elemental of concepts, into another justification for bureaucracy and corporate welfare. The al-Nafisis of the world understand much more clearly than we do that this war has just begun, and that it may indeed prove generational in scope. While we willingly neglect our responsibility to protect ourselves, our enemies are busily working to commit murder on an almost unimaginable scale.

We need to shake ourselves awake and move, as my father used to say, "like we have a purpose in life." MacArthur discovered over sixty years ago that eight hours was all the time he had. Eight years may well prove to be all the time we will get to prepare.

Endnotes

Introduction

1 William H. Bartsch, *MacArthur's Pearl Harbor,* Texas A&M University Press, 2003, x.
2 Bartsch, *MacArthur's Pearl Harbor,* x.
3 Bartsch, *MacArthur's Pearl Harbor,* x.
4 Len Deighton, *Blood, Tears and Folly,* HarperCollins, New York, New York, 1993, 569.

Chapter One: If Even the Military Is Not Safe, What Chance Do the Rest of Us Have?

1 CW4 Randy Gaddo, "The 1983 Beirut Bombing," *Leatherneck Magazine,* Vol. XCI, No. 10 (October 2008), Quantico, Virginia, Marine Corps Association, 42.
2 Gaddo, "The 1983 Beirut Bombing," 48.
3 Lou Michel and Dan Herbeck, *American Terrorist: Timothy McVeigh and the Oklahoma City Bombing* (New York: Regan Books, 2001), 164.
4 Michel and Herbeck, *American Terrorist,* 163.
5 Michel and Herbeck, *American Terrorist,* 231.
6 Michel and Herbeck, *American Terrorist,* 233.
7 Michel and Herbeck, *American Terrorist,* 231.
8 The NEFA Foundation, "The Fort Dix Plot," www.nefafoundation.org, January 2008, 1.
9 Dina Temple-Raston, "Independent Cell Allegedly Hatched Fort Dix Plan," www.npr.org, May 9, 2007.
10 The NEFA Foundation, "The Fort Dix Plot," 1.
11 The NEFA Foundation, "The Fort Dix Plot," 1.
12 Associated Press, "Fort Dix Plotter Spoke of Bombs on Tape," www.cbsnews.com, October 29, 2008.
13 "Fort Dix Plotter Spoke of Bombs on Tape."
14 The NEFA Foundation, "The Fort Dix Plot," 7.
15 The NEFA Foundation, "The Fort Dix Plot," 5.
16 The NEFA Foundation, "The LA Plot to Attack U.S. Military, Israeli Government, and Jewish Targets," www.nefafoundation.org, June 2007, 2.
17 The NEFA Foundation, "The Fort Dix Plot," 20.
18 The NEFA Foundation, "The Fort Dix Plot," 20.

Chapter Two: A Very Slow-Motion Train Wreck

1 Lorenzo Vidino, *Al-Qaeda in Europe* (Amherst, NY: Prometheus Books, 2006), 293.

2 Alphus Hinds, JTIC Terrorism Case Study No. 1: "The Madrid Rail Bombings," Open Source Info, www.opensourceinfo.org, January 29, 2006.

3 Hinds, "The Madrid Rail Bombings."

4 Intelligence and Security Committee (May 2006), "Report into the London Terrorist Attacks on 7 July 2005," (PDF), 11.

5 "Report into the London Terrorist Attacks on 7 July 2005," 11.

6 The Center for Policing Terrorism, "Analysis: Mumbai Train Bombings of 2006," www.cpt-mi.org, www.cpt-mi.org/pdf/Mumbai_report.pdf.

7 CBC News, "190 Dead in Mumbai Railway Bombings," www.cbc.ca, 11 July 2006, www.cbc.ca/world/story/2006/07/11/mumbai-trains.html.

8 Eben Kaplan, "Rail Security and the Terrorist Threat," Council for Foreign Relations, www.cfr.org, 12 March 2007, www.cfr.org/publication/12800/rail_security_and_the_terrorist_threat.html.

9 David S. Ortiz, Brian A. Weatherford, Michael D. Greenberg, Lisa Ecola, "Improving the Safety and Security of Freight and Passenger Rail in Pennsylvania," RAND Corporation, www.rand.org, www.rand.org/pubs/technical_reports/2008/RAND_TR615.pdf, xiv.

10 Mary Beth Betts, "Pennsylvania Station," *The Encyclopedia of New York City.* Ed. Kenneth T. Jackson (New Haven, CT & London & New York: Yale University Press & The New York Historical Society, 1995), 890–891.

11 U.S. Government Accountability Office, "Passenger Rail Security," GAO-05-851, September 2005, 36.

12 Lisa Antonelli-Brown, "Virginia—A Commonwealth Comes of Age," www.amhistpress.com, 2004, www.amhistpress.com.rail.pdf, 1.

13 www.amtrak.com, "Amtrak Fact Sheet Fiscal Year 2008," www.amtrak.com/pdf/factsheets/dc08.pdf.

14 www.unionstationdc.com, "About Union Station," www.unionstationdc.com/about.aspx.

15 Justin Fenton, "Man with Assault Rifle Arrested on Train," www.baltimoresun.com, 19 November 2008, http://mobile.baltimoresun.com/news.jsp?key=231078.

16 www.dhs.com, "Fact Sheet: U.S. Department of Homeland Security Announces 6.8 Percent Increase in Fiscal Year 2009 Budget Request," www.dhs.gov/xnews/releases/pr_1202151112290.shtm.

17 Mary Beth Sheridan, "Planning Agency Approves Homeland Security Complex," *The Washington Post,* January 9, 2009, B1.

18 www.nefafoundation.org, "The New York City Subway Poison Gas Plot," December 2007, 1, www.nefafoundation.org /miscellaneous/nycpoisonplot.pdf.

19 "The New York City Subway Poison Gas Plot," 2.

20 "The New York City Subway Poison Gas Plot," 3.

21 Tom Hays, "Pakistani Immigrant Convicted in New York Subway Bomb Plot," www.nctimes.com, 2006, www.nctimes.com/articles/2006/05/25/news/nation/17_14_295_24_06.txt.

22 The NEFA Foundation, "The PATH Tunnel Plot," www.nefafoundation.org, 2007, 2, www.nefafoundation.org/miscellaneous/PATH/PATH.pdf.

23 Marcia Kramer, "Al-Qaeda's Goal: Cripple Amtrak's N'East Corridor," www.wcbstv.com, 2008, www.wcbstv.com/national/nyc.subway.terror.2.874830.html.

Chapter Three: Nothing More Hideous Could Be Imagined

1   Timothy Phillips, *Beslan* (London, England: Granta Books, 2007), 7.

2   Vladimir Bobrovnikov, "The Beslan Massacre," www.isim.nl, 2005, www.isim.nl/files/Review_15/Review_15-13.pdf.

3   Phillips, *Beslan,* 242.

4   Nick Paton Walsh and Peter Beaumont, "When Hell Came Calling at Beslan's School No. 1," www.guardian.co.uk, 5 September 2004, www.guardian.co.uk/world/2004/sep/05/russia.chechnya.

5   C. J. Chivers, "The School," www.esquire.com, March 14, 2007, www.esquire.com/features/ESQ0606BESLAN_140.

6   Chivers, "The School," March 14, 2007.

7   Frank Borelli, "Terror at Beslan," www.officer.com, November 24, 2006, www.officer.com/web/online/Operations-and-Tactics/Terror-At-Beslan/3$33229.

8   James Jay Carafano, "After Mumbai: Could It Happen Here? What to Do," www.heritage.org, November 28, 2008, www.heritage.org/research/homelandsecurity/wm2147.cfm.

9   Carafano, "After Mumbai."

10 Abdul Hameed Bakier, "Lessons from Al-Qaeda's Attack on the Khobar Compound," www.jamestown.org, August 11, 2006, www.jamestown.org/single/?no_cache=1&tx_ttnews%5Btt_news%5D=871.

11 Jason Burke, "Militants Give Blow-by-Blow Account of Saudi Massacre," www.guardian.co.uk, June 6, 2004.

12 Burke, "Militants Give Blow-by-Blow Account of Saudi Massacre."

13 "HM Announces Measures to Enhance Security," Press Release, Press Information Bureau, Government of India, December 11, 2008, http://pib.nic.in/release.asp?relid=45446.

14 "Tracing the Terrorist Route," IndianExpress.com, December 10, 2008, www.indianexpress.com/news/tracing-the-terror-route/396335/0.

15 Randeep Ramesh, Duncan Campbell, and Paul Lewis, "They Were in No Hurry. Cool and Composed, They Killed and Killed," www.guardian.co.uk,

November 29, 2008, www.guardian.co.uk/world/2008/nov/28/mumbai-terror-attacks-india.

16 Padma Rao Sundarji, "How India Fumbled Response to Mumbai Attack," http://news.yahoo.com, December 3, 2008, http://news.yahoo.com/s/mcclatchy/20081204/wl_mcclatchy/3115227.

17 Ramesh, Campbell, and Lewis, "They Were in No Hurry."

18 Sundarji, "How India Fumbled Response to Mumbai Attack."

19 Sundarji, "How India Fumbled Response to Mumbai Attack."

20 I have chosen deliberately to omit the names of the attackers out of a desire to deny them any claim, even posthumously, to attention and notoriety.

21 David K. Kopel, "What If We Had Taken Columbine Seriously?," Second Amendment Project, April 24, 2000, www.davekopel.com/2A/Mags/WhatIfWeHadTakenColumbineSeriously.htm.

22 James J. Scanlon, "Active Shooter Situations," *Marksman,* Vol. XXVI, No. 4, July/August 2001, www.nasta.ws/police_marksman.htm.

23 Frank Borelli, "A Modern Police Necessity," Police Officers Association of Michigan, 2005, www.poam.net/main/train-educate/active-shooter-response-training.html.

24 Frank Borelli, "Adapting Immediate Response Training to Terrorist Team Tactics," borelliconsulting.com, www.borelliconsulting.com/articles/asevolution.htm.

25 John Giduck, "Lessons Learned from Beslan, Part Two," www.projectwhitehorse.com, 2005, www.projectwhitehorse.com/pdfs/4a.%20PREPARING%20FOR%20THE%20INEVITABLE.pdf.

Chapter Four: It Has Happened Before

1 Dominique Lapierre and Javier Moro, *Five Past Midnight in Bhopal* (New York: Warner Books, 2002), xvii.

2 Lapierre and Moro, *Five Past Midnight in Bhopal,* 50.

3 Lapierre and Moro, *Five Past Midnight in Bhopal,* 300.

4 Lapierre and Moro, *Five Past Midnight in Bhopal,* 375.

5 Lapierre and Moro, *Five Past Midnight in Bhopal,* 377.

6 Lapierre and Moro, *Five Past Midnight in Bhopal,* 378.

7 Lapierre and Moro, *Five Past Midnight in Bhopal,* 49.

8 Paul Orum and Reece Rushing, "Chemical Security 101," Center for American Progress, Washington, D.C., November 2008, 7.

9 www.greenpeace.org, "Map of Vulnerability Zone Reported to the EPA by the Kuehne Chemical Plant in South Kearny, NJ," 2002, www.greenpeace.org/usa/news/does-a-chemical-plant-in-your/view-worst-case-scenario-chemi.

10 www.greenpeace.org, "Terrorism at Los Angeles Area Chemical Plants Could Put Millions at Risk," 2002, www.greenpeace.org/usa/news/does-a-chemical-plant-in-your/view-worst-case-scenario-chemi.

11 Paul Burgarino, "Study: Bay Point Chemical Plant at High Risk of Terrorist Attack," www.contracostatimes.com, November 19, 2008, www.contracostatimes.com/CI_11026233.

12 David Howe, The Homeland Security Council, www.scd.state.hi.us, July 2004, www.scd.state.hi.us/grant_docs/National_Planning_Scenarios_ExecSummaries_ver2.pdf.

13 "Open Letter to Bayer CropScience," www.peopleconcernedaboutmic.com, October 8, 2008, www.peopleconcernedaboutmic.com/openletter/.

14 "Open Letter to Bayer CropScience."

15 "Open Letter to Bayer CropScience."

16 "Bracing for the Worst in Chemicals," *New York Times,* June 4, 1994, www.cbgnetwork.org/985.html.

17 Contra Costa Health Services, "Major Accidents at Chemical Refinery Plants," 2008, www.cchealth.org/groups/hazmat/accident_history.php.

18 Material Safety Data Sheet, Mallinckrodt Baker, Inc., Phillipsburg, New Jersey, www.jtbaker.com/msds/englishhtml/t3913.htm.

19 William L. Holmes, "Thousands Evacuated from North Carolina Town amid Chemical Fire," www.sovereigndeed.com, 2006, www.sovereigndeed.com/PDF/articles_Thousands_Evacuated_from_North_Carolina_Town_Amid_Chemical_Fire.pdf.

20 Meghan Purvis and Julia Bauler, "Irresponsible Care," U.S. Public Interest Research Group Education Fund, Washington, D.C., 2004, 9.

21 International Fluoride Information Network, "Fluoride Release Leads to Evacuation of Texas Neighborhood," July 10, 2001, www2.fluoridealert.org/Pollution/Oil-Refineries/Fluoride-Release-Leads-to-Evacuation-of-Texas-Neighborhood.

22 "High Alert: Workers Warn of Security Gaps on Nation's Railroads," Brotherhood of Locomotive Engineers and Trainmen: A Division of the Teamsters Rail Conference, 2007, 3.

23 Eben Kaplan, "Rail Security and the Terrorist Threat," www.cfr.org, March 12, 2007, www.cfr.org/publication/12800/rail_security_and_the_terrorist_threat.html?breadcrumb=%2Fbios%2F11392%2Feben_kaplan%3Fgroupby%3D2%26page%3D1%26hide%3D1%26id%3D11392.

24 Kaplan, "Rail Security and the Terrorist Threat."

25 David Kocieniewski, "Despite 9/11 Effect, Rail Yards Are Still Vulnerable," *New York Times,* March 27, 2006, http://projectdisaster.com/?cat=11.

26 "High Alert: Workers Warn of Security Gaps on Nation's Railroads," 16.

27 Lisa Kim Bach and Beth Walton, "Las Vegas Dodged a Bullet: Chlorine-Hauling Tanker Rolls Free," reviewjournal.com, August 30, 2007, www.lvrj.com/news/9466232.html.

28 "New York Train Accident Involves Hazardous Chemicals; No Personal Injuries Reported," www.totalinjury.com, March 13, 2007, http://blog.totalinjury.com/archives/personal-injury-cases-in-the-news-new-york-train-accident-involves-hazardous-chemicals-no-personal-injuries-reported.html.

29 "High Alert: Workers Warn of Security Gaps on Nation's Railroads," 16.

30 David Michael Ettlin and Del Quentin Wilber, "Train Fire, Toxic Cargo Shut City," www.baltimoresun.com, July 19, 2001, www.baltimoresun.com/news/local/bal-te.md.train19jul19,0,1133743.story.

31 Michael Dresser, "CSX to Pay $2 Million to Baltimore," www.baltimoresun.com, February 14, 2006, www.baltimoresun.com/news/local/bal-te.md.settle14feb14,0,3079137.story.

32 Ettlin and Wilber, "Train Fire, Toxic Cargo Shut City."

33 Burgarino, "Study: Bay Point Chemical Plant at High Risk of Terrorist Attack."

34 Linda Capuano, *Terrorism and the Chemical Infrastructure* (Washington, DC: National Academies Press, 2006), 116.

35 Orum and Rushing, "Chemical Security 101," 19.

36 "Cleanup Continues at Bay Bridge Crash Site," www.wbaltv.com, August 10, 2008, www.wbaltv.com/news/17148398/detail.html.

37 Information Bulletin, "Potential Threat to Homeland Using Heavy Transport Vehicles," Department of Homeland Security and Federal Bureau of Investigation, July 30, 2004, 1.

38 Department of Homeland Security, "Risk-Based Performance Standards Guidance," October 2008, Department of Homeland Security, Washington, D.C., 7.

39 "Risk-Based Performance Standards Guidance," 27.

40 "Risk-Based Performance Standards Guidance," 29.

41 "Risk-Based Performance Standards Guidance," 37.

42 Orum and Rushing, "Chemical Security 101," 40.

43 Orum and Rushing, "Chemical Security 101," 2.

44 Material Safety Data Sheet, Mallinckrodt Baker, Inc.

45 Carina Rose, "Train Derailment Results in Hydrochloric Acid Leak in Lafayette, Louisiana," www.topnews.in, 2008, www.topnews.in/usa/train-derailment-causes-hydrochloric-acid-leak-lafayette-louisiana-2390.

46 Material Safety Data Sheet, Mallinckrodt Baker, Inc.

47 Saeed Ahmed and Janet DiGiacomo, "Toxic Cloud Passes," www.cnn.com, October 12, 2008, http://edition.cnn.com/2008/U.S./10/12/chemical.leak/?iref=mpstoryview.

48 Material Safety Data Sheet, Mallinckrodt Baker, Inc.

49   Kocieniewski, "Despite 9/11 Effect, Rail Yards Are Still Vulnerable."

50   Carl Prine, "Terror on the Tracks," www.pittsburghlive.com, January 14, 2007, www.pittsburghlive.com/x/pittsburghtrib/news/specialreports/s_487117.html.

51   Matthew Weinstock, "Easy Targets," www.govexec.com, February 15, 2003, www.govexec.com/features/0203/0203s2.htm.

52   Rebecca Lang, "U.S. Plants: Open to Terrorists," www.cbsnews.com, June 13, 2007, www.cbsnews.com/stories/2003/11/13/60minutes/main583528.shtml.

53   Press Release of Senator Menendez, www.menendez.senate.gov, March 30, 2006, http://menendez.senate.gov/newsroom/record.cfm?id=253453.

54   Denise Patel, "New Dangers Found at Nation's Most Potentially Hazardous Chemical Plant," www.njwec.org, December 13, 2008, www.njwec.org/PDF/Kuehne%20OSHA_Dec%2008.pdf.

55   Anthony D. Weiner and Jeff Flake, "Security or Pork?," U.S. House of Representatives, Washington, D.C., March 1, 2007, www.house.gov/list/press/ny09-weiner/boondoggles.pdf.

56   Weiner and Flake, "Security or Pork?"

57   Ian S. Lustick, "The War on Terror Feeding Frenzy," www.theindependentinstitute.com, April 22, 2008.

58   Representatives Tom Davis and Henry Waxman, "Waste, Abuse and Mismanagement in Department of Homeland Security Contracts," U.S. House of Representatives, Committee on Government Reform, Washington, D.C., July 2006, http://oversight.house.gov/documents/20060727092939-29369.pdf.

59   www.gsnmazazine.live.netconcepts.com/cms/resources/contracts/617.html.

60   Elena Herrero-Beaumont and Rachel Monahan, "Big-Time Security," www.forbes.com, August 28, 2006, www.forbes.com/2006/07/27/homeland-security-contracts-cx_wl_0728homeland.html.

Chapter Five: From the Frying Pan into the Fire—LNG

1   "The East Ohio Gas Company Explosion and Fire," The Encyclopedia of Cleveland History, 1998, www.ech.cwru.edu/ech-cgi/article.pl?id=eogceaf.

2   Virginia L. Thorndike, *LNG: A Level-Headed Look at the Liquefied Natural Gas Controversy* (Camden, ME: Down East Books, 2007), 24.

3   "Delivery of 140,000 CBM Type LNG Carrier *Arctic Discoverer*," www.kline.co, February 15, 2006, www.kline.co.jp/news/2006/060215_e.htm.

4   "Federal Efforts Needed to Address Challenges in Preventing and Responding to Terrorist Attacks on Energy Commodity Tankers," General Accounting Office, Washington, D.C., December 2007, www.gao.gov/new.items/d08141.pdf, 8.

5 Shinhye Kang and Dinakra Sethuraman, "Samsung to Deliver World's Biggest LNG Tanker for Exxon Project," July 8, 2008, www.bloomberg.com, www.bloomberg.com/apps/news?pid=20601080&sid=ayn7XSw1Ktg4& refer=asia.

6 Paul W. Parfomak and Adam S. Vann, Congressional "Liquefied Natural Gas (LNG) Import Terminals: Siting, Safety and Regulation," http:// assets.opencrs.com, October 7, 2008, http://assets.opencrs.com/rpts/ RL32205_20081007.pdf.

7 Richard A. Clarke, "LNG Facilities in Urban Areas," Good Harbor Consulting, Arlington, Virginia, May 2005, 36.

8 Armory B. Lovins and L. Hunter Lovins, *Brittle Power* (Andover, MA: Brick House Publishing, 2001), 87.

9 "Federal Efforts Needed to Address Challenges in Preventing and Responding to Terrorist Attacks on Energy Commodity Tankers," 31.

10 Lovins and Lovins, *Brittle Power,* 91.

11 Lovins and Lovins, *Brittle Power,* 91.

12 Lovins and Lovins, *Brittle Power,* 88.

13 Lovins and Lovins, *Brittle Power,* 88.

14 Tim Riley and Hayden Riley, "Risks and Dangers of LNG," LNGdanger .com, 2006, www.emediawire.com/releases/2006/5/emw380147.htm.

15 Lovins and Lovins, *Brittle Power,* 88.

16 Clarke, "LNG Facilities in Urban Areas," 47.

17 James A. Fay, "Spills and Fires from LNG Tankers in Fall River," www .greenfutures.org, August 26, 2003, www.greenfutures.org/projects/LNG/Fay .html.

18 Bart S. Fisher, "Comments of the LNG Opposition Team Requesting Denial of Permit of AES Sparrows Point LNG, LLC AND Mid-Atlantic Express, LLC," Sparrows Point LNG Opposition Team, Sparrows Point, Maryland, 2008, 93.

19 "AES Project Overview," www.aessparrowspointlng.com, 2009, www .aessparrowspointlng.com/sparrowspoint.asp#anchor1, 2.

20 "AES Project Overview," 3.

21 "AES Project Overview," 9.

22 Richard A. Clarke, "AES Sparrows Point: A Risk Assessment," Good Harbor Consulting, Arlington, Virginia, 2007, 1.

23 Tom Albert, "Liquefied Natural Gas: An Overview of the LNG Industry for Fire Marshals and Emergency Responders," National Association of State Fire Marshals, Washington, D.C., 2005, 11.

24 Jacob Dweck and Sonia Boutilon, "Deadly LNG Incident Holds Key Lessons for Developers, Regulators," www.sutherland.com, January 2004, 1.

25 "Pirates Storm Indonesian Tanker," www.bbc.co.uk, March 14, 2005, http:// news.bbc.co.uk/2/hi/asia-pacific/4347167.stm.

26 Keith Wallis, "Another Tanker Hijacked as Stolt Valor is Released," www
.lloydslist.com, November 18, 2008, www.lloydslist.com/ll/news/another-
tanker-hijacked-as-stolt-valor-is-released/1226798185542.htm?highlight=
true&containingAll=stolt+valor&containingPhrase=&containingAnyWords.

27 "Somali Pirates Free Tanker after Ransom," www.cnn.com, January 10,
2009, http://edition.cnn.com/2009/WORLD/africa/01/10/pirates.tanker/
index.html.

28 David Dieudonne, "Somali Pirates Seize Oil and Chemical Tanker," www
.nationalpost.com, November 28, 2008, www.nationalpost.com/story
.html?id=1005316.

29 "Somali Pirates Seize German Tanker," www.thelocal.com, January 29, 2009,
www.thelocal.de/national/20090129-17083.html.

30 "IMB Reports Unprecedented Increase in Maritime Hijackings," www
.eyefortransport.com, January 19, 2009, www.eyefortransport.com/content/
imb-reports-unprecedented-increase-maritime-hijackings.

31 "Somalia: Pirates Continuing Evolution," www.stratfor.com, October 1,
2008, www.stratfor.com/analysis/20081016_somalia_pirates_continuing_
evolution.

32 Martin Plaut, "Pirates Working with Islamists," www.bbc.com, November
19, 2008, http://news.bbc.co.uk/2/hi/7737375.stm.

33 Abdul Hameed Bakier, "Jihadis Question Al-Qaeda's Relationship with
Israel," www.jamestown.org, *Terrorism Monitor,* Vol. VII, Issue 5, March 13,
2009.

34 Michael G. Frodl, "Choke Point," *National Defense* magazine, Arlington,
Virginia, March 2009, 18.

35 Andrea Elliott, "A Call to Jihad, Answered in America," *New York Times,* July
12, 2009, 1.

36 Andrew Marshall, "Surge in Piracy Raises Concerns over Maritime
Terrorism," www.iht.com, November 25, 2008, www.iht.com/
articles/2008/11/25/asia/pirates.php.

37 Stephen Flynn, *The Edge of Disaster* (New York: Random House, 2007), 34.

38 "LNG Information," www.aessparrowspointlng.com, 2007, www
.aessparrowspointlng.com/powerpoint/aes_pp_testimony_milsten_
annapolis.ppt.

39 Senator Barbara A. Mikulski, "Mikulski Testifies on Opposition to LNG
Facility at Sparrows Point," www.mikulski.senate.gov, April 23, 2007, http://
mikulski.senate.gov/Newsroom/PressReleases/record.cfm?id=274078.

40 Senator Benjamin L. Cardin, "Maryland Delegation Calls on FERC to
Delay LNG Decision until Obama Administration Takes Office," www
.cardin.senate.gov, January 13, 2009, http://cardin.senate.gov/issues/record
.cfm?id=306612&.

41   "Waterway Suitability Report for AES Sparrows Point LNG," U.S. Coast
      Guard Sector Baltimore, Baltimore, Maryland, 2008, 4.
42   "Waterway Suitability Assessment for the Dominion Cove Point LNG
      Expansion Project," U.S. Coast Guard Sector Baltimore, Baltimore,
      Maryland, 2007, www.dhs.gov/xnews/gc_1179776352521.shtm, 2.
43   "Waterway Suitability Assessment for the Dominion Cove Point LNG
      Expansion Project," www.dhs.gov/xnews/gc_1179776352521.shtm, 2.
44   "Fact Sheet: National Infrastructure Protection Program Sector-
      Specific Plans," www.dhs.gov, October 8, 2008, www.dhs.gov/xnews/
      gc_1179776352521.
45   "FERC Approves AES Sparrows Point LNG Terminal; Mid-Atlantic Express
      Pipeline," www.ferc.gov, January 15, 2009, www.ferc.gov/news/news-
      releases/2009/2009-1/01-15-09-C-1.pdf.

Chapter Six: Noah Knew

1   David McCullough, *The Johnstown Flood* (New York: Simon and Schuster,
      1968), 107.
2   McCullough, *The Johnstown Flood,* 122.
3   McCullough, *The Johnstown Flood,* 146.
4   McCullough, *The Johnstown Flood,* 102.
5   McCullough, *The Johnstown Flood,* 102.
6   Kevin G. Coleman, "U.S. Dams: Is Security Seeping Through the Cracks?,"
      www.govtsecurity.com, December 1, 2005, www.govtsecurity.com/mag/u.s._
      dams_security/.
7   Committee on the Assessment of the Bureau of Reclamation's Security
      Program, "Assessment of the Bureau of Reclamation's Security Program"
      (Washington, D.C.: The National Academies Press, 2008), 9.
8   Claudia Copeland, "Terrorism and Security Issues Facing the Water
      Infrastructure Sector," Congressional Research Service, Washington, D.C.,
      November 16, 2007, 5.
9   "Assessment of the Bureau of Reclamation's Security Program," 38.
10   "The U.S. Army Corps of Engineers Wolf Creek Dam Seepage
      Rehabilitation Project," www.lrn.usace.army.mil, July 23, 2008, www.lrn
      .usace.army.mil/WolfCreek/.
11   "Center Hill Dam Seepage Reduction," www.lrn.usace.army.mil, October
      30, 2008, www.lrn.usace.army.mil/centerhill/.
12   "Wolf Creek Dam Preparedness Information," www.nashville.gov, 2009,
      www.nashville.gov/oem/preparedness/wcd.htm.
13   Amelia A. Pridemore, "Bluestone Dam," www.register-herald.com, February
      7, 2009, www.register-herald.com/homepage/local_story_038222841
      .html?keyword=leadpicturestory.

14 "Infrastructure Report Card: Dams," www.infrastructurereportcard.org, www
    .infrastructurereportcard.org/fact-sheet/dams.
15 "Dam Safety and Security in the United States: A Progress Report on
    the National Dam Safety Program, Fiscal Years 2004 and 2005," Federal
    Emergency Management Administration, Washington, D.C., 9.
16 "How Dams Fail," www.probeinternational.org, 2009, http://probe
    international.org/how-dams-fail.
17 "Taum Sauk Pumped Storage Project No. P-2277 Dam Breach Incident,"
    www.ferc.gov, July 8, 2008, www.ferc.gov/industries/hydropower/safety/
    projects/taum-sauk.asp.
18 News Release December 21, 2005, "Commission Conducts Investigation of
    Taum Sauk Dam Breach," www.ferc.gov, December 21, 2005, www.ferc.gov/
    news/news-releases/2005/2005-4/12-21-05.asp.
19 "Secrets of the Dead Case File: Bombing Nazi Dams," www.pbs.org, 2003,
    www.pbs.org/wnet/secrets/previous_seasons/case_nazidams/index.html.
20 Lou Michel and Dan Herbeck, *American Terrorist: Timothy McVeigh and the
    Oklahoma City Bombing* (New York: Regan Books, 2001), 164.
21 Alfred R. Pagan, "Catastrophic Dam Failures," www.cenews.com, December
    1, 2005, www.cenews.com/article.asp?id=982.
22 Pagan, "Catastrophic Dam Failures."
23 Erich Rathfelder, "Dangerous Forces: Dams, Dikes and Nuclear Stations,"
    www.crimesofwar.org, 1999–2003, www.crimesofwar.org/thebook/
    dangerous-forces.html.
24 Matthew Harwood, "Boise Most Vulnerable City in Western U.S. to
    Terroist Attack," www.securitymanagement.com, April 1, 2008, www
    .securitymanagement.com/news/boise-most-vulnerable-city-western-us.
25 Robert Allen, "Dillon Dam: Target for Terror?," www.summitdaily.com, July
    14, 2008, www.summitdaily.com/article/20080714/NEWS/709184279-
    terrorist-attack.
26 "Mohammedan Terrorists Target Bhakra Dam in the Punjab," www
    .islamicterrorism.wordpress.com, March 18, 2009, http://islamicterrorism
    .wordpress.com/2009/03/18/mohammedan-terrorists-target-bhakra-dam-in-
    punjab/.
27 Nishit Dholabhai, "Terror Threat to Seize Dams and Cause Flood," www
    .telegraphindia.com, February 8, 2009, www.telegraphindia.com/1090209/
    JSP/frontpage/story_10506891.JSP.
28 www.quqnooos.com and Pan, "Terrorists Target Dams," www.quqnooos
    .com, July 29, 2008, http://quqnooos.com/index.php?option=com_
    content&task=view&id=1258.
29 Saeed Ali Achakzai, "Hundreds of Taliban Massing to Attack Dam: Official,"
    www.reuters.com, February 12, 2007, www.reuters.com/article/topNews/
    idUSSP23361820070212.

30 "Unclassified Summary of Evidence for Administrative Review Board in the Case of Abdullah Al-Matrafi," DOD Office for the Administrative Review of the Detention of Enemy Combatants at U.S. Naval Base Guantanamo Bay, Cuba, March 22, 2006, www.dod.mil/pubs/foi/detainees/csrt_arb/ARB_Round_2_Factors_1-99.pdf#7.

31 Barton Gellman, "U.S. Fears Al-Qaeda Cyber Attacks," *The Washington Post,* June 26, 2006, www.securityfocus.com/news/502.

32 MSNBC Staff and Wire Reports, "The Threat of Terrorism," www.ionizers.org, January 31, 2002, www.ionizers.org/water-terrorism.html.

33 Justin Hall, "Who Is Dispensing Gratuitous Fear?" www.whitenuclearsnowflake.blogspot.com, 2008, whitenuclearsnowflake.blogspot.com/2007/04/who-is-dispensing-gratuitous-fear.html.

34 Clark Kent Ervin, *Open Target* (New York: Palgrave Macmillan, 2006), 151.

Chapter Seven: Remembering Caffa Bio Labs

1   Rosemary Horrox, *The Black Death* (New York: Manchester University Press, 2003) 26.

2   Clark Kent Ervin, *Open Target,* 178.

3   Elisa D. Harris, "The Killers in the Lab," www.nytimes.com, August 12, 2008, www.nytimes.com/2008/08/12/opinion/12harris.html.

4   Judith Miller, "Bioterrorism's Deadly Math," www.city-journal.org, Autumn 2008, www.city-journal.org/2008/18_4_bioterrorism.html.

5   "NIH Asks for More Time to Complete Safety Review of Boston U's Germ Lab," www.chronicle.com, April 15, 2009, http://chronicle.com/news/article/6322/nih-asks-for-more-time-to-complete-safety-review-of-boston-us-germ-lab.

6   U.S. Department of Justice, Application and Affidavit for Search Warrant, www.usdoj.gov, October 31, 2007, www.usdoj.gov/amerithrax/docs/07-524-m-01.pdf.

7   U.S. Department of Justice, Application and Affidavit for Search Warrant.

8   U.S. Department of Justice, Application and Affidavit for Search Warrant.

9   Nelson Hernandez, "Inventory Uncovers 9,200 More Pathogens," www.washingtonpost.com, June 18, 2009, www.washingtonpost.com/wp-dyn/content/article/2009/06/17/AR2009061703271.html?referrer=emailarticle.

10 Kenneth Chang, "Split Verdicts in Texas Trial of Professor and the Plague," www.nytimes.com, December 2, 2003, www.nytimes.com/2003/12/02/us/split-verdicts-in-texas-trial-of-professor-and-the-plague.html.

11 Adam Rawnsley, "Army Biolab's Missing Vials May Never Be Found," www.wired.com, April 23, 2009, www.wired.com/dangerroom/2009/04/ft-detricks-bug/.

12 David Goodhue, "Plague-Infested Mice Missing from New Jersey Research Lab," www.prisonplanet.com, February 7, 2009, www.prisonplanet.com/plague-infested-mice-missing-from-new-jersey-research-lab.html.

13 "Plague Mice Escape Newark Lab," www.defensetech.org, September 16, 2005, www.defensetech.org/archives/001811.html.

14 Emily Ramshaw, "Boom in Biodefense Labs Sparks Security Debate," www.dallasnews.com, October 26, 2007, www.dallasnews.com/sharedcontent/dws/dn/latestnews/stories/102707dntexbioterrorism.366092c.html.

15 Harris, "The Killers in the Lab."

16 "Foot and Mouth Outbreak Traced to Lab Pipe," Associated Press, September 7, 2007, www.msnbc.msn.com/id/20643204/from/ET.

17 Alan Schofield, Jonathan Leake, and Robert Booth, "Virus Lab Behind Foot and Mouth Outbreak," www.timesonline.co.uk, August 5, 2007, www.timesonline.co.uk/tol/news/uk/article2199149.ece.

18 Jack Dolan and Dave Altimari, "Anthrax Missing from Army Lab," *The Hartford Courant,* January 20, 2002, www.ph.ucla.edu/epi/bioter/anthraxmissingarmylab.html.

19 Ramshaw, "Boom in Biodefense Labs Sparks Security Debate."

20 GAO: Biosafety Laboratories: Perimeter Security Assessment of the Nation's Five BSL-4 Laboratories GAO-08-1092, September 2008, www.gao.gov/products/gao-08-1092.

21 "Biomedical Research Laboratory," http://brl.gmu.edu, August 4, 2009, http://brl.gmu.edu/page2.cfin?menu_id=16&SUB_menu_id=0.

22 Annie Jacobsen, "Al-Qaeda Targets Lethal Disease Research Facility on NY Island," www.pajamasmedia.com, September 14, 2008, www.pajamasmedia.com/blog/al-qaeda-operative-targets-lethal-disease-research-island-in-connecticut/.

23 Bob Graham and Jim Talent, *World at Risk* (New York: Vintage Books, 2008), 10.

24 "MI-5 Investigating Al-Qaeda Attempt to Infiltrate British Labs, Get Killer Viruses," www.jihadwatch.org, March 30, 2008, www.jihadwatch.org/archives/020502.php.

25 Graham and Talent, *World at Risk,* 24.

26 Spencer Hsu, "Homeland Security Pulls Experimental Biosensors from New York City," *The Washington Post,* May 7, 2009, www.globalsecuritynewswire.org/gsn/nw_20090507_9427.php.

27 Jon Fox, "DHS Auditors Fault Biowatch Program," www.gsn.nti.org, February 8, 2007, http://gsn.nti.org/gsn/GSN_20070208_323043AD.php.

28 Graham and Talent, *World at Risk,* xv.

Chapter Eight: We Have Been Warned

1   "Fact Sheet on the Three Mile Island Incident," Nuclear Regulatory Commission, www.nrc.gov, March 9, 2009, www.nrc.gov/reading-rm/doc-collections/fact-sheets/3mile-isle.html.

2   "Three Mile Island: How a Nuclear Reactor Works," www.pbs.org, April 2009, www.pbs.org/wgbh/amex/three/sfeature/tmihow.html.

3   Mike Gray and Ira Rosen, *The Warning* (New York: W. W. Norton, 2003), 276.

4   "The Chernobyl Disaster," www.bbc.co.uk, 2006, http://news.bbc.co.uk/2/shared/spl/hi/guides/456900/456957/html/nn2page1.stm.

5   Nuclear Energy Agency, Organisation for Economic Co-Operation and Development, "Chernobyl—Assessment of Radiological and Health Impacts," www.nea.fr, 2002, www.nea.fr/html/rp/reports/2003/nea3508-chernobyl.pdf.

6   "Chernobyl Blast's Health Impact Varies According to Source," www.voanews.com, April 26, 2006, www.voanews.com/english/archive/2006-04/Chernobyl-Health-Impact-Varies-According-to-Source.cfm.

7   Paul Gunter, "Chernobyl: Basic Facts," www.nirs.org, December 5, 1995, www.nirs.org/reactorwatch/accidents/cherfact.htm.

8   Edwin S. Lyman, "Chernobyl on the Hudson?," www.ucsusa.org, September 2004, www.ucsusa.org/assets/documents/nuclear_power/indianpointhealthstudy.pdf.

9   Lyman, "Chernobyl on the Hudson?"

10   Mark Thompson, "Why America's Nuclear Power Plants Are Still So Vulnerable to Terrorist Attack and How to Make Them Safer," www.healthandenergy.com, June 12, 2005.

11   Thompson, "Why America's Nuclear Power Plants Are Still So Vulnerable."

12   Julian West, "Al-Qaeda Sought Nuclear Scientists," *The Washington Times,* April 11, 2002, www.nci.org/02/04f/12-03.htm.

13   Jacobsen, "Al-Qaeda Targets Lethal Disease Research Facility on NY Island."

14   Andrew Norfolk, "The Unexpected Profile of the Modern Terrorist," www.timesonline.co.uk, July 7, 2007, www.timesonline.co.uk/tol/news/uk/crime/article2039865.ece.

15   Author's interview of confidential source, March 2009.

16   Author's interview of confidential source, June 2009.

17   Author's interview of confidential source, June 2009.

18   Peter D. H. Stockton, "Vulnerability of Spent Fuel Pools and the Design Basis Threat," presented to the National Academy of Sciences, May 10, 2004.

19   "Pakistan: A Tactical Assessment of the Pearl Continental Attack," www.stratfor.com, June 10, 2009, www.stratfor.com/analysis/20090609_pakistan_tactical_assessment_pearl_continental_attack.

20 "Saudi Arabia: Anatomy of the Abqaiq Bombing Attempt," www.stratfor
   .com, February 24, 2006, www.stratfor.com/saudi_arabia_anatomy_abqaiq_
   bombing_attempt.

21 "Abqaiq Attack," www.globaljihad.net, 2007, www.globaljihad.net/view_
   page.asp?id=1214.

22 Author's interview of confidential source, Spring 2009.

23 Ray Walser, "Mexico, Drug Cartels and the Merida Initiative: A Fight We
   Cannot Afford to Lose," www.heritage.org, July 23, 2008, www.heritage.org/
   research/latinamerica/bg2163.cfm.

24 "Nuclear Power Plant Security: Voices from Inside the Fences," www.pogo
   .org, September 12, 2002, www.pogo.org/pogo-files/reports/nuclear-
   security-safety/voices-from-inside-the-fences/.

25 Thompson, "Why America's Nuclear Power Plants Are Still So Vulnerable."

26 Gray and Rosen, *The Warning*, 273.

27 Gray and Rosen, *The Warning*, 273.

28 Thompson, "Why America's Nuclear Power Plants Are Still So Vulnerable."

29 Author's interview of confidential source, Summer 2009.

30 Author's interview of confidential source, Summer 2009.

31 John Dorschner, "FPL Fined Over Sleeping Security Guards," www.a4nr.org,
   2008, http://a4nr.org/library/security/04.10.2008-miamiherald.

32 Jim Warren, "Harris Nuclear Plant Fined for Security Violations," www
   .ncwarn.org, August 30, 2007, www.ncwarn.org/docs/news%20rels/2007/
   nr%208-30-07-HarrisFinedForSecurityViolations.htm.

33 Author's interview of confidential source, Summer 2009.

34 Gray and Rosen, *The Warning*, 272.

35 Thompson, "Why America's Nuclear Power Plants Are Still So Vulnerable."

36 Steven Mufson, "Nuclear Agency: Air Defenses Impractical," *The Washington
   Post*, January 30, 2007, www.washingtonpost.com.

37 "What Is Nuclear Waste?," www.whatisnuclear.com, 2009, www
   .whatisnuclear.com/articles/waste.html.

38 "Security," www.pilgrimwatch.org, August 31, 2009, www.pilgrimwatch.org/
   sec4.html#land.

39 "Risks to Spent Fuel Ponds," www.riverkeeper.org, 2009, www.riverkeeper
   .org/campaign.php/indianpoint_waste/the_facts/1259-risks-to-spent-fuel-
   pools.

40 Robert Alvarez, Jan Beyea, Klaus Janberg, Jungmin Kang, Ed Lyman, Allison
   Macfarlane, Gordon Thompson, Frank N. von Hippel, "Reducing the
   Hazards of Stored Spent Fuel," Science and Global Security, May 28, 2003,
   http://mothersforpeace.org/data/20030122ReducingTheHazards.

41 "Dry Cask Storage," Indian Point Energy Center, www.safesecurevital.org/
   safe-secure-vital/dry-cask-storage.html.

42 "Spent Fuel Storage," www.nucleartourist.com, March 15, 2001, www .nucleartourist.com/systems/spfuel1.htm.

43 Author's interviews of confidential sources, Summer 2009.

44 Thompson, "Why America's Nuclear Power Plants Are Still So Vulnerable."

45 "Al-Qaeda Plotted Nuclear Attacks," www.bbc.co.uk, September 8, 2002, http://news.bbc.co.uk/2/hi/middle_east/2244146.stm.

Chapter Nine: Making It Safe

1 "NC Terror Suspects Had Arms, Ammo, FBI 'Playbook,' Agent Says," www .cnn.com, August 4, 2009, www.cnn.com/2009/crime/08/04/carolina.terror .suspects/.

2 "Unspent Funds for Train Safety, Make N.J. Lawmakers Furious," *Star-Ledger*, March 16, 2009, www.homelandsecurityforsale.org/node/118.

3 Kathleen Lucadamo, "Homeland Security Department Terror Trucker Training a Waste, Rep. Weiner," www.nydailynews.com, March 26, 2008, www.nydailynews.com/news/2008/03/26/2008-03-26_homeland_security_ department_terror_truc-1.html.

4 John Steele Gordon, "Nazi Saboteurs Land on Long Island," www .americanheritage.com, March 26, 2008, www.americanheritage.com/ articles/web/20070627-nazis-sabotage-world-war-II-coast-guard-long-island- amagansett_print.shtml.

5 "BSL-4 Laboratories Improved Perimeter Security Despite Limited Action by CDC," www.gao.gov, July 2009, www.gao.gov/new.items/d09851.pdf.

6 Sara A. Carter, "Al-Qaeda Eyes Bio Attack from Mexico," www.washington times.com, June 3, 2009, www.washingtontimes.com/news/2009/jun/03/al- qaeda-eyes-bio-attack-via-mexico-border/print/.

Index

Abqaiq oil processing facility, 178–79
active shooters, 52–53, 60. *See also* mass-
    casualty attacks
AES Corporation, 102–3, 109
Ahmad, Rauf, 159
Ahmed, Shirwa, 107
Al Jazeera, 46, 203
American Society of Civil Engineers,
    117–18, 120
Amtrak, 32, 34
amusement parks, 55, 56
Annapolis Naval Academy, 7–9, 11–13
anthrax, 135, 137–44, 145, 148, 154,
    159, 203–4
Army Corps of Engineers, 118, 120
Atta, Mohamed, 192

bag checks, 29, 30, 31, 37, 38, 39, 56
Baltimore Ravens stadium, 55–56
Baltimore Washington International rail
    station, 25, 27, 30
barriers, vehicle, 78–79, 81
Bayer CropScience, 69–71
Beirut marine barrack attacks, 9–10
Beslan school, 43, 54
Bhakra Dam, 125
Bhopal chemical leak, 66–67, 70
Biden, Joe, 87
Binalshibh, Ramzi, 192
bin Laden, Osama, 126, 173
biodefense laboratories
    biological attacks originating from,
        138–44
    in Britain, 159
    internal procedures and security in,
        144–49
    levels and descriptions, 136–38
    physical security issues, 149–51
    security assessments of, 151–58
    security measures implemented,
        200–202
    terrorist psychology and, 159–61
    as terrorist targets, 158–59
biological attacks
    anti-terrorism planning scenarios
        for, 135
    biodefense programs, overview, 135–
        38 (*see also* biodefense laboratories)
    examples of, 138–44
    expectation of, 162
    illness disasters in history, 133–34
    as terrorists' plans, 158–59, 161,
        203–4
Biomedical Research Laboratory (BRL),
    154–56
Biowatch, 162
Biscaglia (chemical tanker), 105
Black Cats, 49
Black Death, 133–34
Bluestone Dam, 120
Boise, Idaho, 124
bombs (explosives). *See also* VBIEDs
    devices and materials used for, 10, 22,
        23, 24, 41, 44
    effects of, 9–11, 22, 23, 24
    for nuclear reactor waste building
        attacks, 189
    WWII dam explosions, 123
Borelli, Frank, 64
Brucella, 148
BSL 3 (Biosafety Level 3) labs, 136,
    137–38, 151–56, 160
BSL 4 (Biosafety Level 4) labs, 136–37,
    138, 149–51, 156–58, 160,
    200–201
Buffalo Mining Company, 121
Burguillo Dam, 123
Butler, Thomas C., 146–47

cancer, due to radiation exposure, 169,
    170, 171
Cardin, Benjamin, 110–11

Center Hill Dam, 120
Centers for Disease Control (CDC), 147, 200–201
Chemical Facility Anti-Terrorism Standards (CFATS), 80
chemical plants
    anti-terrorism planning scenarios for, 69
    flooding damage potential and, 120
    government risk management requirements, 68
    hazard potential, 71
    industrial accidents, examples of, 66–68, 69–72, 83, 84
    population proximity to, 68–69
    security assessments of, 85–90
    security legislation regarding, 87
    terrorist assessment scenario, 75–82
chemical toxins. *See also* chemical plants
    effects of, 66–67, 71, 72, 74, 83
    homeland security funding *vs.* security against, 90–92
    rail transportation of, 72–74, 85–86
    rail yard storage of, 83, 85
    tanker transportation of, and piracy, 105–7
    water treatment plants using, 82–83
Chemstar Venus (chemical tanker), 105
Chernobyl nuclear power plant, 168–69
"China Syndrome, The," 166, 168
chlorine and chlorine gas
    anti-terrorism planning scenarios addressing, 69
    chemical plant accidents with, 70, 71–72
    description and use, 68
    rail transportation accidents with, 73, 74
    risk-based performance standards and, 81
    sites for, 75, 82, 83, 87
citizens' alert directives, 33, 35
Clarke, Richard A., 98–99, 103, 109
Clark Field attack, vi
Columbine High School, 50–52, 58, 59

Commission on the Prevention of WMD Proliferation and Terrorism reports, 162
ConocoPhillips, 72
containment procedures, 50–51, 60
Cove Point LNG terminal, 101, 112–15
Croatian War, 124
Cullen, John, 199–200
Customs and Border Protection Division (CBP), 91
cyanide gas, 40–41, 70

dams
    cities most vulnerable to terrorist attacks on, 124
    construction types of, 121
    failure causes due to design, 121–22
    flooding catastrophes, examples of, 116–17, 118–20
    Homeland Security classification of, 124
    location statistics and hazard potential, 117–18
    private *vs.* government ownership of, 118
    safety issues of at-risk, 120
    security assessments of, 126–32
    terrorist threats and attacks, 123, 124–26
    wartime attacks on, 123–24
Daschle, Tom, 138
Davidson, Kathy, 184
DBT (Design Basis Threat), 174–81
Delta Force, 64
Department of Homeland Security (DHS)
    anti-terrorism planning scenarios, 69, 135
    biological weapon sensors utilized by, 162
    budget of, 40
    chemical facility anti-terrorism standards of, 80
    chemical transportation statements, 73
    core priority of, 114

dam vulnerability and security, 124
expenditures and funding priorities,
40, 90–92, 135–36, 196–98
passenger railway directives, 32–36
VBIED reports, 79–80
Dillon Dam, 124–25
Dnjeprostroj Dam, 124
Dobbins Air Reserve Base, 20
dogs, explosive-sniffing, 17, 27, 29, 31,
34, 36, 37, 38
Dover Air Force Base, 19

East Ohio Gas Company, 95
Ebola virus, 137, 145, 148
Edge of Disaster, The (Flynn), 108
encephalitis, 138, 145, 147
Environmental Protection Agency,
68, 87

Falkenrath, Richard, 73
Fay, James, 99–100
FBI (Federal Bureau of Investigation),
64, 79–80, 107, 126, 138–44, 195
Federal Energy Regulatory Commission
(FERC), 115
Ferreira, Frank and Rosa, 86–87
fight or flight victim responses, 58–62
floods, 116–21. *See also* dams
Flynn, Stephen, 108
foot-and-mouth disease, 148–49, 158
Forbes (magazine), 91–92
Fort Detrick BSL 4 laboratory, 138–44,
147, 149, 156–58, 160
Fort Dix Army Base, 18–20
Fort Monmouth, 19
Fort Myer, 14–18
Fouda, Yosri, 192

General Chemical Bay Point, 68
General Chemical Corp., 74
George Mason University laboratory,
154–56
Giduck, John, 61, 64
Glen Canyon Dam, 118
Good Harbor Counseling, 102–3

Government Accountability Office
(GAO), 72–73, 149–51, 200, 201
Greenpeace, 86, 87, 169
guards, security
"active shooter" responses, 49, 56, 57,
61–62
at biodefense labs, 152
at dams, 131
at military installations, 13, 15–16
at nuclear power plants, 182–85,
191–92
at public events and entertainment
places, 56–57
at rail stations, 25, 27–29, 30, 37,
38, 39

Hammoud, Assem, 41–42
hijackers, 58
homeland security
capitalism and, 198–99
common sense and, 198
methodology requirements, 201–2
national perceptions of threat and, 21,
194–97, 201, 202–4
Honeywell Facility, 72
Hoover, J. Edgar, 132
Hoover Dam, 118, 126–27
Hostage Rescue Team (HRT), 64
hostages. *See also* mass-casualty attacks
law enforcement procedures and
training, 50–51, 52, 60, 63–64
national rescue forces and
effectiveness, 64
negotiations, 58, 59, 62–63
piracy and, 105
terrorists' objectives with, 53–54
victim reaction suggestions, 57–60
worldwide situation examples, 43–45
Hurricane Katrina, 91
Hurst, Dana R., 120
Hussain (Khobar terrorist), 45–46
hydrochloric acid, 82, 83
hydrogen cyanide/hydrocyanic acid,
67, 68

identification checks, 3, 34, 35–36, 37, 203
Indian Point nuclear power plant, 169–71
infectious diseases. *See* biodefense laboratories; biological attacks
influenza, 134, 148, 154
InfraGard program, 126
International Maritime Bureau, 106
Ivins, Bruce Edward, 138–44

Johnstown, Pennsylvania, 116–17

Kajaki Dam, 125
Karim, Sajjad, 48
Kensico Dam, 130–32
Khobar, Saudi Arabia, mass-casualty attacks in, 45–46
Kimmel, Husband E., vi
Kuehne Chemical Plant, 86–90

Lakehurst Naval Air Station, 19
Lashkar-e-Taiba (LeT), 24, 47–49, 125
Laurel Station, Maryland, 38–39
Leahy, Patrick, 138
Leopold Cafe, 47–48
Limburg (tanker), 97
LNG (liquid natural gas). *See also* LNG tankers
    description and use, 96
    explosions from, examples of, 95, 103–4
    facilities for, 97, 100–105, 107–15, 194–95
    importation of, 96–97
    safety record for, 95
    storage of, 97
LNG (liquid natural gas) tankers
    at-sea attack potential, 105–6
    hazard potential and risk studies, 97–100
    liquid natural gas transportation, 96–97
    safety of, 97
    terrorist attacks on, examples of, 97
    during transit in shipping channels, 107–12
LNG (liquid natural gas) terminals, 97, 100–105, 107–15, 194–95
London Underground bombings, 23
Long Island Railroad, 32, 42
Lucky Peak Dam, 124

MacArthur, Douglas, vii
Madrid train bombings, 22–23, 27, 202
Mahmood, Bashiruddin, 173
MARC (Maryland Area Regional Commuter), 38–40
Marriott Hotel, Islamabad, 179
Maryland Pathogen Research Institute (MPRI), 152–54
Massachusetts Institute of Technology studies, 99–100
mass-casualty attacks. *See also* hostages
    defensive preparations for, 55–57, 60, 61–64
    examples of, 43–49, 50–52, 58, 59
    potential targets for, 55, 173
    security personnel reaction suggestions, 61–62
    terrorist objective for, 53–54
    victim reaction suggestions, 57–62
mass transit, 196. *See also* railways, passenger
Material Safety Data Sheet (MSDS), 83–84
Al-Matrafia, Abdullah, 126
McVeigh, Timothy, 10
metal detectors, 27, 28, 31, 37, 38, 49, 56
Mexican drug cartels, 181–82
MIC (methyl isocyanate), 66–68, 70, 71
Middlemiss, John, 183
Mikulski, Barbara, 110
military installations
    army base assessments, 14–18
    marine base assessments, 1–7
    naval base assessments, 7–9, 11–13
    terrorist attacks planned for, 18–21
    worldwide attacks on, 9–10

military recruiting stations, 20, 21
Mishra, Pappu, 48
"mobtaker," 41
Mohammed, Khalid Sheikh, 192
Morrison, Samuel B., viii
Moteiri, Turki, 45–46
Mumbai attacks (India), 24, 47–49
Murphy, Diane and Michael, 47

Nader (Khobar terrorist), 45
al-Nafisi, Abdullah, 203–4
Naghlu Dam, 125
National Counter Terrorism Security
    Office (Great Britain), 159
National Institutes of Health, 136
Nazi saboteurs, 199
negotiations, hostage, 58, 59, 62–63
Nemer al-Baqmi (Khobar terrorist),
    45–46
New York City
    dams in proximity to, 130–32
    mass transit in, 32
    nuclear power plants near, 169–70
    rail traffic statistics, 32
    security in, 30–31, 132
    subway system, 38, 41–42
New York Times, 85
Nielson, Patti, 50
9/11, viii–ix, 58, 170–71, 176, 192
North Carolina Waste Awareness and
    Reduction Network, 185
nuclear energy, 175
nuclear power plants
    aerial attack scenarios, 186–87
    hazard potential, 166–67, 171–72
    industrial accidents at, 164–66, 168–69
    nationwide location statistics, 171
    physical security systems for, 174–81
    risk studies, 169–71
    security guards and training, 181–86
    spent-fuel storage at, 187–92
    terrorist attack scenarios, 172–73
    as terrorist target, 192
nuclear reactor waste and storage
    facilities, 187–92

Nuclear Regulatory Commission (NRC),
    170, 174, 176, 185–87, 189, 192

Oasis Resort, 46
Obama, Barack, 87
Oberoi Trident Hotel, 48
Oklahoma City bombing, 10–11
Omar, Mahmoud, 19
Ordunte Dam, 123

Parris Island, 1–7
Peach Bottom Nuclear Power Plant, 185
Pearl Continental Hotel, 178
Pearl Harbor attacks, vi, vii–viii, xii
Penn Station, New York City, 30,
    32–33, 42
Peruca Dam, 124
PETN, 10
Philadelphia train stations, 32
phosgene, 67–68, 70
Pilgrim Nuclear Station, 184
piracy, 105–7
Pittsburgh Tribune-Review, 85
plague, 133–34, 146–47, 148, 154
Plum Island Animal Disease Research
    Center, 158
Point Plant (chemical plant pseudonym),
    75–82
police officers
    "active shooter" policies and training,
        50–51, 52, 60, 61–64
    in India, 49
    nuclear power plant attacks and, 191
    rail station presence of, 37, 38
Port Authority Trans-Hudson
    Corporation (PATH), 42
"Potential Threat to Homeland Using
    Heavy Transportation Vehicles"
    (DHS and FBI), 79–80
Prine, Carl, 85
Project on Government Oversight
    (POGO), 177
propane, 73–74, 74, 96
public events and places, 55–56, 59,
    173. *See also* mass-casualty attacks

Al-Qaeda. *See also* terrorist mind-set
  biological attack targets, 135, 158–59,
    203–4
  dams as targets, 126
  education and backgrounds of,
    172–73
  hostage massacres, 45–46
  Lashkar-e-Taiba connections, 125
  methodology contrasts between U.S.
    and, 202
  New York City subway plots, 41, 42
  nuclear power plant as targets, 192
  Somali pirates and, 106
  tactics and capabilities, 5, 178–80
QUAD (Quick Action Deployment),
    51–52

radiation exposure, 165, 167, 168–69,
    171, 187–88. *See also* nuclear power
    plants
"Rail Security" (Government
    Accountability Office), 72–73
railways, freight, 72–74, 83, 85–86
railways, passenger
  attack deterrents, 27–29, 31–32
  Homeland Security directives for,
    33–36
  security assessments, 25, 27, 30–31,
    36–40
  terrorist plans for, 40–42
  travel statistics, 32, 37
  worldwide attacks on, examples,
    22–24, 27, 47
rail yards, 83, 85
Rao-Sundarji, Padma, 49
RDX (explosive compound), 24
Reaction Products, 71
Rhodes, Keith, 149
risk-based performance standards
    (RBPSs), 80
Risk-Based Performance Standards
    Guidance, 80–81
Risk Management Plans (RMPs), 68, 75
rocket-propelled grenades (RPGs), 177
Russia, mass-casualty attacks in, 43–45

Samsung Corporation, 97
Sana'a embassy, 179–80
Sandia Laboratories, 98, 170
SARS, 138, 148, 154
Sawt al-Jihad (magazine), 45
school buses, 44
schools, 43–45, 50–52, 58, 59
Seabrook Nuclear Power Plant, 183–84
Securitas, 185
security vulnerability assessments
    (SVAs), 80
Al-Shabaab, 106, 107
Shareef, Derrick, 21
Shearon Harris Nuclear Power
    Plant, 185
Shnewer, Mohamad, 19
Short, Walter C., vi
Al-Siba'i, Hani, 106
Siddiqui, Aafia, 158–59, 173
Siege, The (movie), 63
Siraj, Shahawar Matin, 41
Sirius Star (supertanker), 105, 107
Six Flags Park, 56
smallpox, 150
Somali pirates, 105, 106–7
South Fork Dam, 117
Southwest Foundation for Biomedical
    Research, 151
Sparrows Point LNG Opposition
    Team, 100
Sparrows Point LNG terminal, 102–5,
    107–12, 115, 194–95
Squadron 617, 123
stadiums and sports events, 55–56, 59
State Homeland Security Grant
    Program, 90
Stolt Valor (chemical tanker), 105
subways, 23, 38, 41–42
Sufaat, Yazid, 159
suicide bombers, 5, 23, 44, 75–79, 107
sulfuric acid, 74, 83–84
surveillance cameras, 25, 34, 39
suspicious behavior alerts, 33, 35, 37
SWAT teams, 50, 51, 52, 60, 64
swine flu, 134

Taj Mahal Palace Hotel, 47, 48
Taliban, 125–26, 178, 179, 193
tankers, 105–7. *See also* LNG (liquid
   natural gas) tankers
Taum Sauk Dam, 121–22
Teamsters Union, 85–86
terminals, LNG (liquid natural gas), 97,
   100–105, 107–15, 194–95
terrorist mind-set
   biodefense laboratories and, 159–61
   composure during attacks, 48
   mass-casualty attacks and, 62
   military security *vs.*, 11–12
   objectives, 47, 53–54, 58
   planning psychology, 18–21, 31, 56,
      59, 89–90
   rail security and, 27–29
   tactics and capabilities, 5
Teton Dam, 119–20
Texas Tech University, 146–47
theaters, 45, 55
30th Street Station, Philadelphia, 32
Three Mile Island Nuclear Power Plant,
   164–66, 167–68, 172
toluene, 70, 71
Transportation Security Administration
   (TSA), 33–34
trash cans, 33–34, 35, 202
truckers, commercial, 197–98
tularemia, 145, 148, 154, 162
Turkey Point Nuclear Power Plant, 185

Union Carbide, 66–67, 70
Union of Concerned Scientists, 170, 185
Union Station, Washington, D.C.,
   36–37

unpredictability, as deterrent, 28
U.S. Coast Guard, 19, 109–12, 114
U.S. consulates, 180
U.S. embassies, 17, 179–80

VBIEDs (vehicle-borne improvised
   explosive devices)
   attack scenarios using, 5, 78–79, 127,
      129, 131, 177
   chemicals used with, 68
   deterrents/defense against, 11–13
   explosive effects of, 9–10
   as prime terrorist tool, 79–80
   two-phased attack approaches using,
      178–79
vehicle inspections, 6, 15–17, 203
victim response procedures, 57–60
Viral Immunology Center (Georgia State
   University), 150
Virginia Railway Express (VRE), 36–37

"war on terror" concept, 21, 59–61
water treatment plants, 82–83
Waterway Suitability Report (U.S. Coast
   Guard), 112, 114
West Nile virus, 138, 154
Wolf Creek Dam, 120
World Health Organization, 169
World War II, vi–ix, xii, 123–24,
   199–200, 201

Yemeni Islamic Brigades, 179–80

Zulu War, 197

About the Author

Charles S. Faddis served twenty years in the Central Intelligence Agency as an operations officer, holding positions as a department chief at the CIA's Counterterrorism Center in Washington, D.C., and as a chief of station in the Middle East. He is the author of *Beyond Repair* (Lyons Press), a scathing critique of today's CIA, and the coauthor of *Operation Hotel California* (Lyons Press), which recounts how he led the first CIA mission into Iraq in 2002 in preparation for the pending invasion. He lives in Davidsonville, Maryland.